I will neve

Cardboard Crack

Counterspell.

A collection of comics about the world's most addictive game.

I will never quit
Cardboard Crack

Copyright © 2014

This book collects comics that originally appeared online between
August 6, 2013 and January 29, 2014 and can also be viewed at:
cardboard-crack.com
facebook.com/CardboardCrack

For information write:
cardboardcrack.mtg@gmail.com

Printed in the U.S.A.

For PEC.
I still remember driving at 4 a.m. for that
Mox Emerald like it was yesterday.

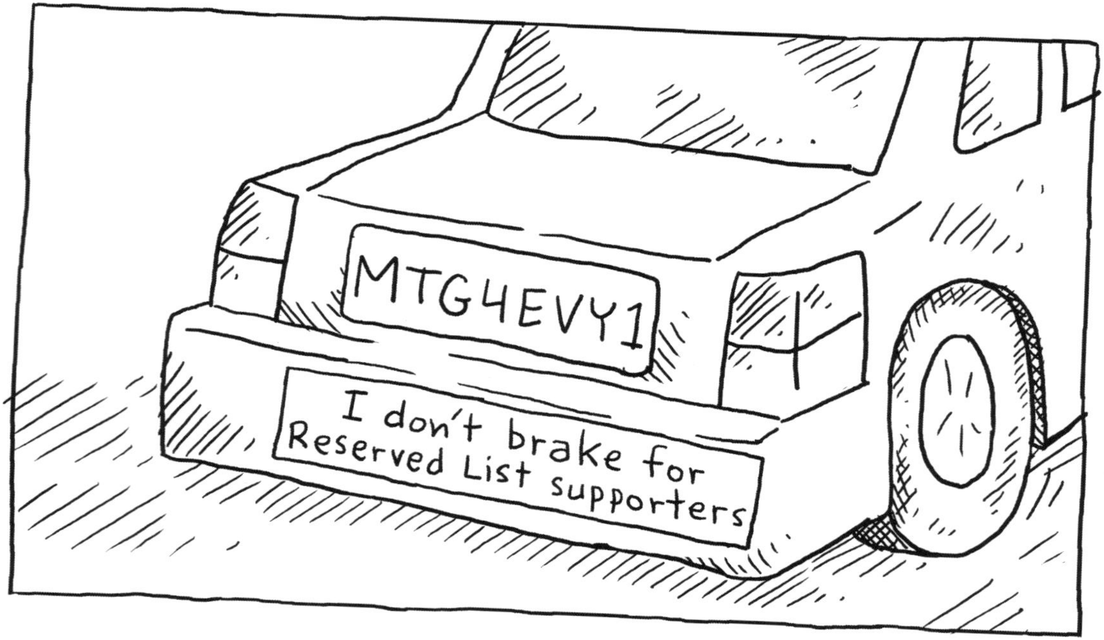
MTG4EVY1
I don't brake for Reserved List supporters

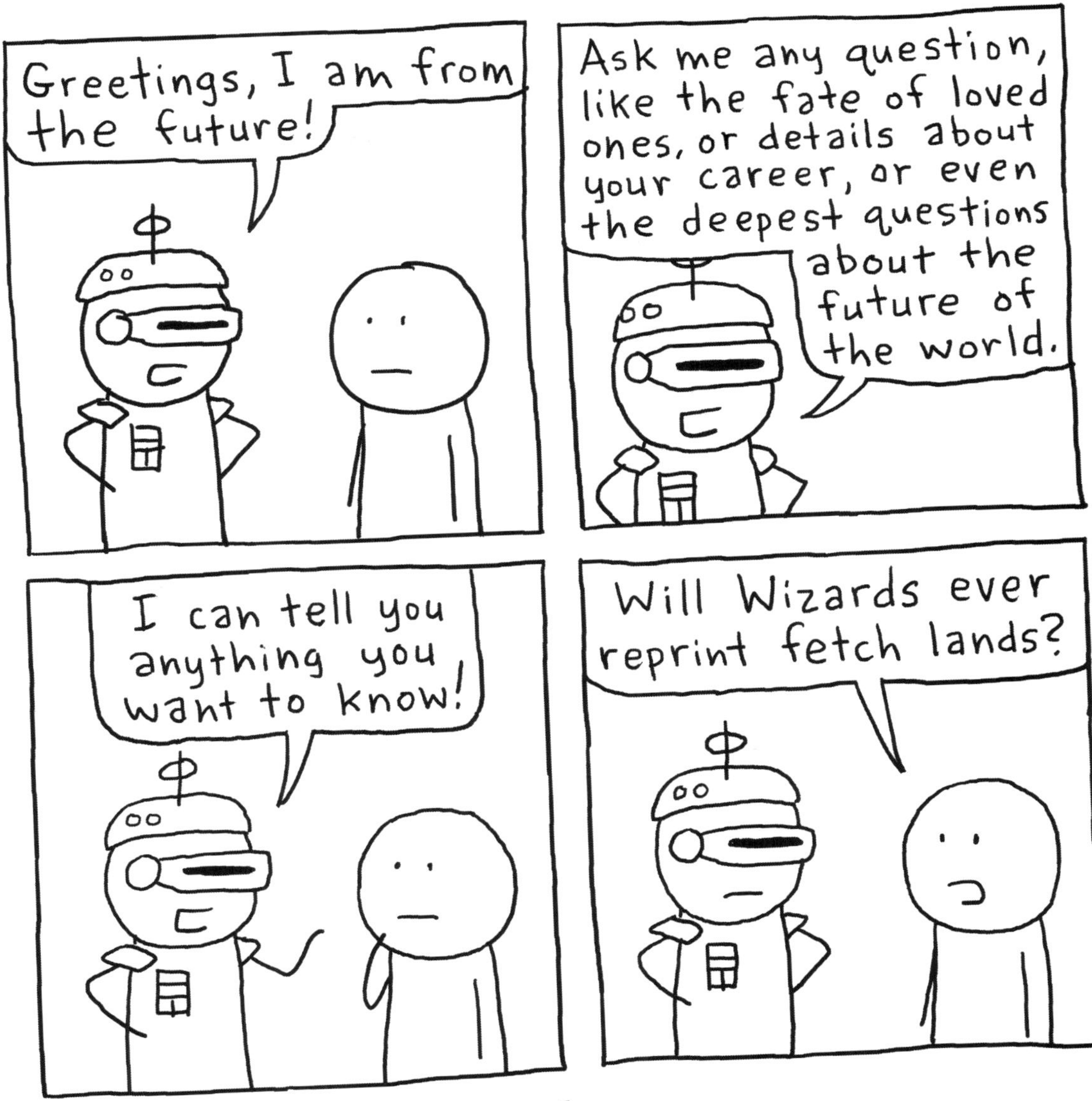
Greetings, I am from the future!
Ask me any question, like the fate of loved ones, or details about your career, or even the deepest questions about the future of the world.
I can tell you anything you want to know!
Will Wizards ever reprint fetch lands?

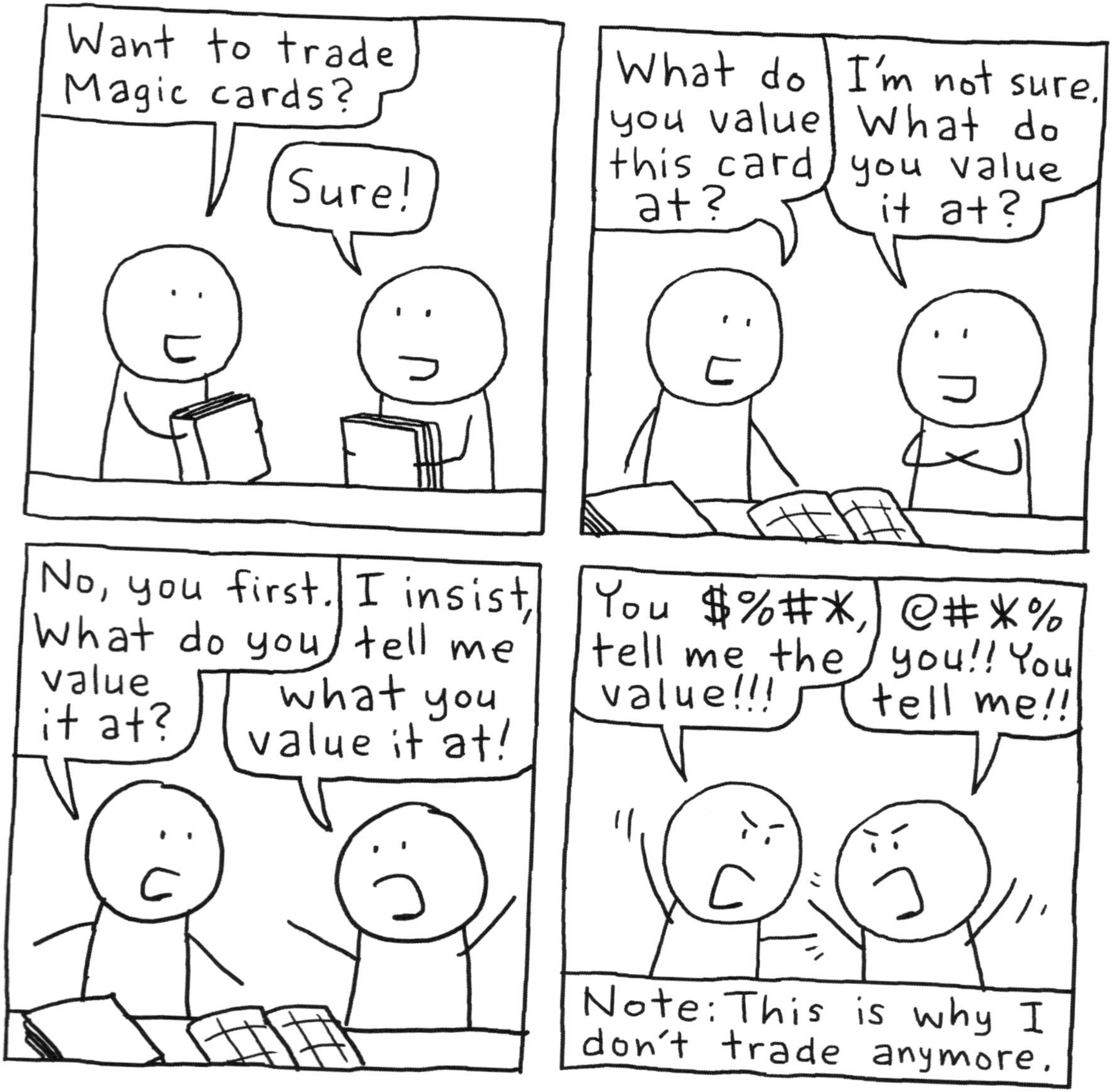
Want to trade Magic cards?
Sure!
What do you value this card at?
I'm not sure. What do you value it at?
No, you first. What do you value it at?
I insist, tell me what you value it at!
You $%#*, tell me the value!!!
@#*% you!! You tell me!!
Note: This is why I don't trade anymore.

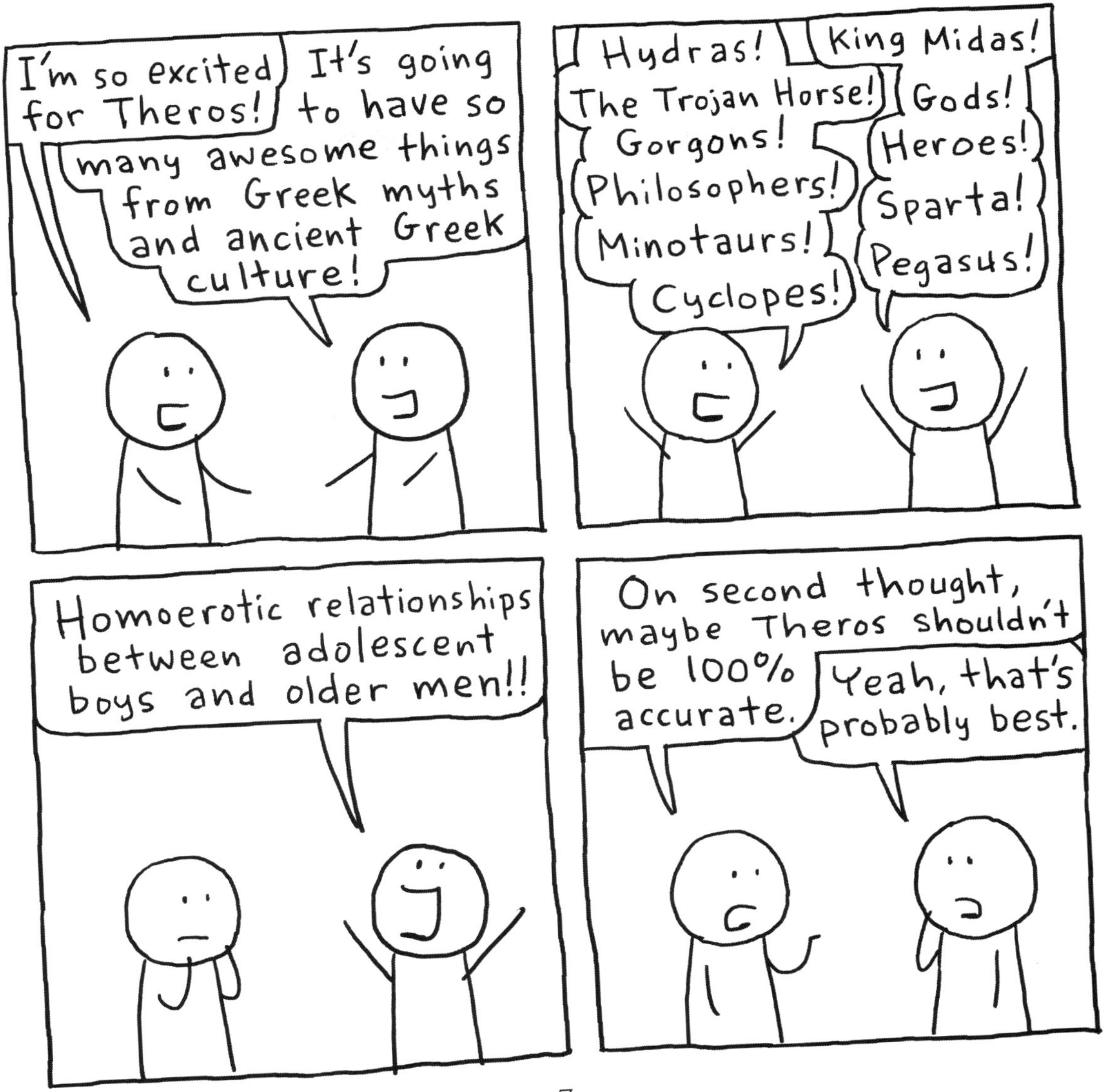
I'm so excited for Theros!
It's going to have so many awesome things from Greek myths and ancient Greek culture!
Hydras!
King Midas!
The Trojan Horse!
Gods!
Gorgons!
Heroes!
Philosophers!
Sparta!
Minotaurs!
Pegasus!
Cyclopes!
Homoerotic relationships between adolescent boys and older men!!
On second thought, maybe Theros shouldn't be 100% accurate.
Yeah, that's probably best.

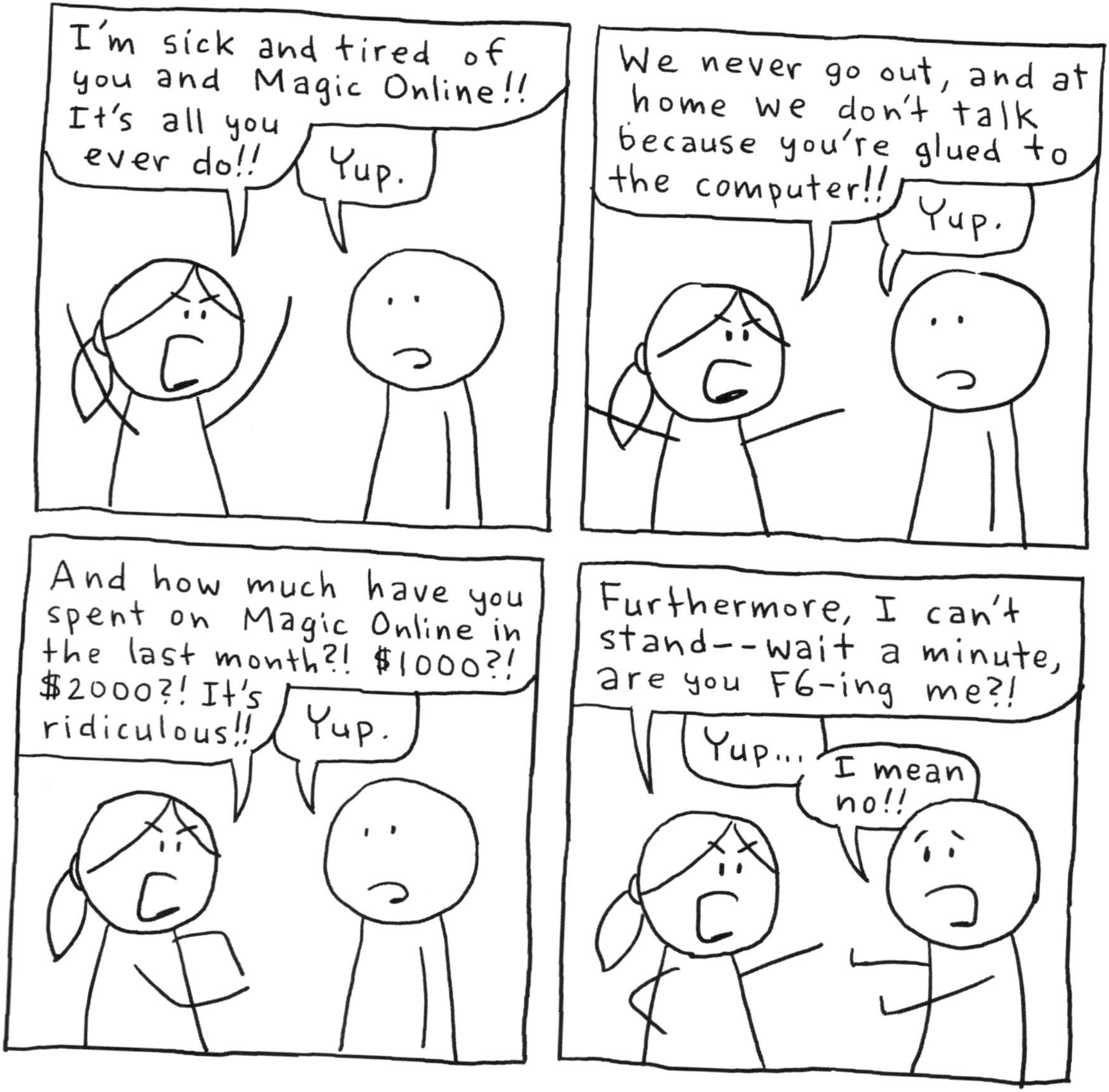
I'm sick and tired of you and Magic Online!! It's all you ever do!!
Yup.
We never go out, and at home we don't talk because you're glued to the computer!!
Yup.
And how much have you spent on Magic Online in the last month?! $1000?! $2000?! It's ridiculous!!
Yup.
Furthermore, I can't stand--wait a minute, are you F6-ing me?!
Yup...
I mean no!!

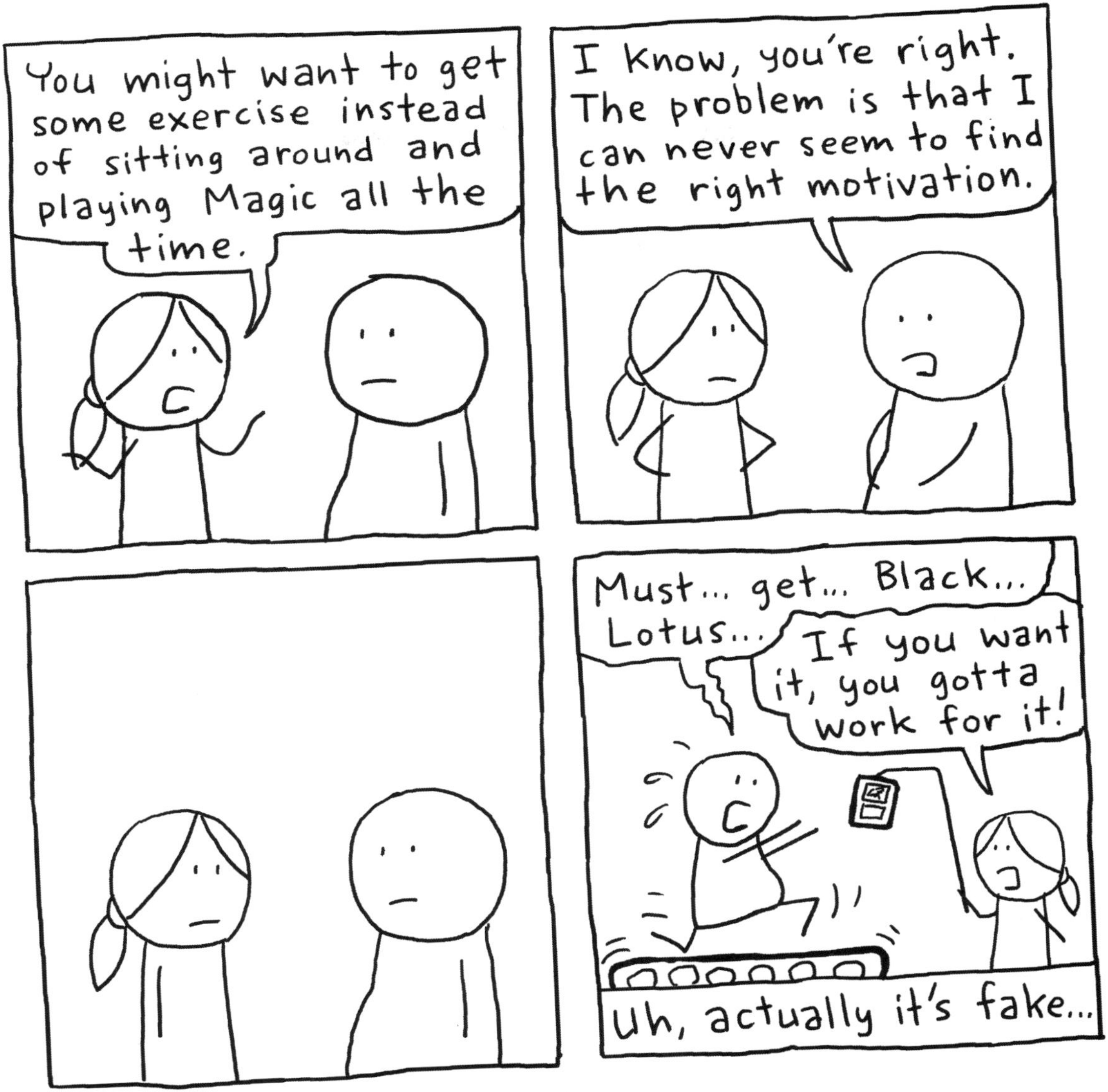
You might want to get some exercise instead of sitting around and playing Magic all the time.
I know, you're right. The problem is that I can never seem to find the right motivation.
Must... get... Black... Lotus...
If you want it, you gotta work for it!
Uh, actually it's fake...

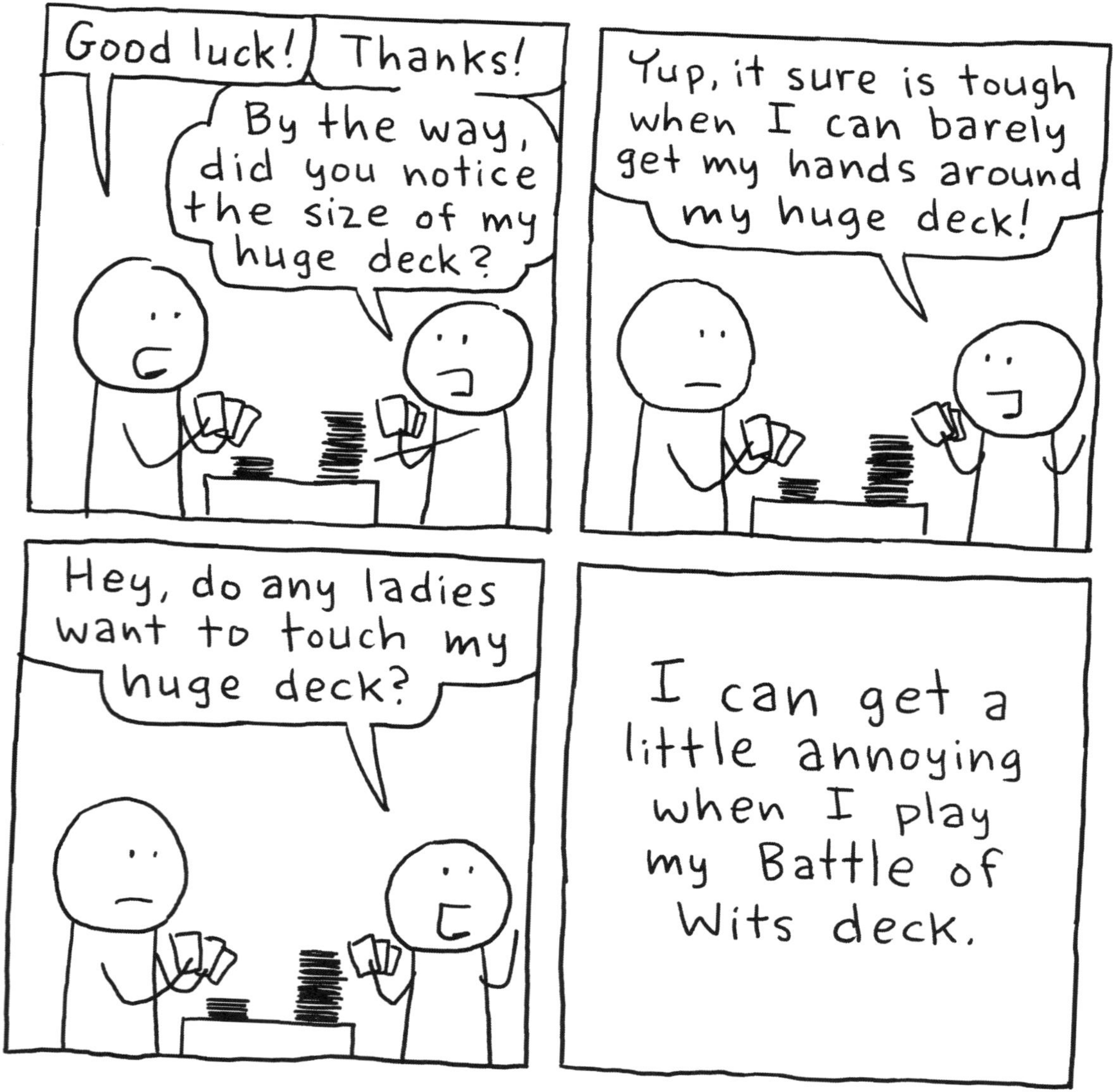
Good luck!
Thanks!
By the way, did you notice the size of my huge deck?
Yup, it sure is tough when I can barely get my hands around my huge deck!
Hey, do any ladies want to touch my huge deck?
I can get a little annoying when I play my Battle of Wits deck.

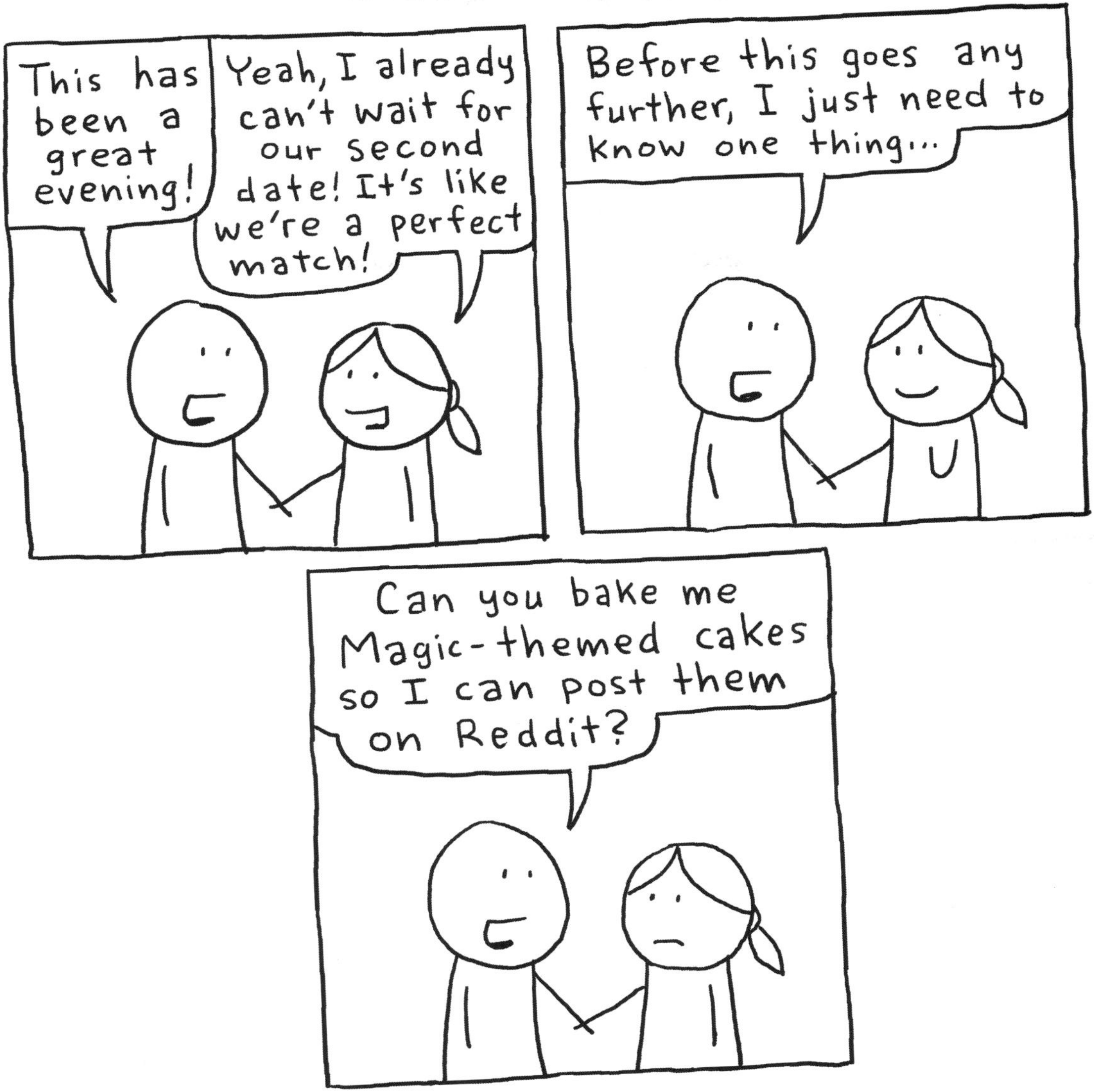
This has been a great evening!
Yeah, I already can't wait for our second date! It's like we're a perfect match!
Before this goes any further, I just need to know one thing...
Can you bake me Magic-themed cakes so I can post them on Reddit?

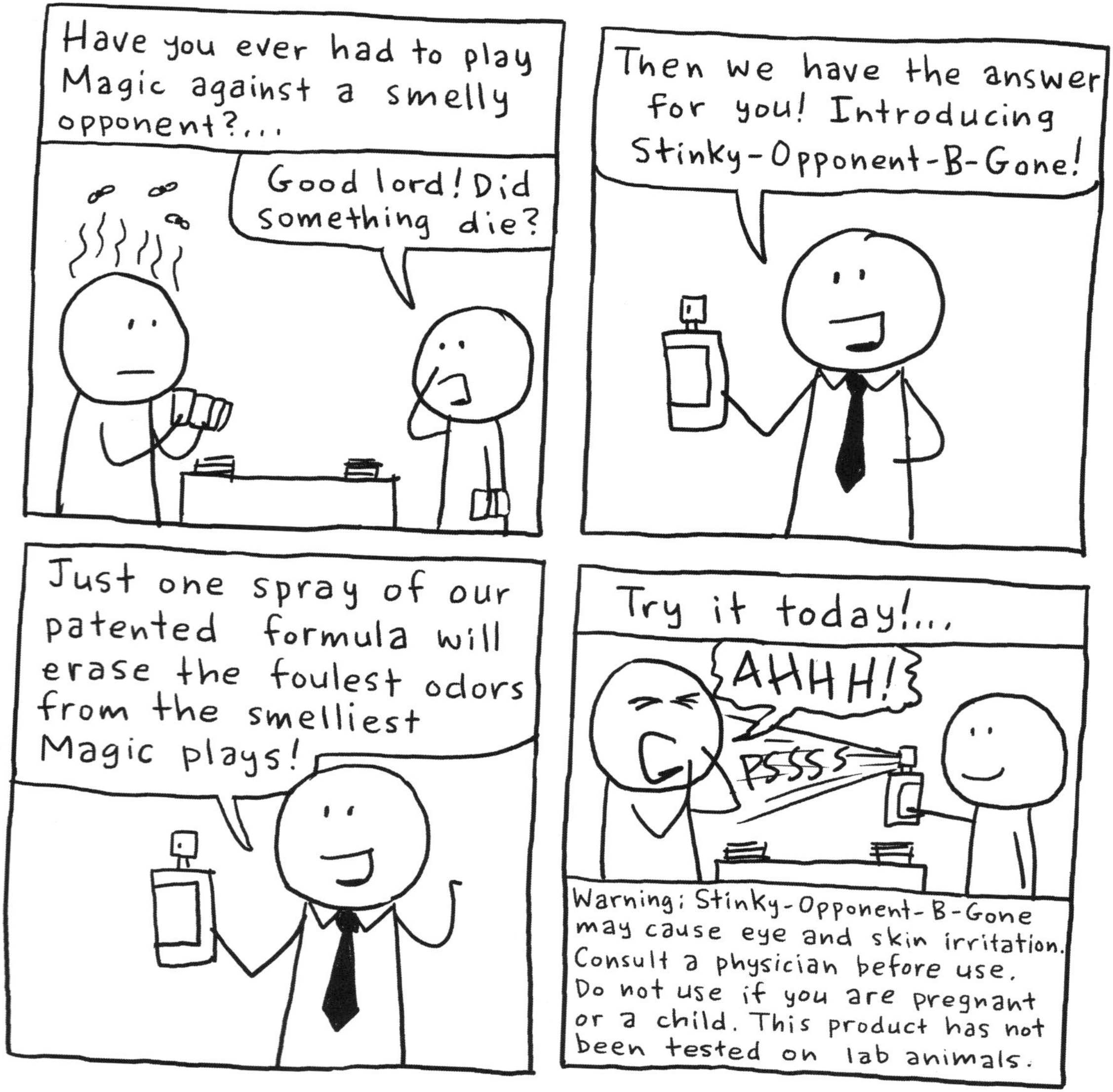
Have you ever had to play Magic against a smelly opponent?...
Good lord! Did something die?
Then we have the answer for you! Introducing Stinky-Opponent-B-Gone!
Just one spray of our patented formula will erase the foulest odors from the smelliest Magic plays!
Try it today!...
AHHH!
PSSSS
Warning: Stinky-Opponent-B-Gone may cause eye and skin irritation. Consult a physician before use. Do not use if you are pregnant or a child. This product has not been tested on lab animals.

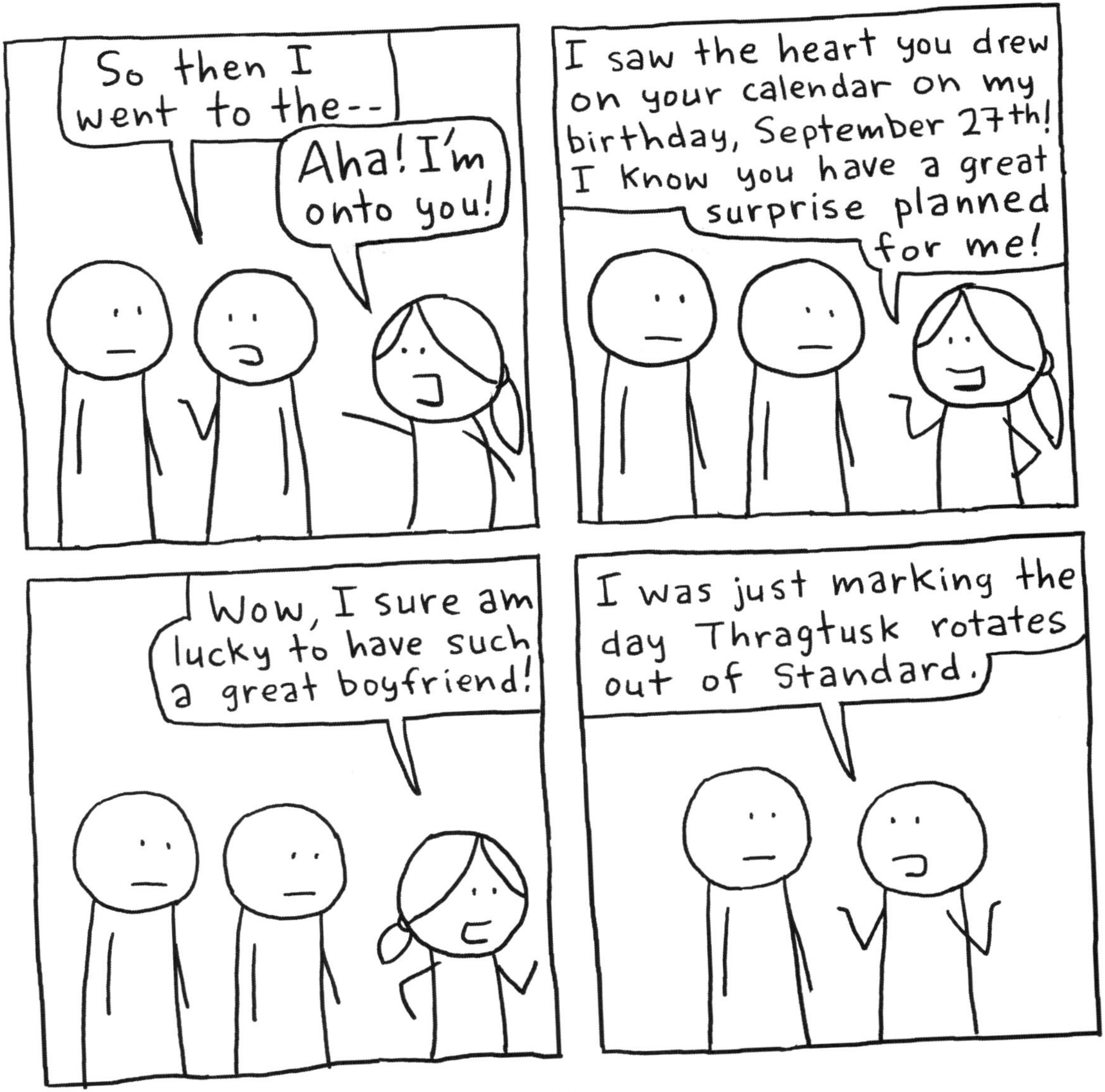
So then I went to the--
Aha! I'm onto you!
I saw the heart you drew on your calendar on my birthday, September 27th! I know you have a great surprise planned for me!
Wow, I sure am lucky to have such a great boyfriend!
I was just marking the day Thragtusk rotates out of Standard.

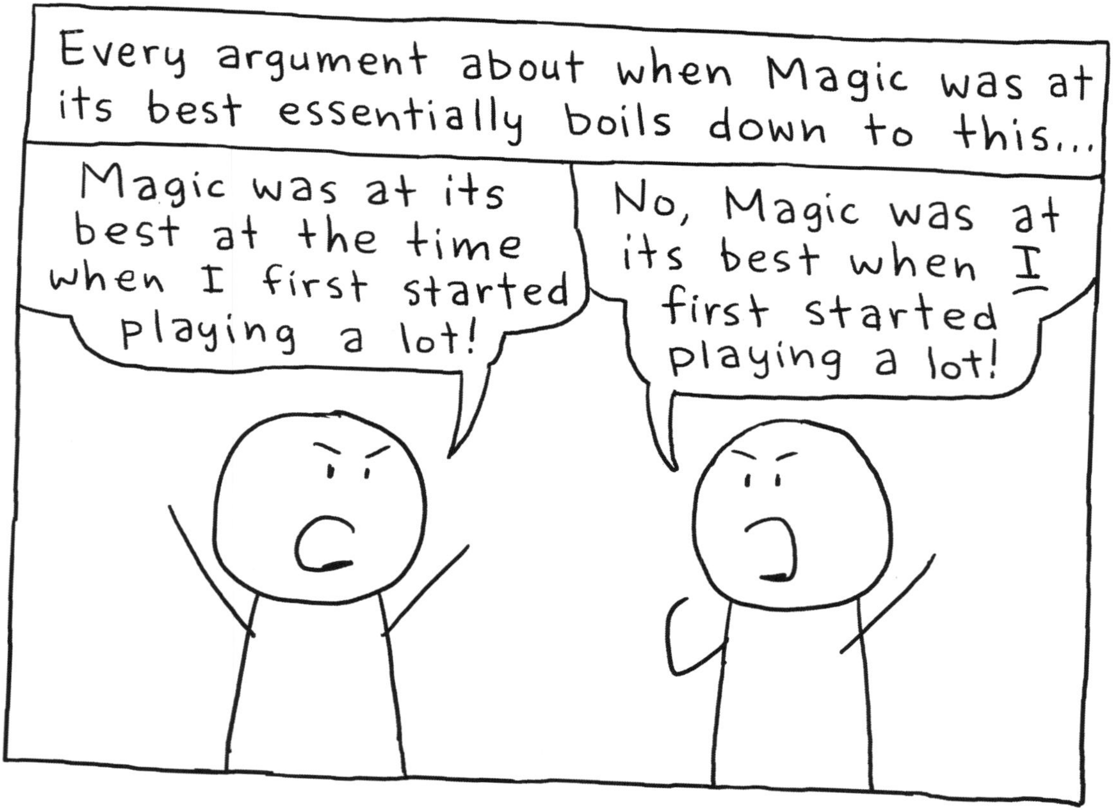
Every argument about when Magic was at its best essentially boils down to this...
Magic was at its best at the time when I first started playing a lot!
No, Magic was at its best when I first started playing a lot!

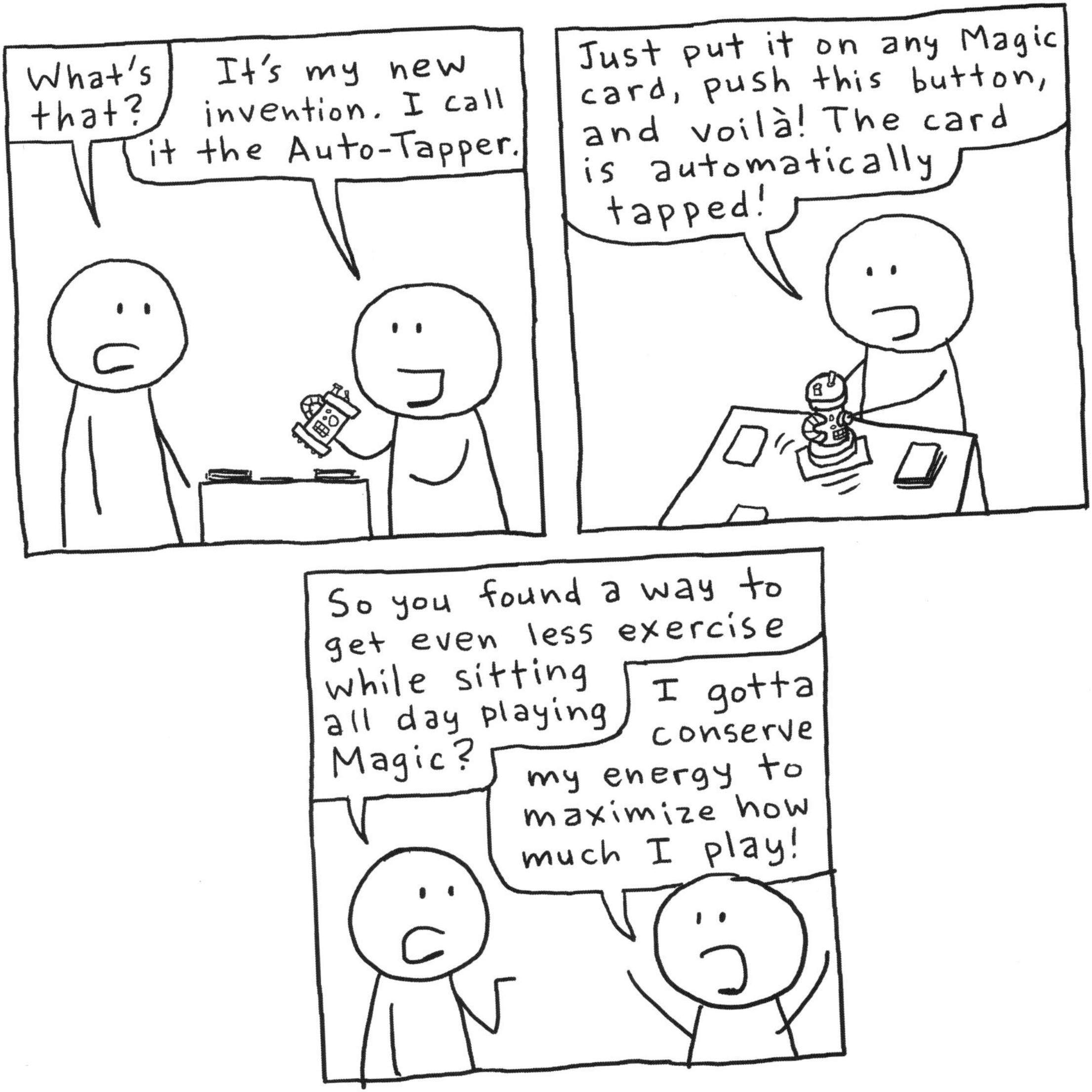
What's that?
It's my new invention. I call it the Auto-Tapper.
Just put it on any Magic card, push this button, and voilà! The card is automatically tapped!
So you found a way to get even less exercise while sitting all day playing Magic?
I gotta conserve my energy to maximize how much I play!

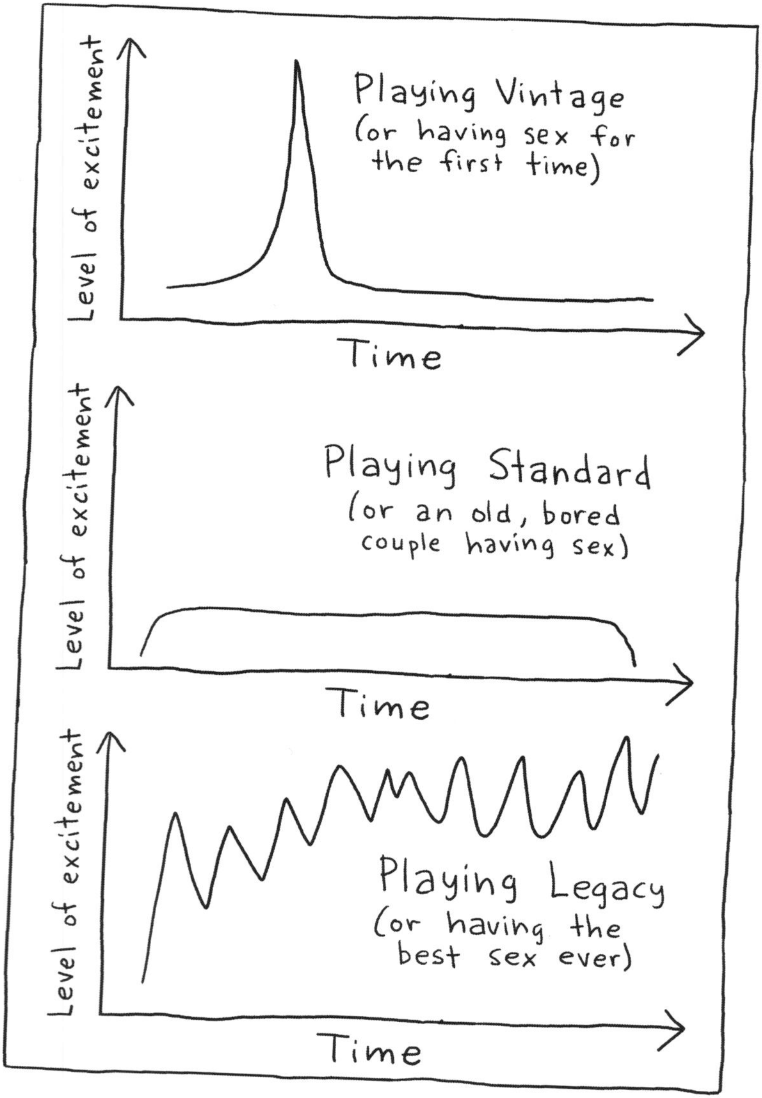

Level of excitement
Playing Vintage
(or having sex for the first time)
Time
Level of excitement
Playing Standard
(or an old, bored couple having sex)
Time
Level of excitement
Playing Legacy
(or having the best sex ever)
Time

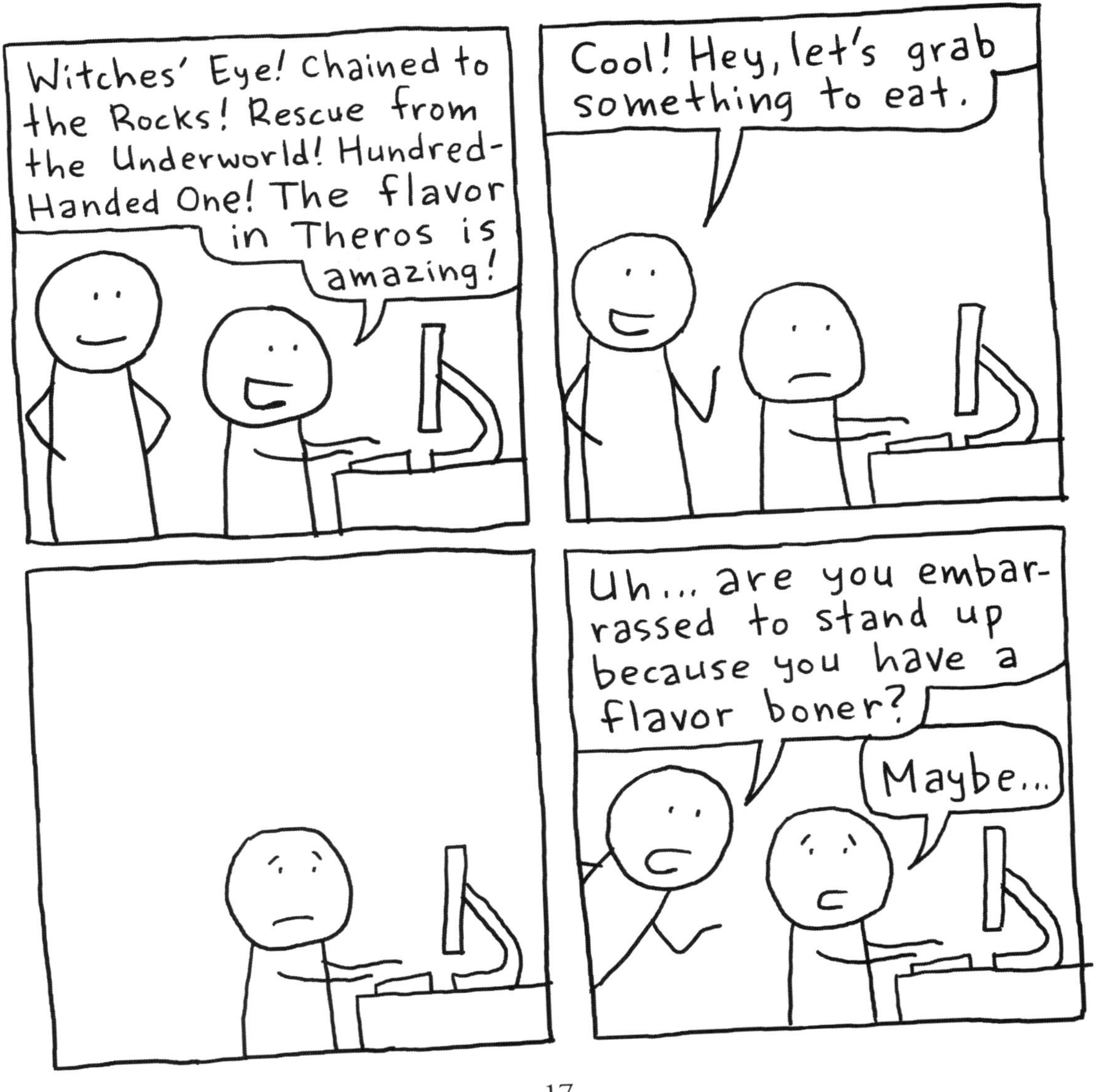
Witches' Eye! Chained to the Rocks! Rescue from the Underworld! Hundred-Handed One! The flavor in Theros is amazing!
Cool! Hey, let's grab something to eat.
Uh... are you embarrassed to stand up because you have a flavor boner?
Maybe...

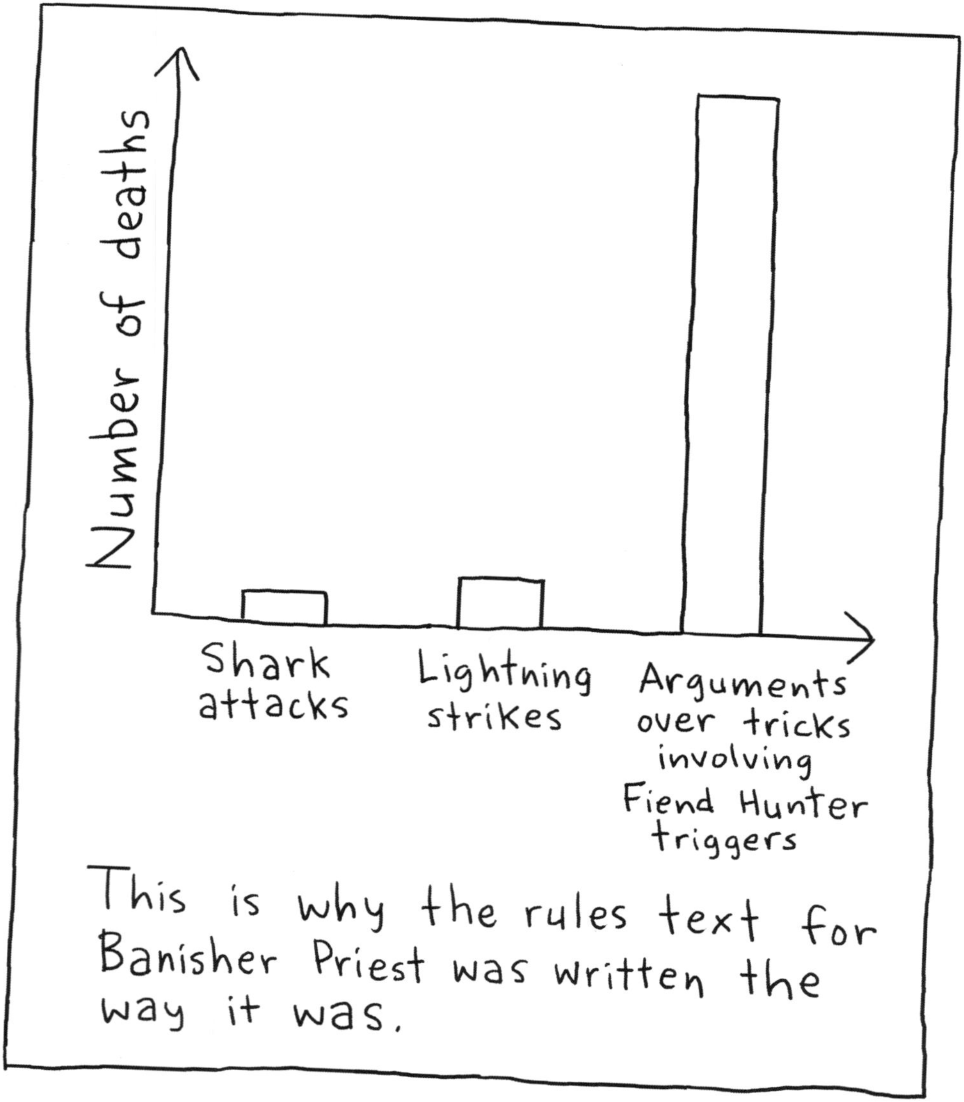
Number of deaths
Shark attacks
Lightning strikes
Arguments over tricks involving Fiend Hunter triggers
This is why the rules text for Banisher Priest was written the way it was.

Top 5 things that will be overheard when playing "Curse of the Swine"...

⑤ "You played an indestructible god? I'll pigify it!"

④ "Dreadboar your team!"

③ "Rapid baconization!"

② "Why are you complaining? Look how cute your creatures are now!"

① "Sorry I exiled your army. Here's some bacon."

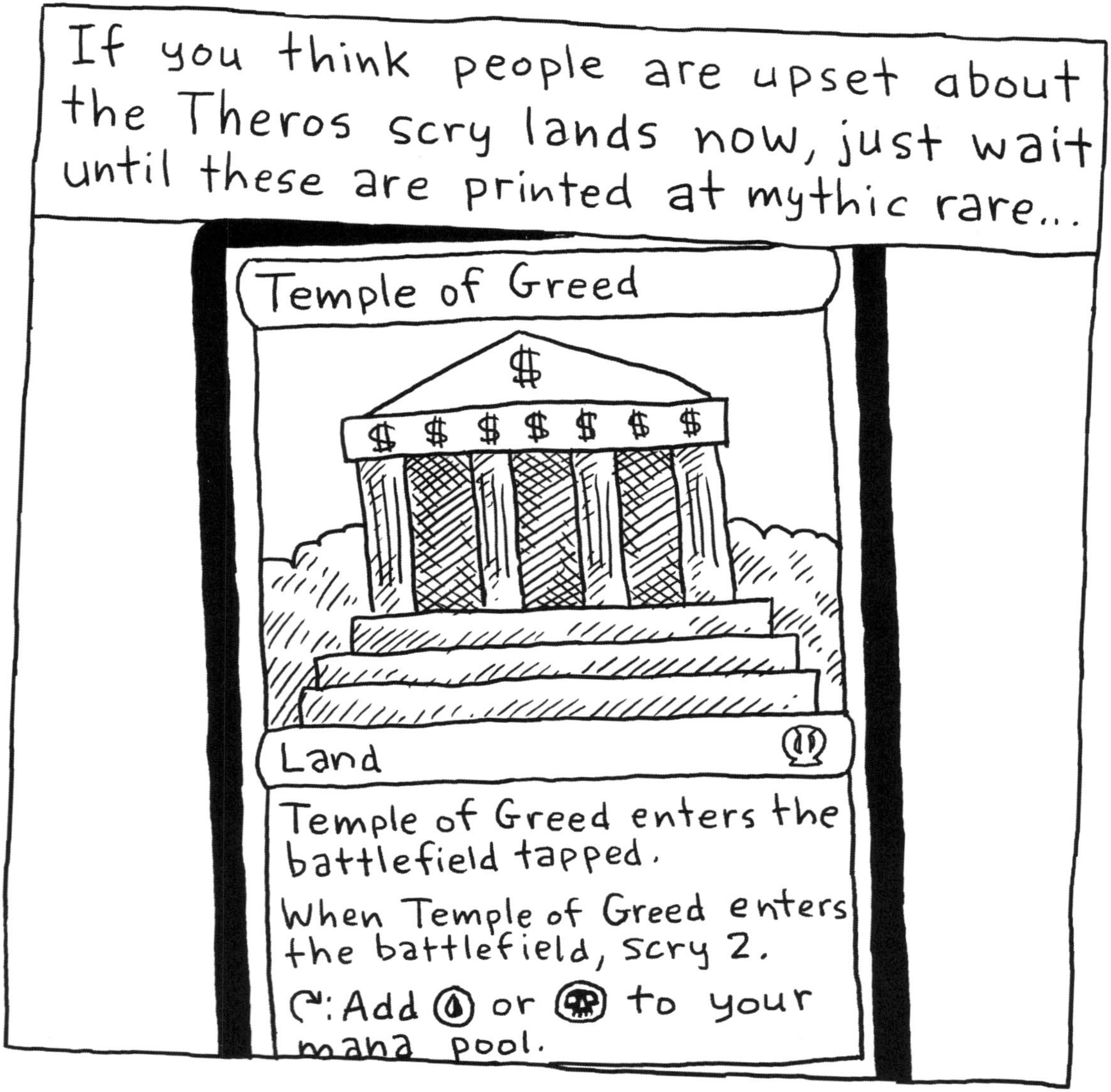
If you think people are upset about the Theros scry lands now, just wait until these are printed at mythic rare...
Temple of Greed
$
$ $ $ $ $ $ $
Land
Temple of Greed enters the battlefield tapped.
When Temple of Greed enters the battlefield, scry 2.
: Add or to your mana pool.

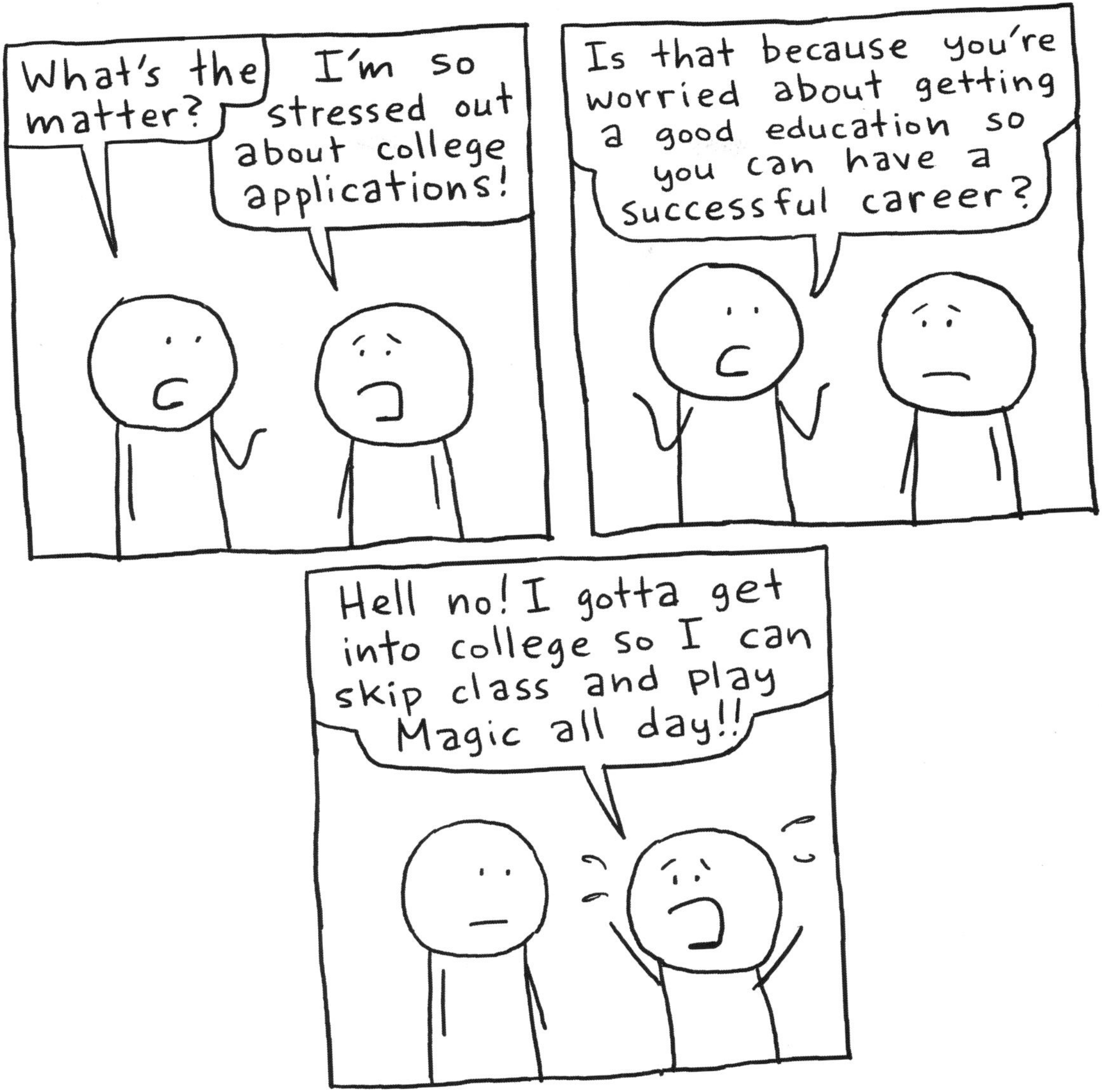
What's the matter?
I'm so stressed out about college applications!
Is that because you're worried about getting a good education so you can have a successful career?
Hell no! I gotta get into college so I can skip class and play Magic all day!!

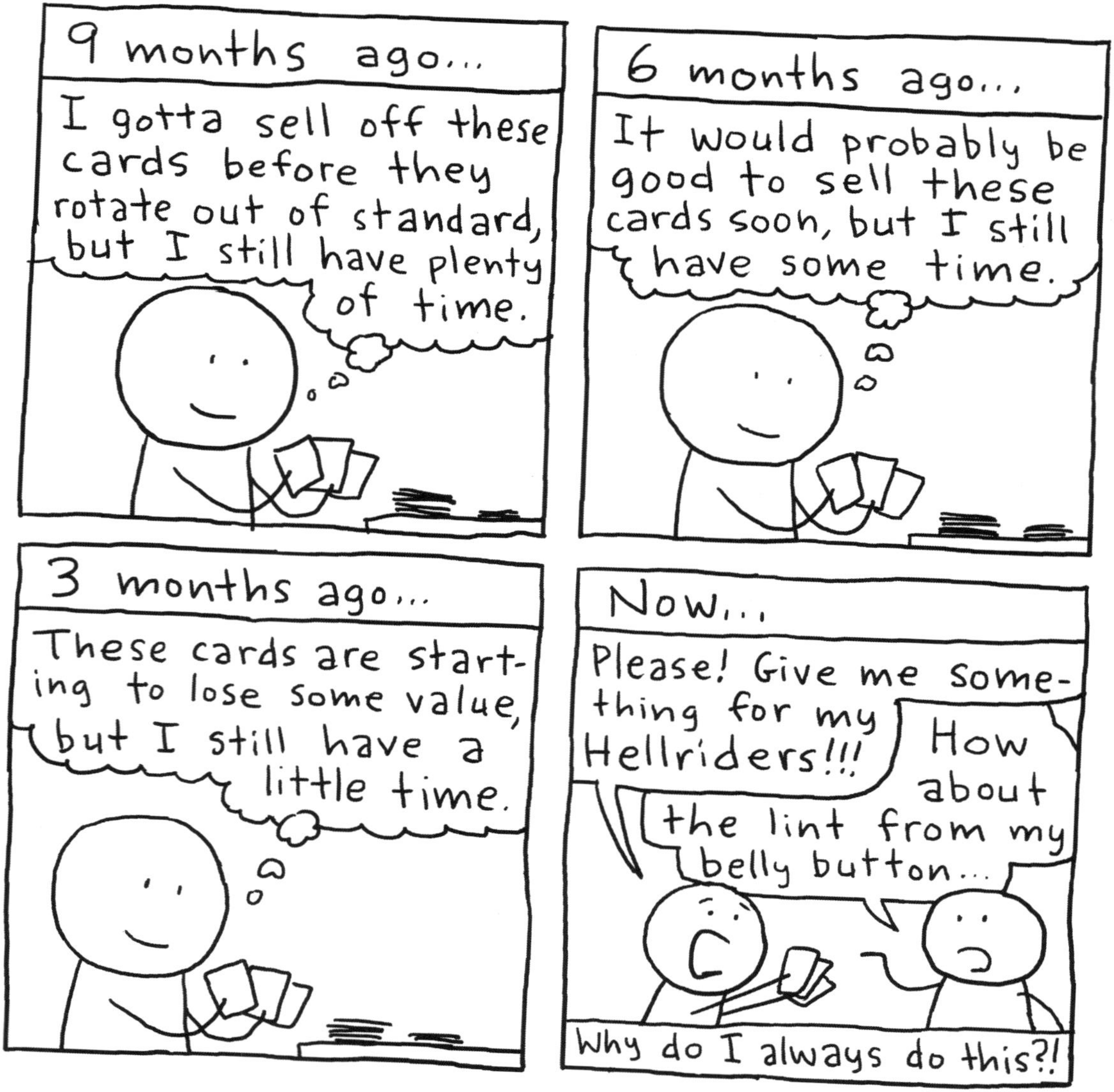
9 months ago...
I gotta sell off these cards before they rotate out of standard, but I still have plenty of time.
6 months ago...
It would probably be good to sell these cards soon, but I still have some time.
3 months ago...
These cards are starting to lose some value, but I still have a little time.
Now...
Please! Give me something for my Hellriders!!!
How about the lint from my belly button...
Why do I always do this?!

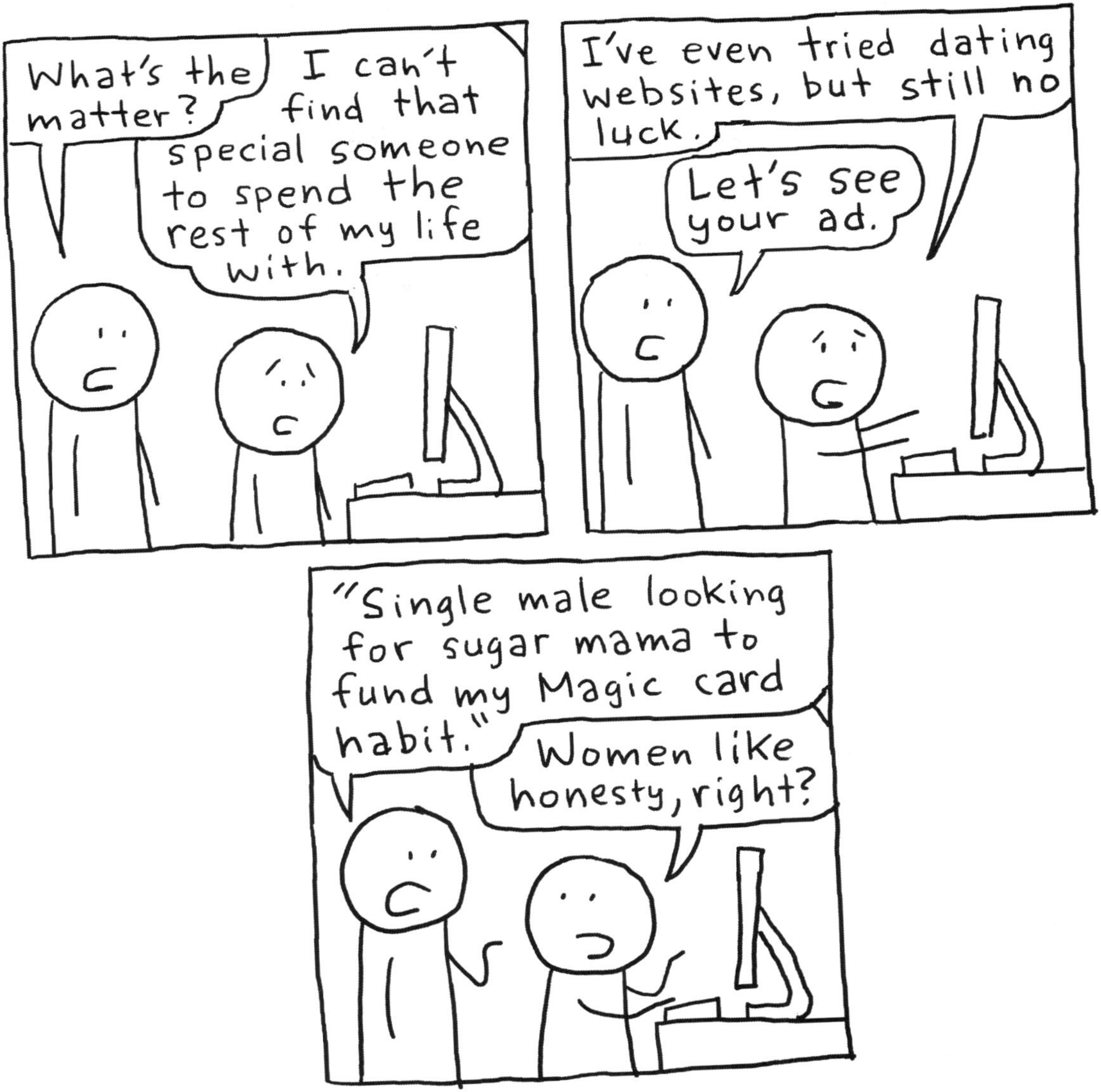
What's the matter?
I can't find that special someone to spend the rest of my life with.
I've even tried dating websites, but still no luck.
Let's see your ad.
"Single male looking for sugar mama to fund my Magic card habit."
Women like honesty, right?

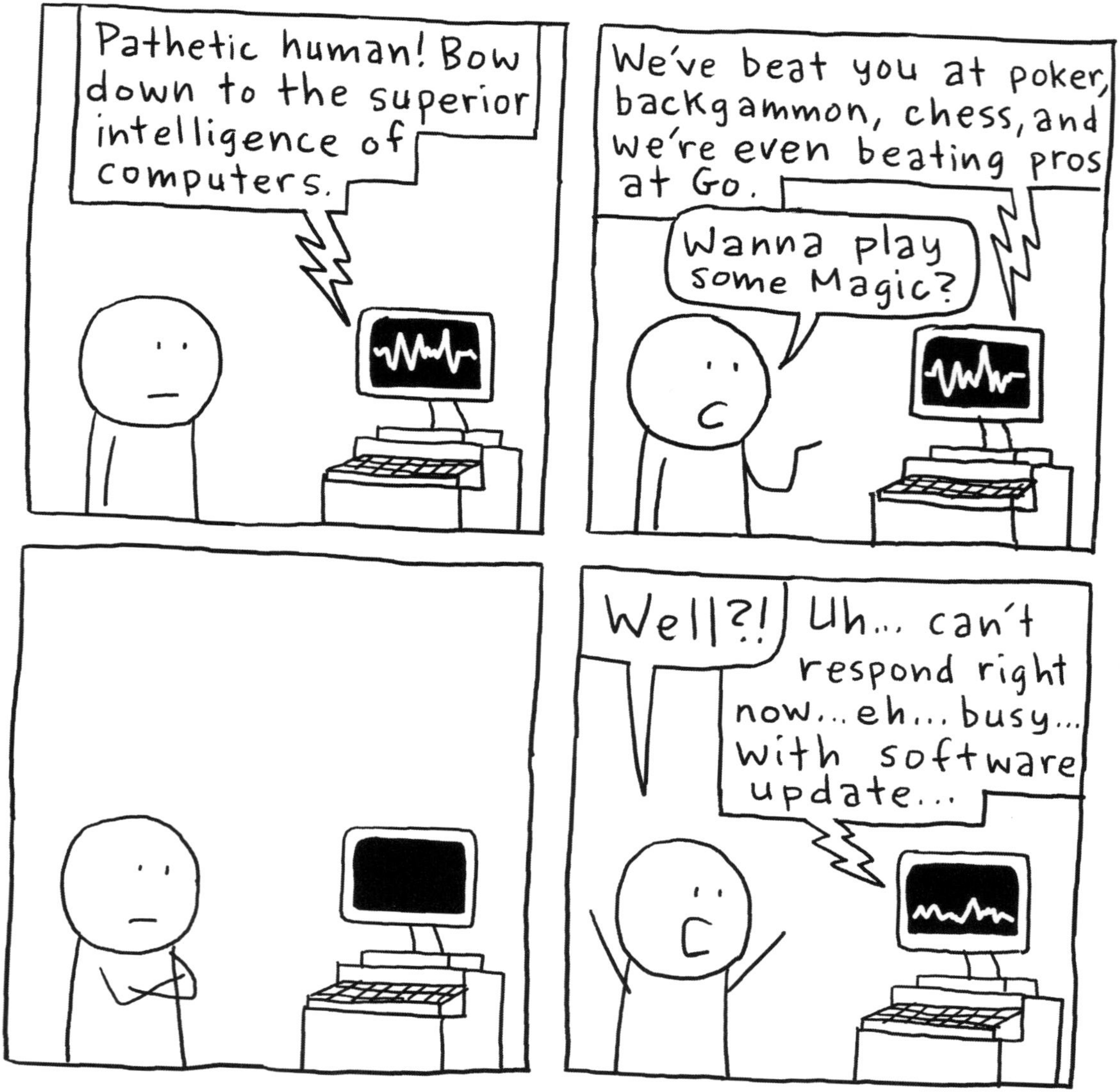
Pathetic human! Bow down to the superior intelligence of computers.
We've beat you at poker, backgammon, chess, and we're even beating pros at Go.
Wanna play some Magic?
Well?!
Uh... can't respond right now... eh... busy... with software update...

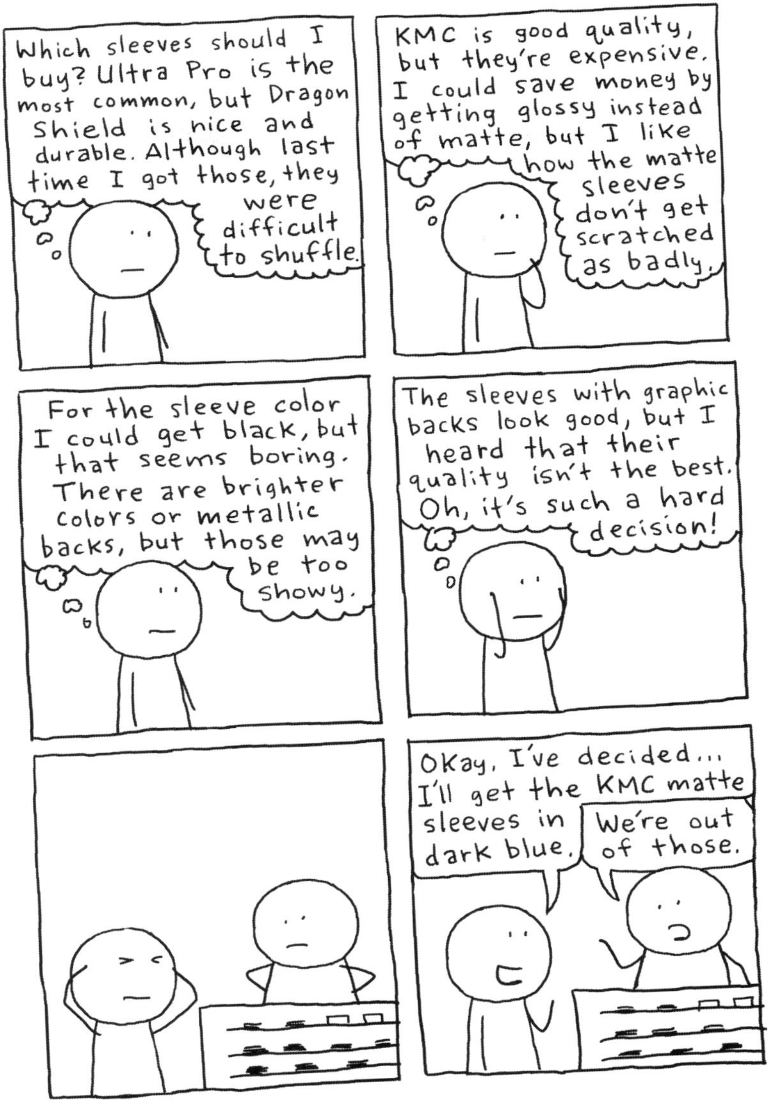
Which sleeves should I buy? Ultra Pro is the most common, but Dragon Shield is nice and durable. Although last time I got those, they were difficult to shuffle.
KMC is good quality, but they're expensive. I could save money by getting glossy instead of matte, but I like how the matte sleeves don't get scratched as badly.
For the sleeve color I could get black, but that seems boring. There are brighter colors or metallic backs, but those may be too showy.
The sleeves with graphic backs look good, but I heard that their quality isn't the best. Oh, it's such a hard decision!
Okay, I've decided... I'll get the KMC matte sleeves in dark blue.
We're out of those.

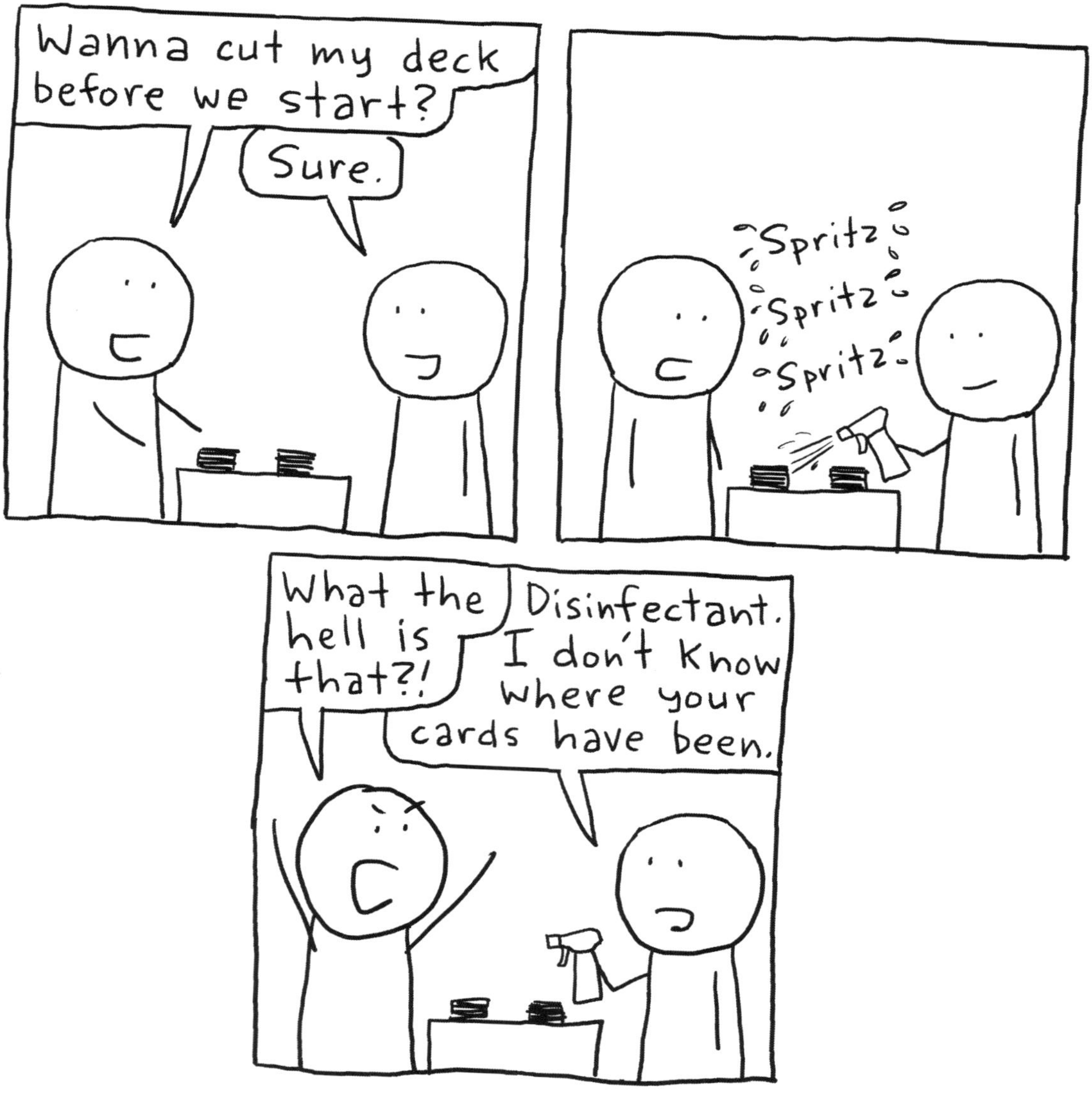
Wanna cut my deck before we start?
Sure.
Spritz
Spritz
Spritz
What the hell is that?!
Disinfectant. I don't know where your cards have been.

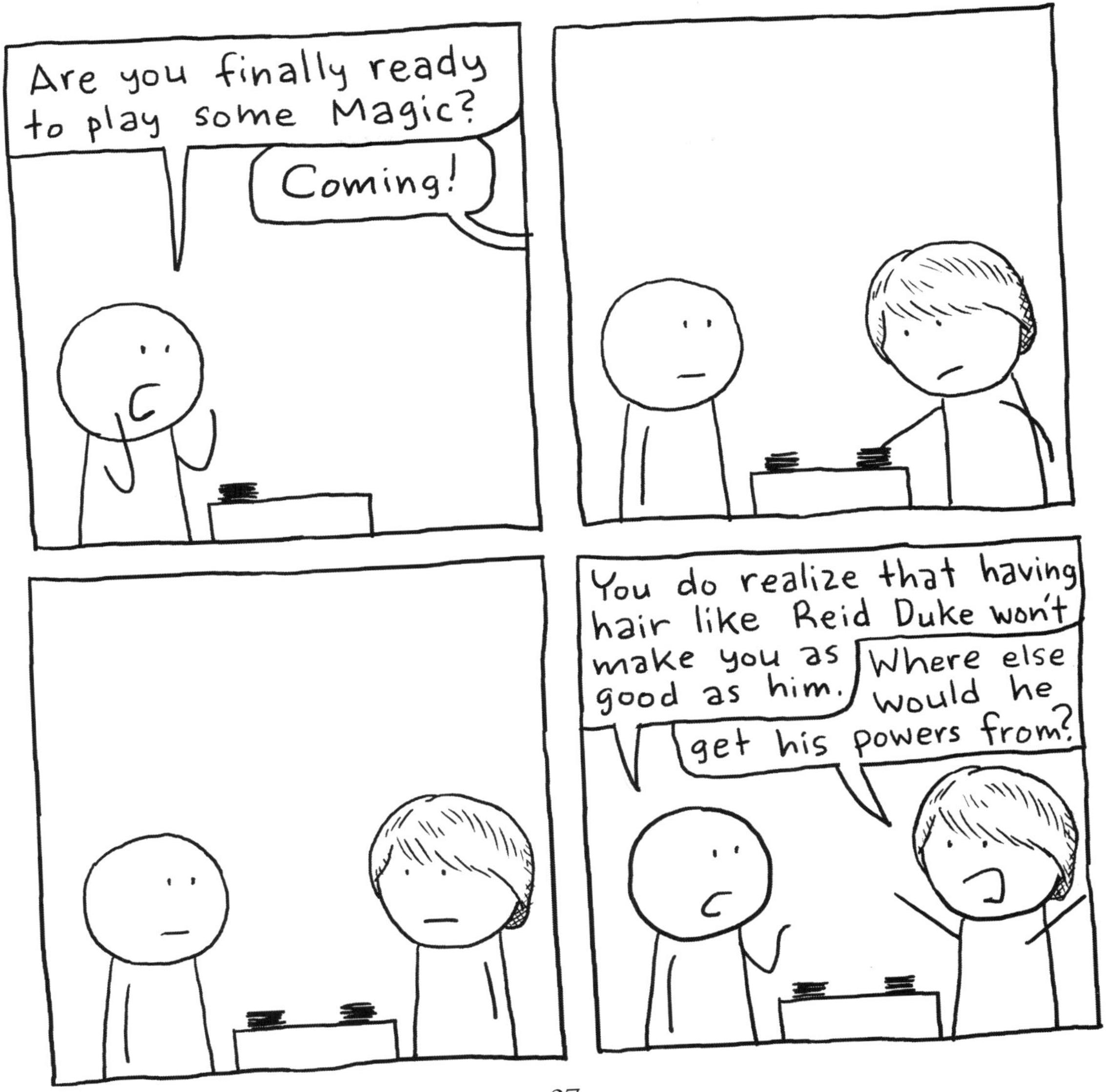
Are you finally ready to play some Magic?
Coming!
You do realize that having hair like Reid Duke won't make you as good as him.
Where else would he get his powers from?

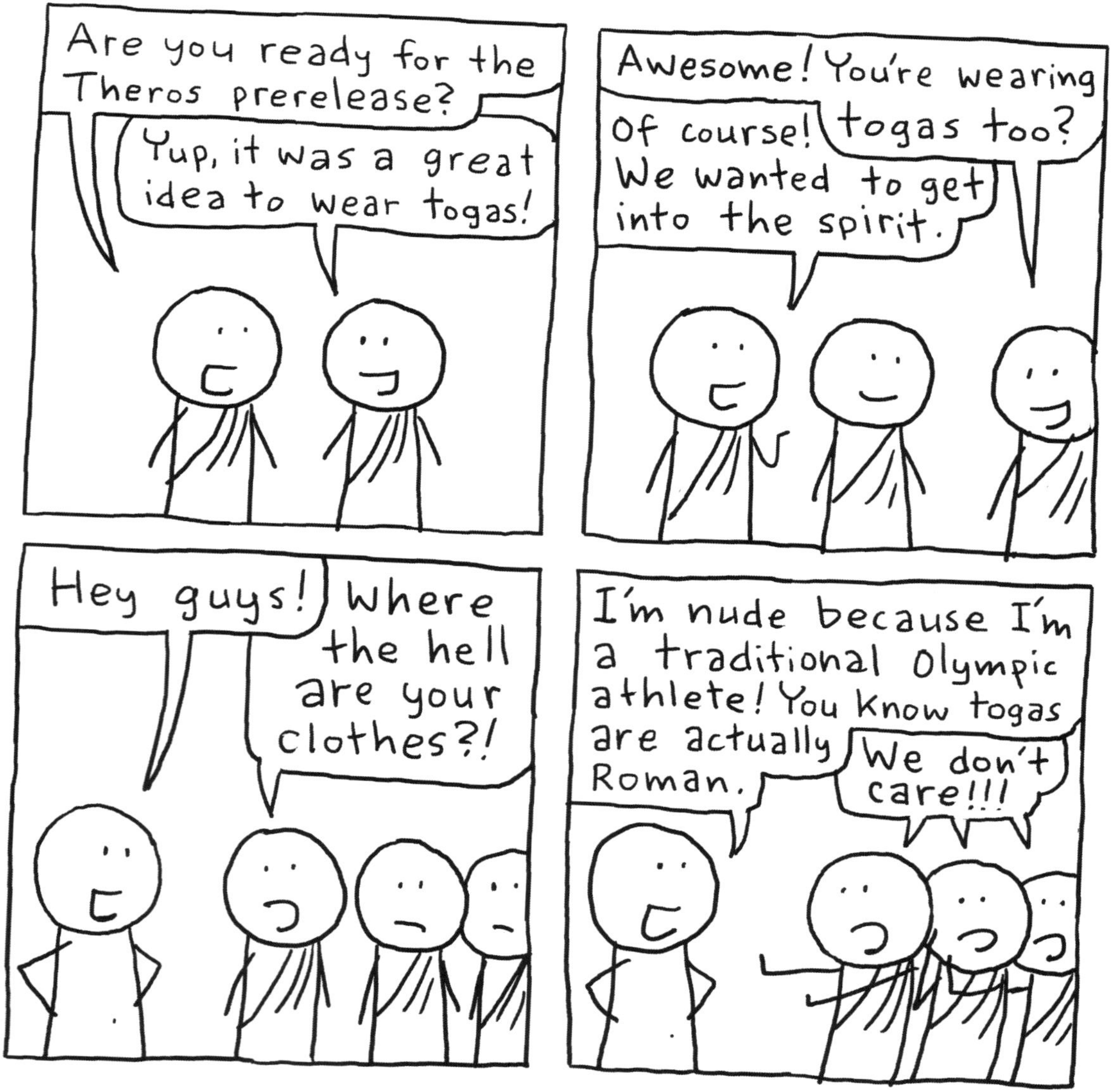
Are you ready for the Theros prerelease?
Yup, it was a great idea to wear togas!
Awesome! You're wearing togas too?
Of course! We wanted to get into the spirit.
Hey guys!
Where the hell are your clothes?!
I'm nude because I'm a traditional Olympic athlete! You know togas are actually Roman.
We don't care!!!

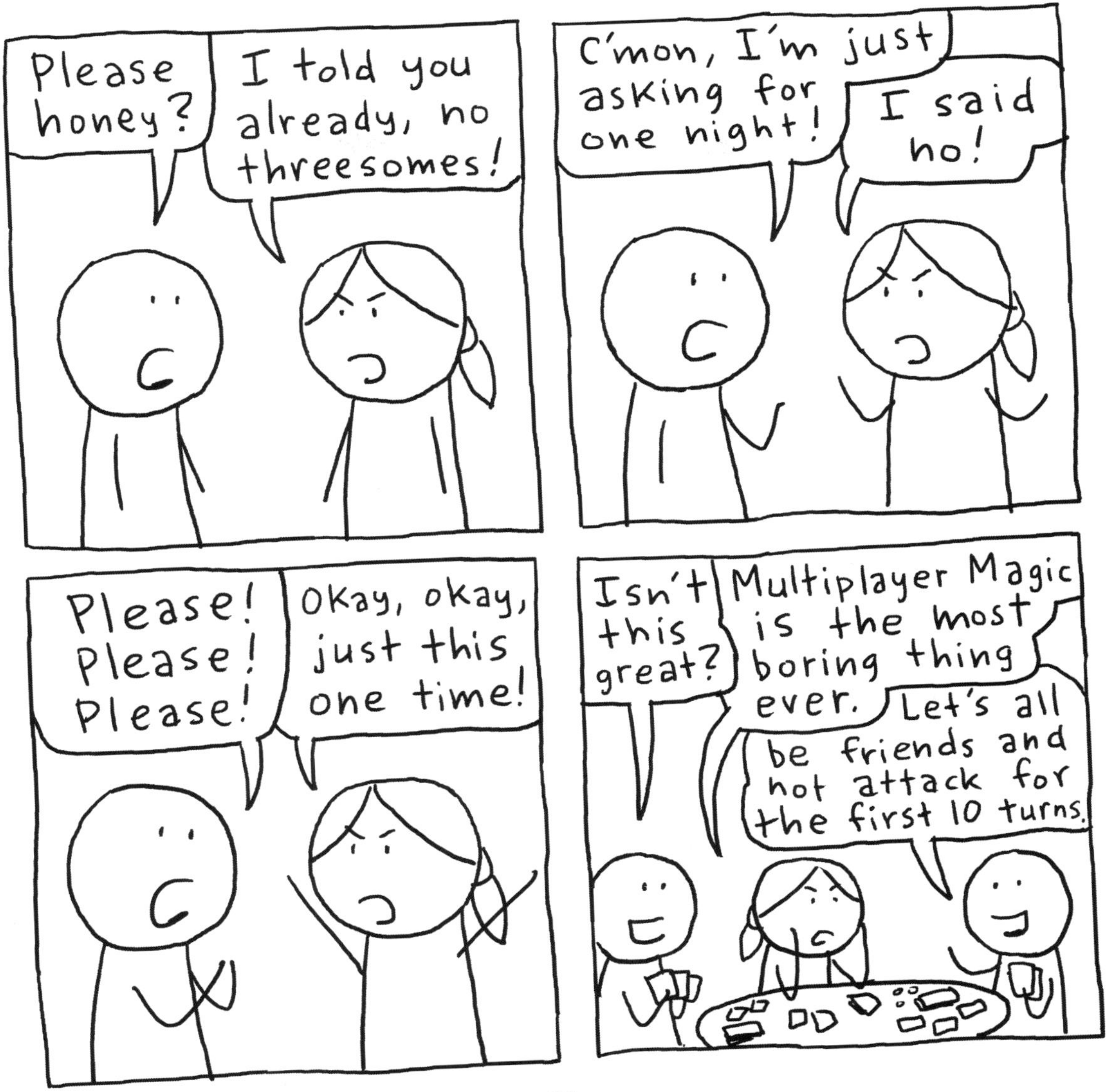
Please honey?
I told you already, no threesomes!
C'mon, I'm just asking for one night!
I said no!
Please! Please! Please!
Okay, okay, just this one time!
Isn't this great?
Multiplayer Magic is the most boring thing ever.
Let's all be friends and not attack for the first 10 turns.

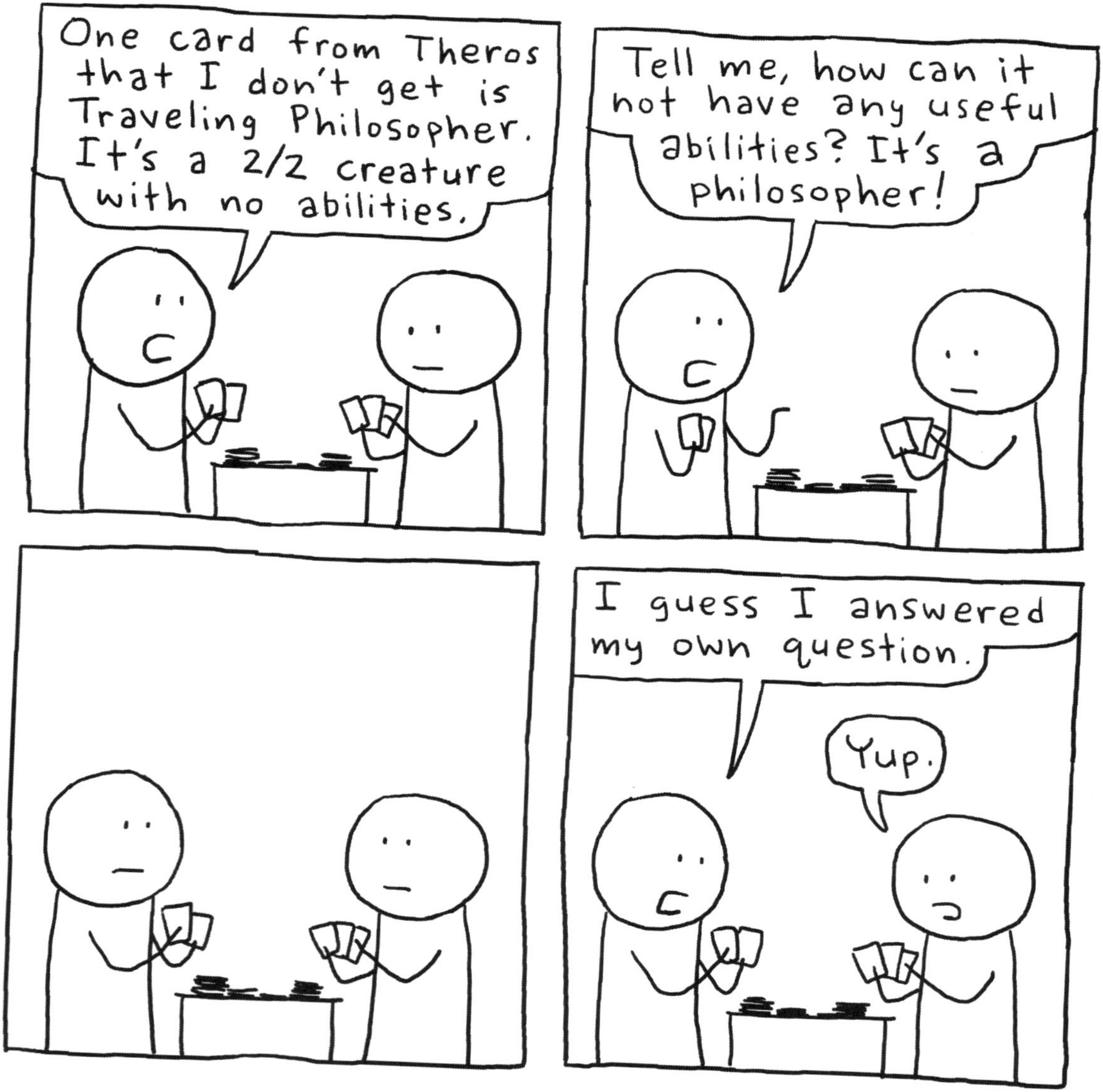
One card from Theros that I don't get is Traveling Philosopher. It's a 2/2 creature with no abilities.
Tell me, how can it not have any useful abilities? It's a philosopher!
I guess I answered my own question.
Yup.

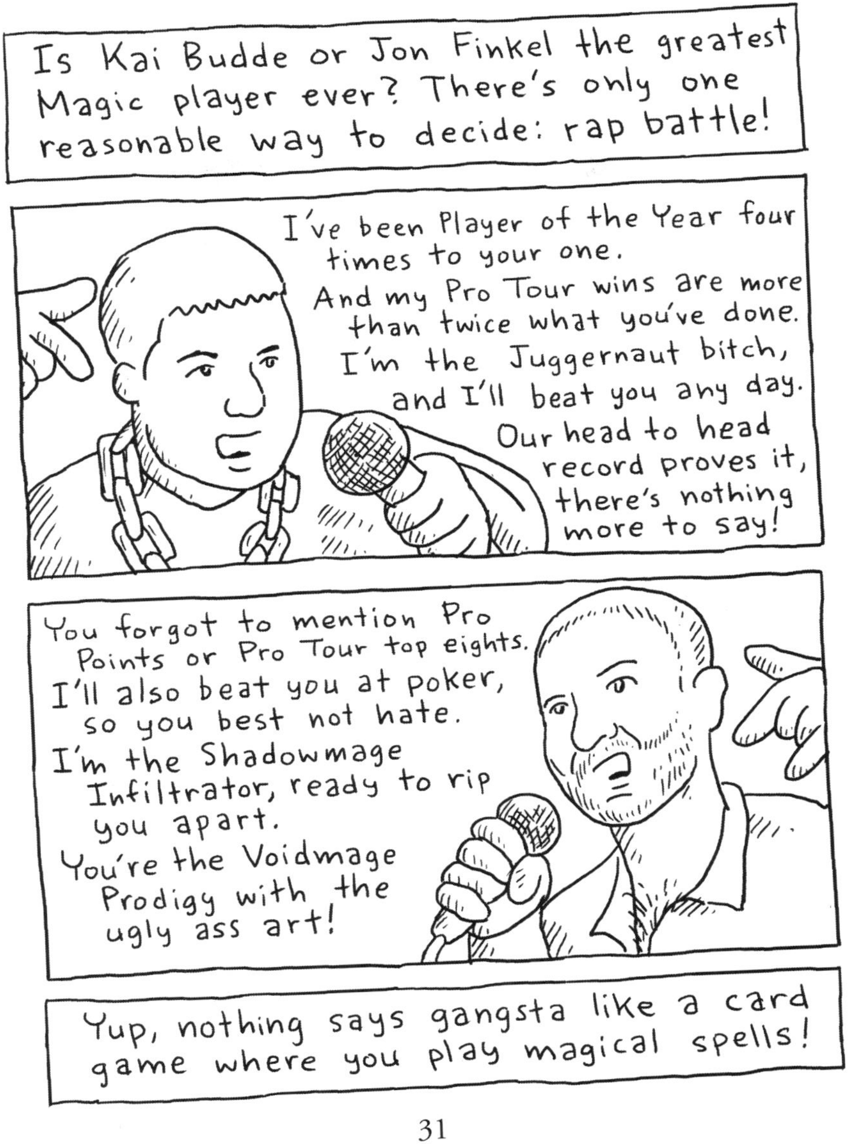
Is Kai Budde or Jon Finkel the greatest Magic player ever? There's only one reasonable way to decide: rap battle!
I've been Player of the Year four times to your one.
And my Pro Tour wins are more than twice what you've done.
I'm the Juggernaut bitch, and I'll beat you any day.
Our head to head record proves it, there's nothing more to say!
You forgot to mention Pro Points or Pro Tour top eights.
I'll also beat you at poker, so you best not hate.
I'm the Shadowmage Infiltrator, ready to rip you apart.
You're the Voidmage Prodigy with the ugly ass art!
Yup, nothing says gangsta like a card game where you play magical spells!

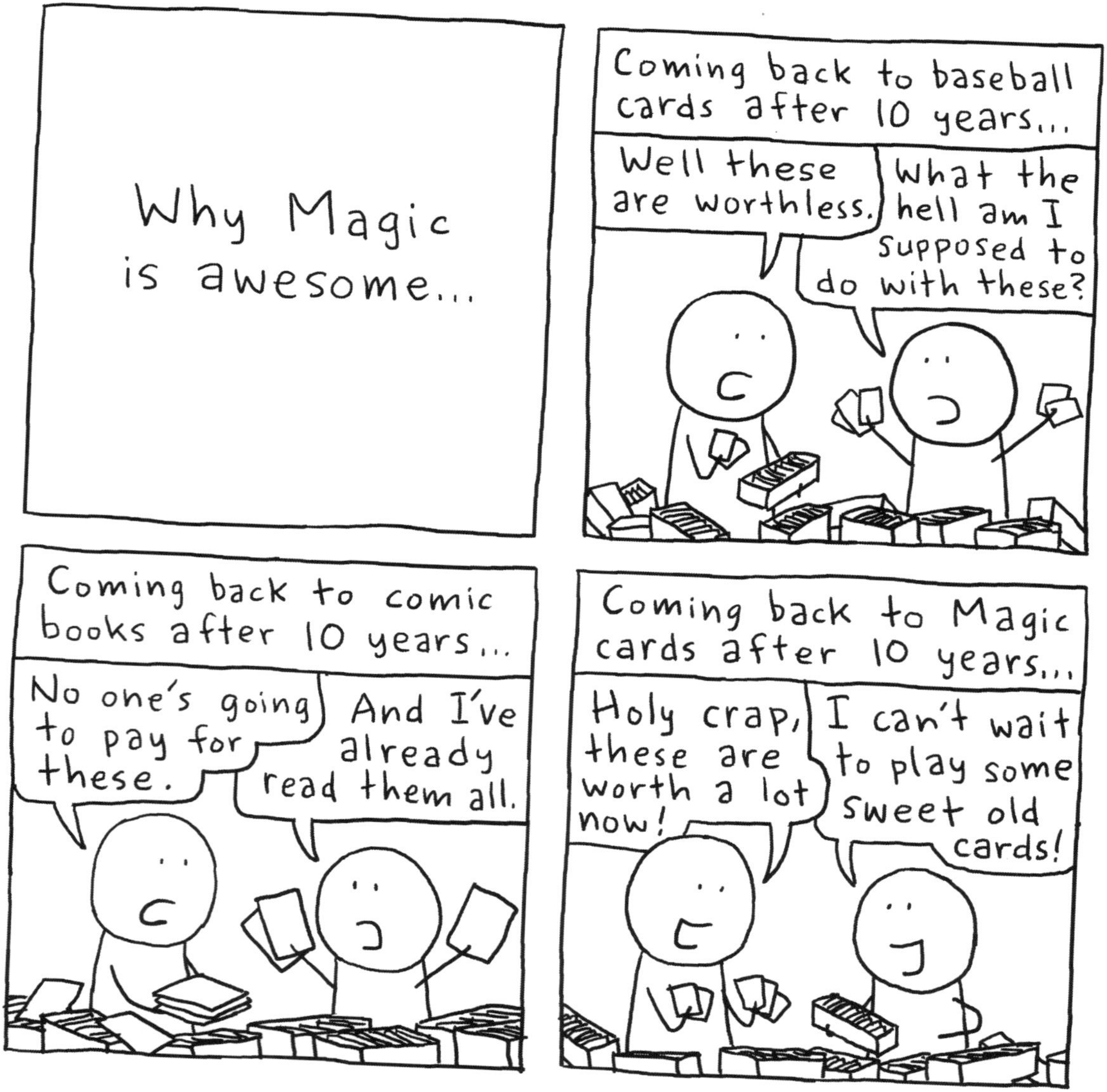
Why Magic is awesome...
Coming back to baseball cards after 10 years...
Well these are worthless.
What the hell am I supposed to do with these?
Coming back to comic books after 10 years...
No one's going to pay for these.
And I've already read them all.
Coming back to Magic cards after 10 years...
Holy crap, these are worth a lot now!
I can't wait to play some sweet old cards!

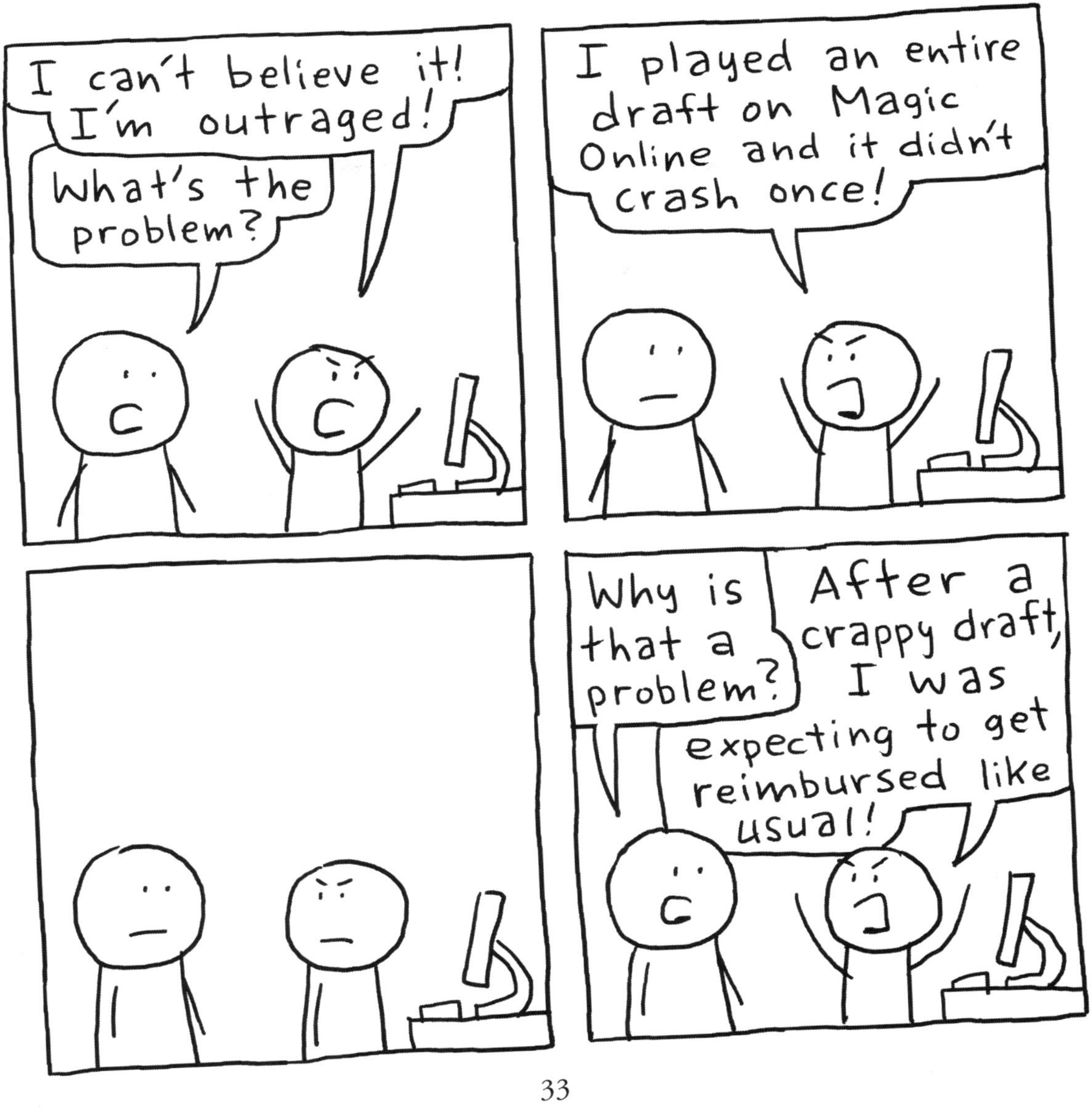
I can't believe it! I'm outraged!
What's the problem?
I played an entire draft on Magic Online and it didn't crash once!
Why is that a problem?
After a crappy draft, I was expecting to get reimbursed like usual!

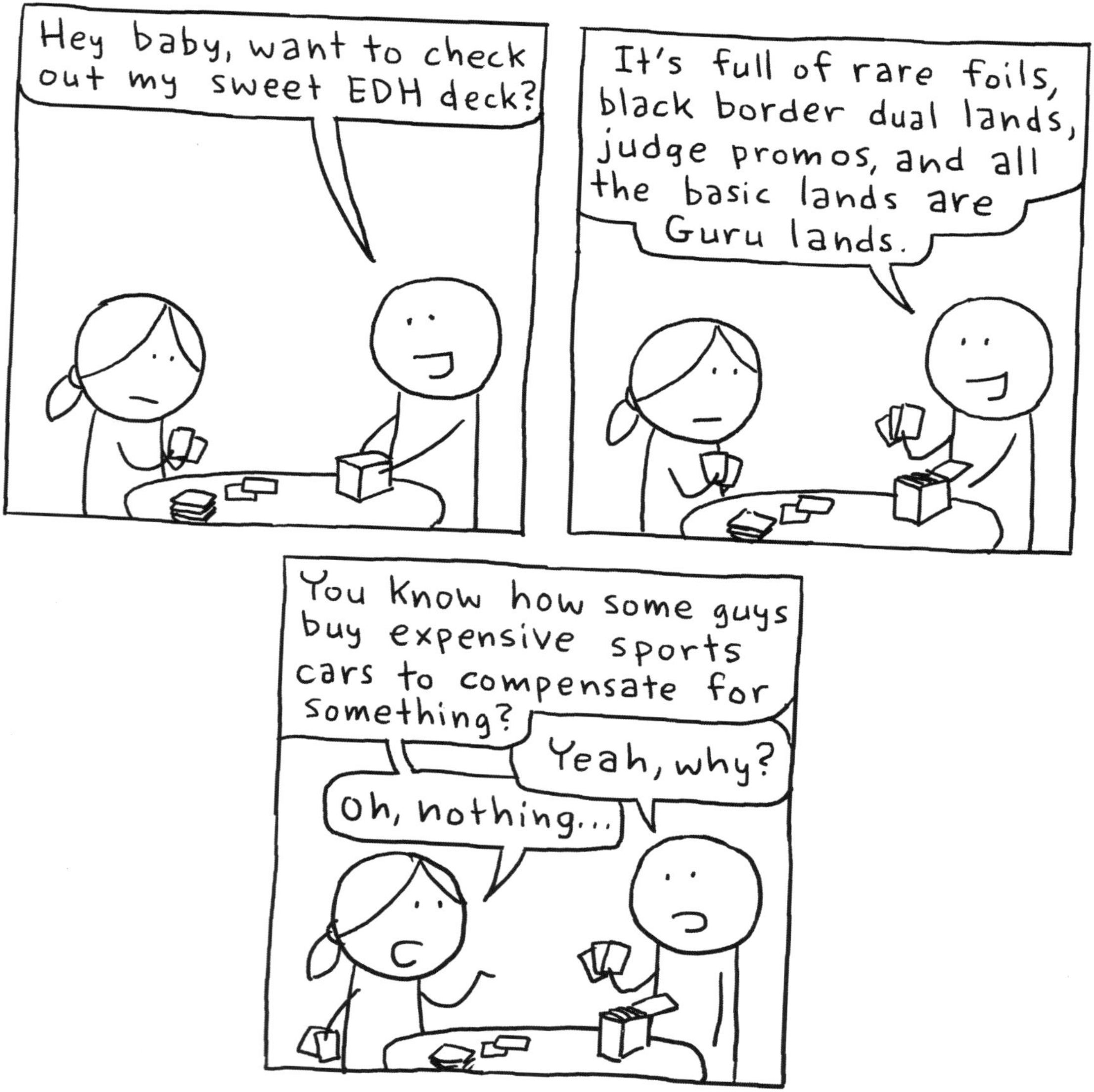
Hey baby, want to check out my sweet EDH deck?
It's full of rare foils, black border dual lands, judge promos, and all the basic lands are Guru lands.
You know how some guys buy expensive sports cars to compensate for something?
Yeah, why?
Oh, nothing...

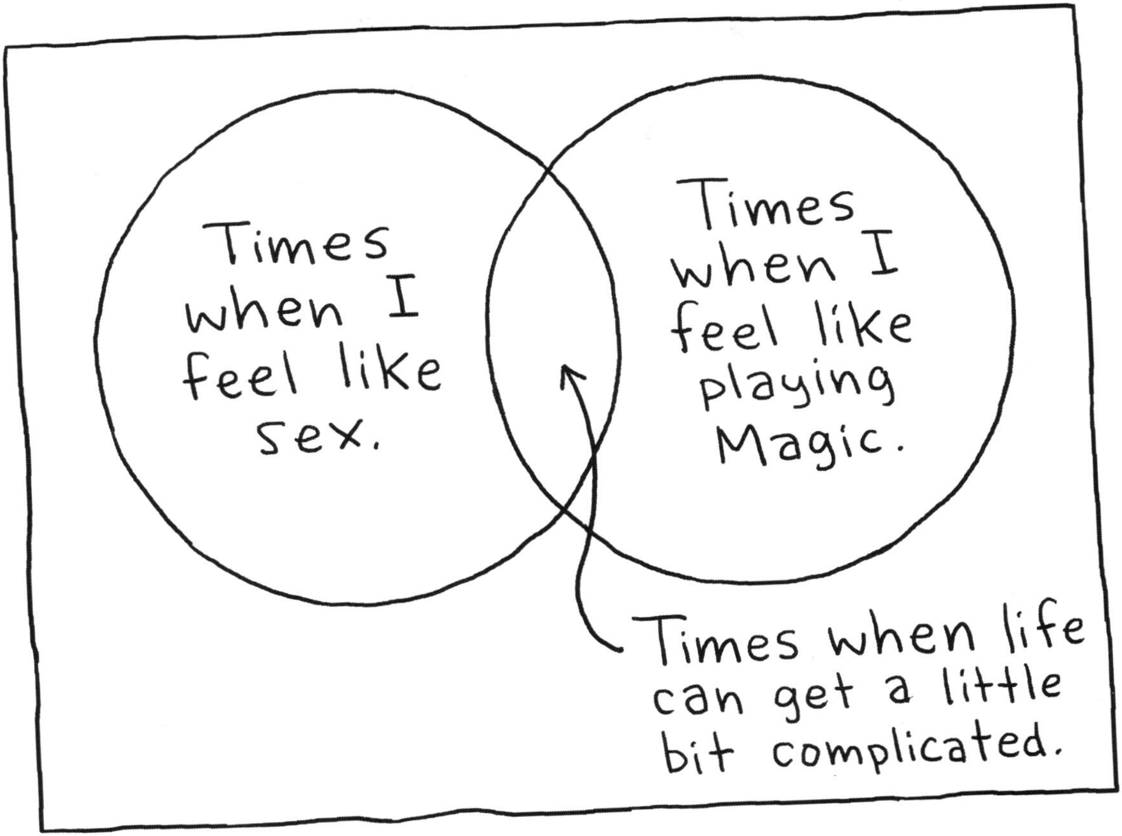
Times when I feel like sex.
Times when I feel like playing Magic.
Times when life can get a little bit complicated.

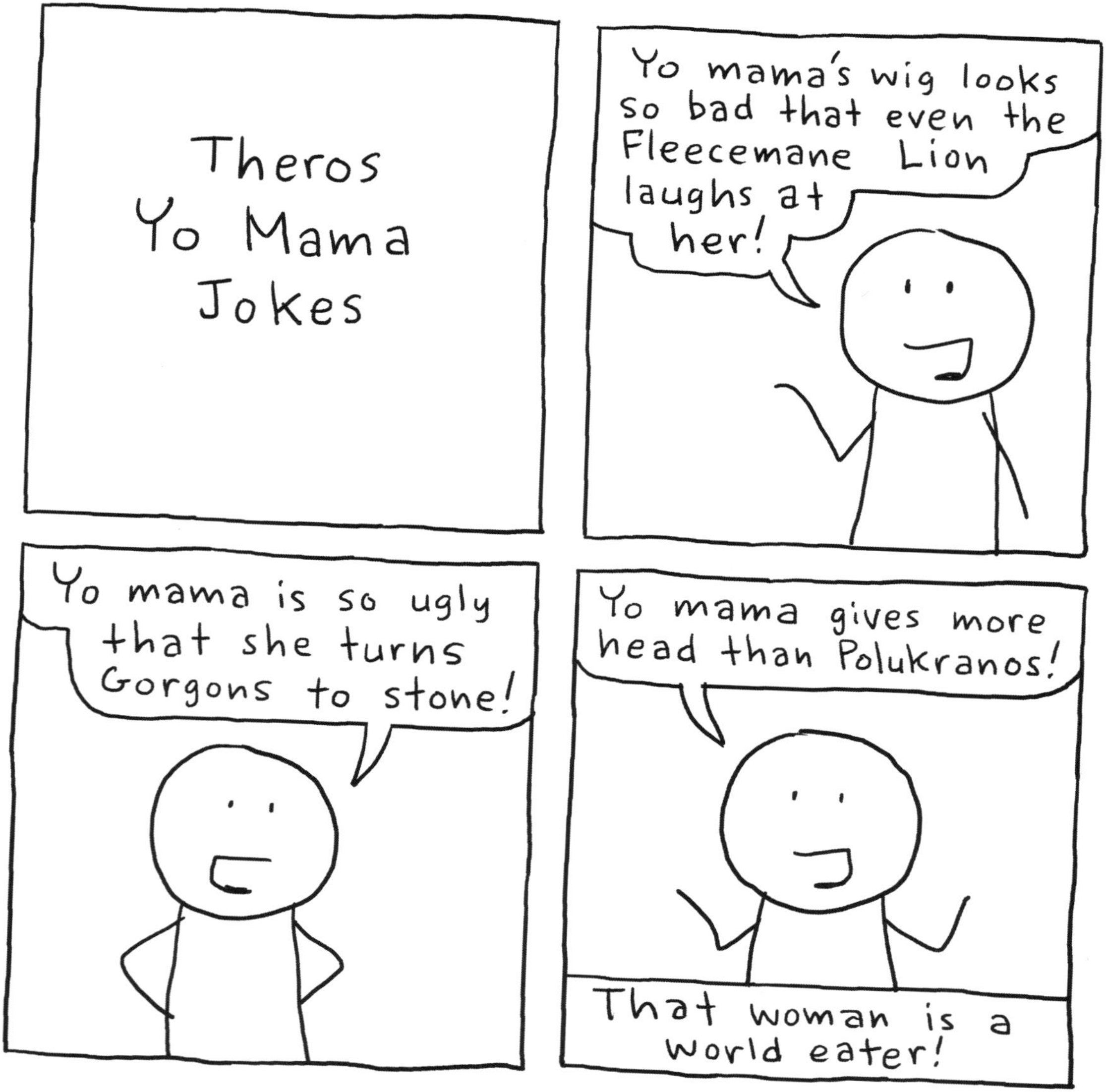
Theros Yo Mama Jokes
Yo mama's wig looks so bad that even the Fleecemane Lion laughs at her!
Yo mama is so ugly that she turns Gorgons to stone!
Yo mama gives more head than Polukranos!
That woman is a world eater!

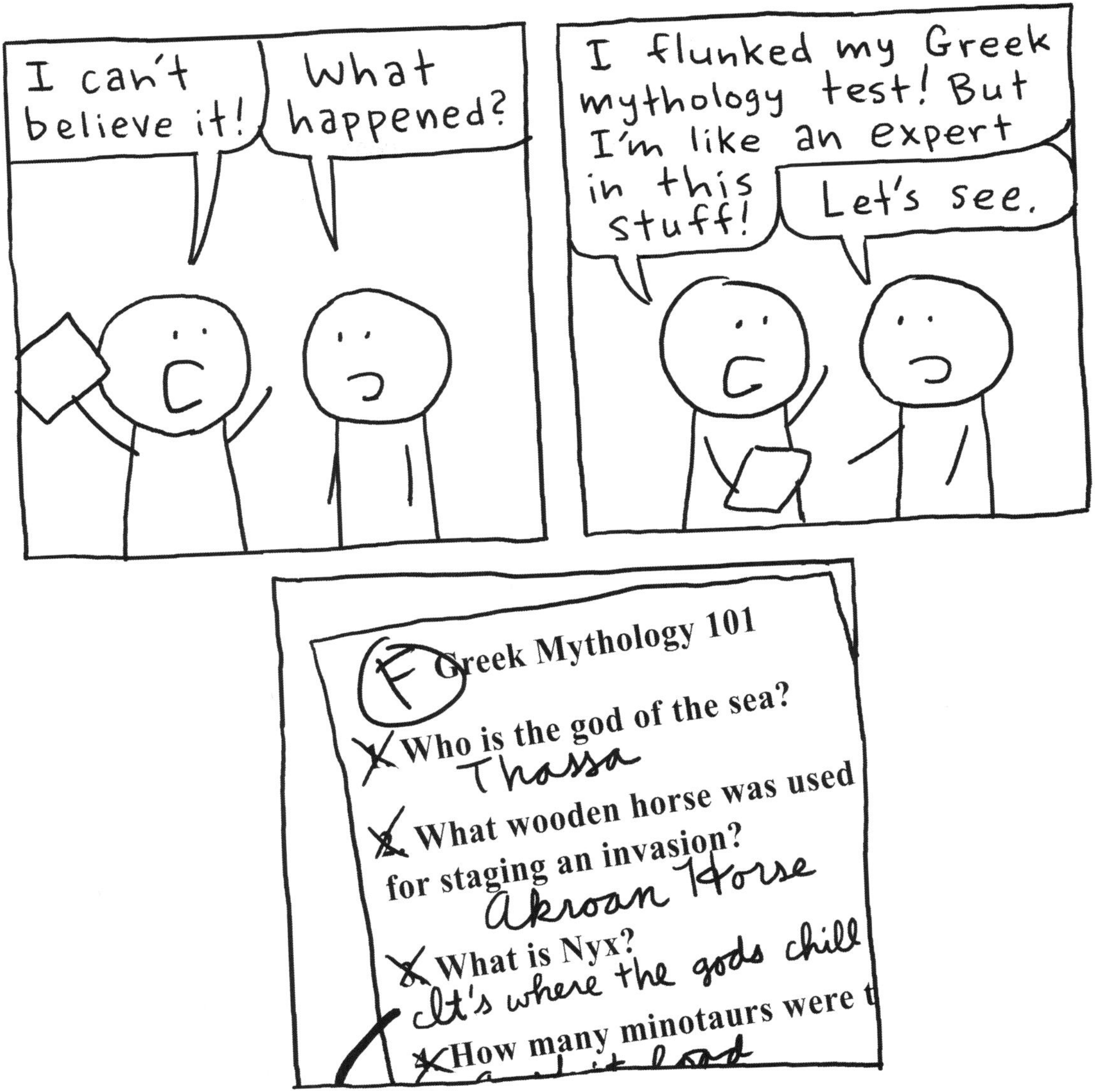
I can't believe it!
What happened?
I flunked my Greek mythology test! But I'm like an expert in this stuff!
Let's see.
F
Greek Mythology 101
1. Who is the god of the sea?
Thassa
2. What wooden horse was used for staging an invasion?
Akroan Horse
3. What is Nyx?
It's where the gods chill
How many minotaurs were t

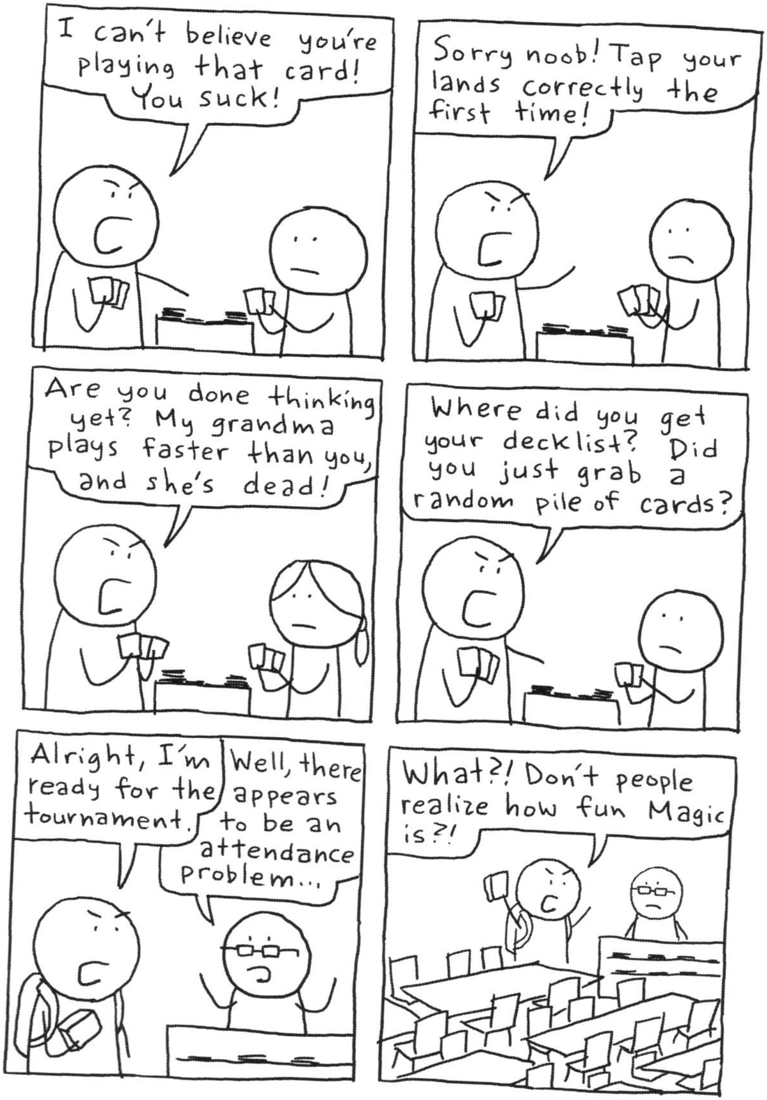
I can't believe you're playing that card! You suck!
Sorry noob! Tap your lands correctly the first time!
Are you done thinking yet? My grandma plays faster than you, and she's dead!
Where did you get your decklist? Did you just grab a random pile of cards?
Alright, I'm ready for the tournament.
Well, there appears to be an attendance problem...
What?! Don't people realize how fun Magic is?!

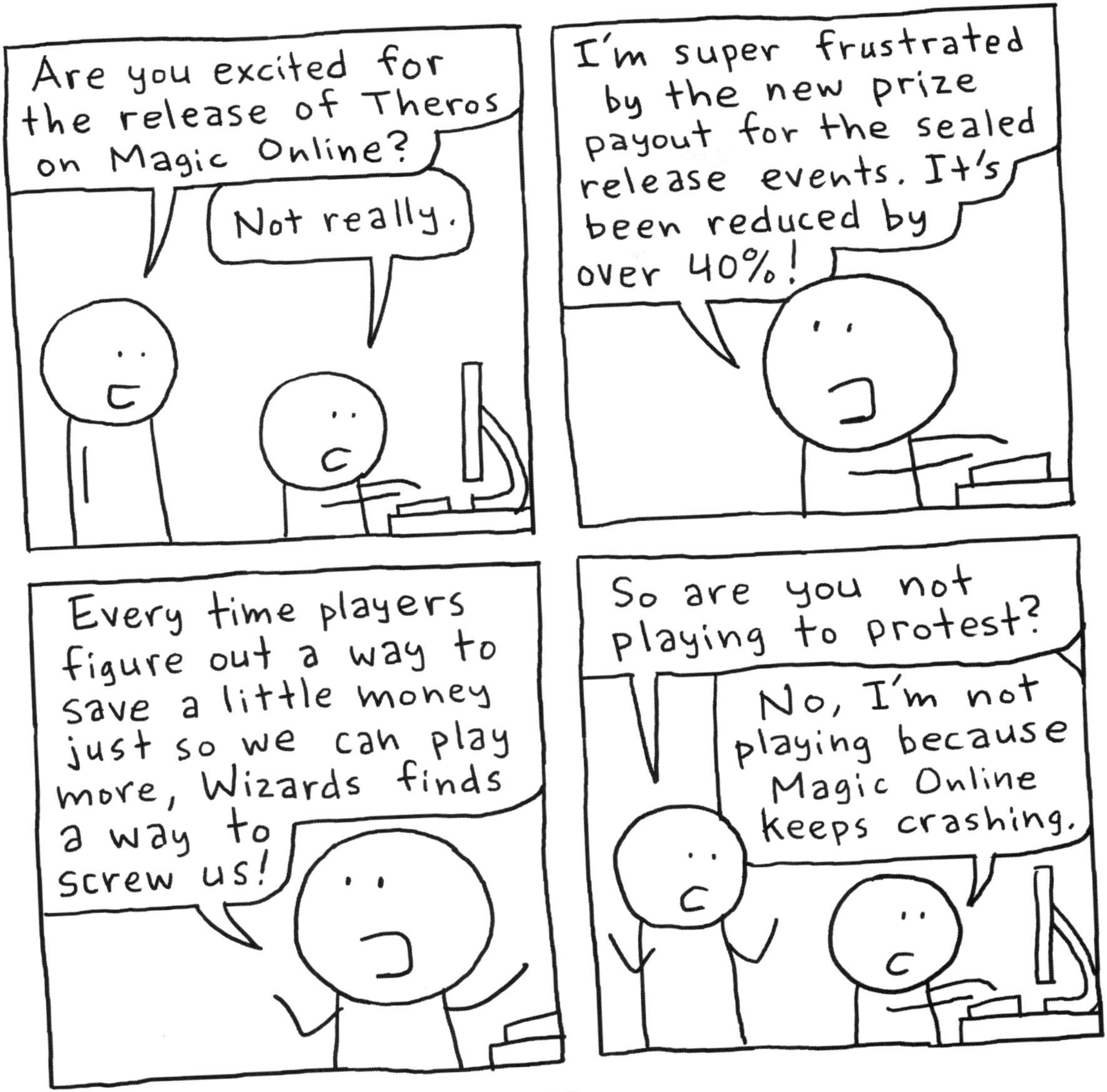
Are you excited for the release of Theros on Magic Online?
Not really.
I'm super frustrated by the new prize payout for the sealed release events. It's been reduced by over 40%!
Every time players figure out a way to save a little money just so we can play more, Wizards finds a way to screw us!
So are you not playing to protest?
No, I'm not playing because Magic Online keeps crashing.

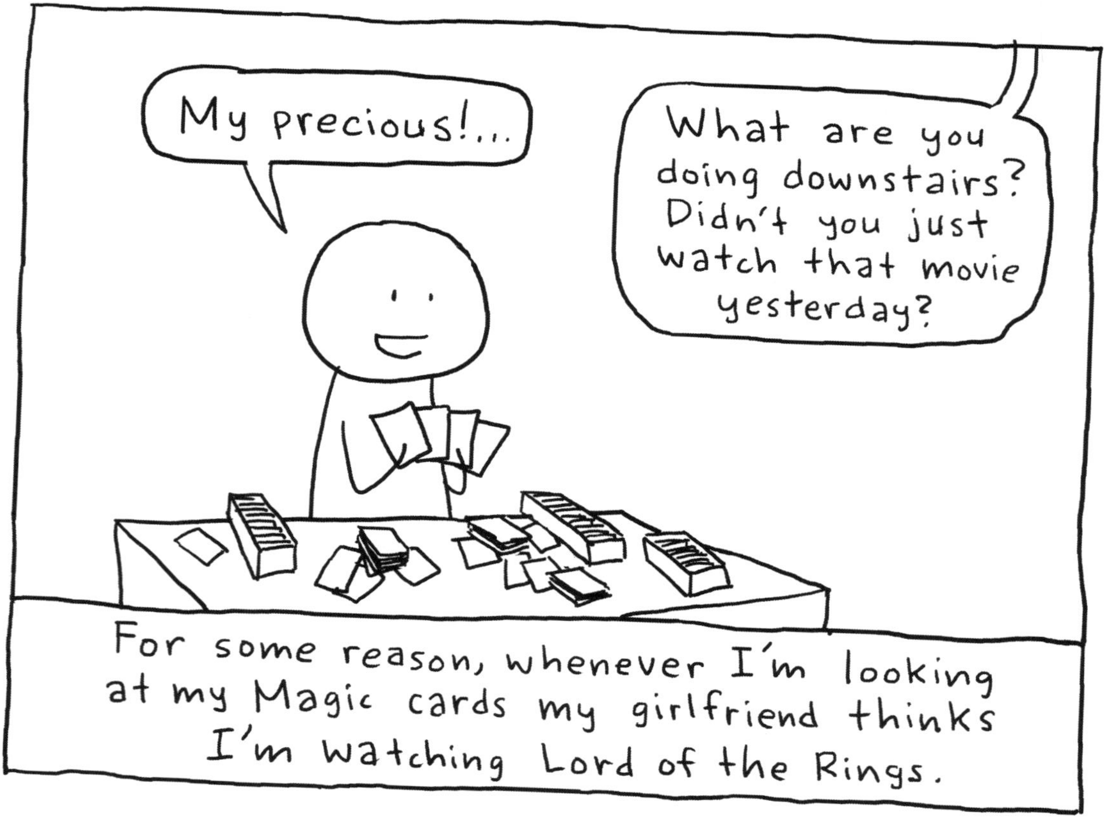
My precious!...
What are you doing downstairs? Didn't you just watch that movie yesterday?
For some reason, whenever I'm looking at my Magic cards my girlfriend thinks I'm watching Lord of the Rings.

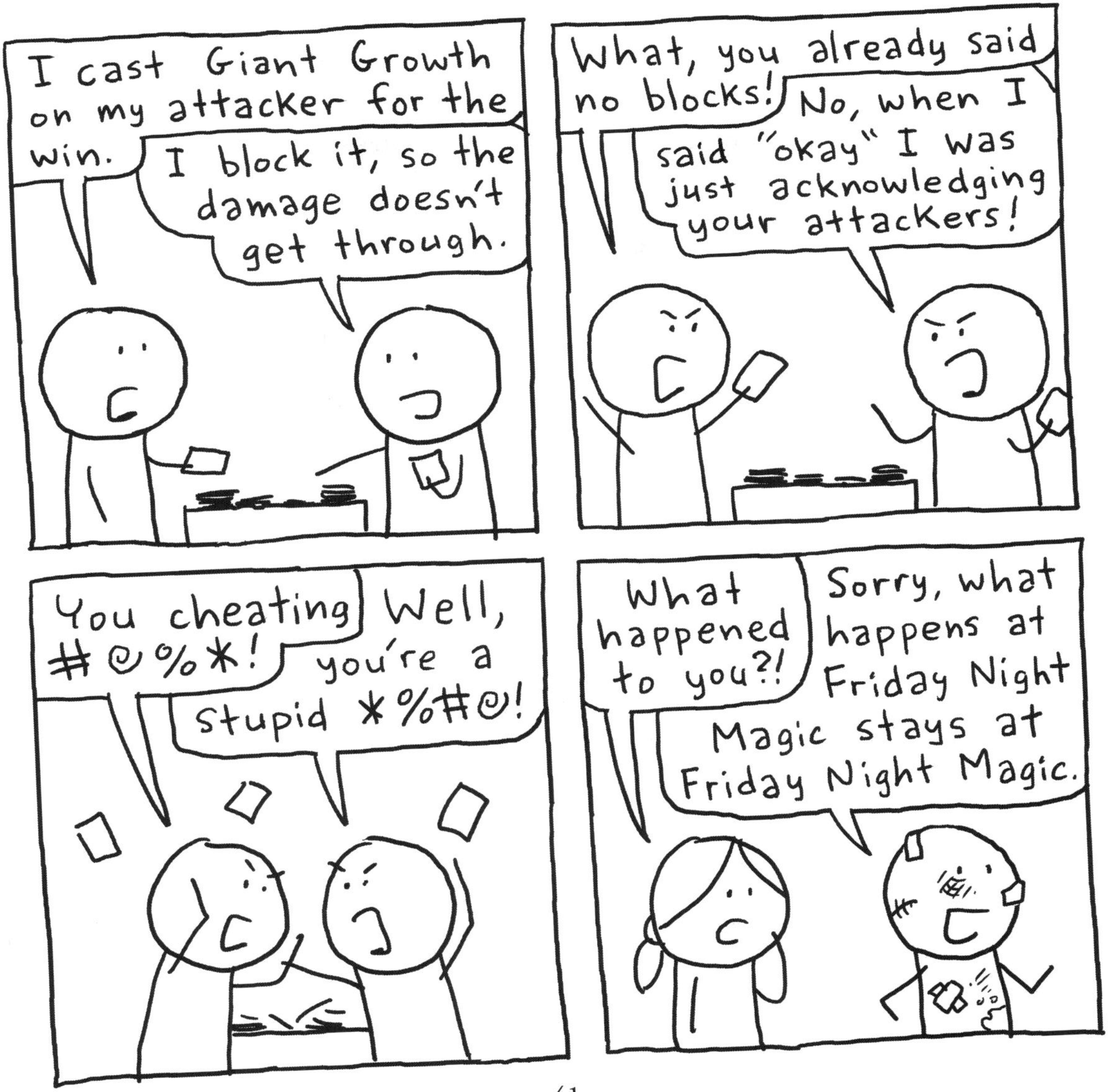
I cast Giant Growth on my attacker for the win.
I block it, so the damage doesn't get through.
What, you already said no blocks!
No, when I said "okay" I was just acknowledging your attackers!
You cheating #@%*!
Well, you're a stupid *%#@!
What happened to you?!
Sorry, what happens at Friday Night Magic stays at Friday Night Magic.

...and so class, that is why they say "no man is an island."
Yes Johnny?
But if you have a Mutavault with a Stormtide Leviathan in play, then a human can be an island!

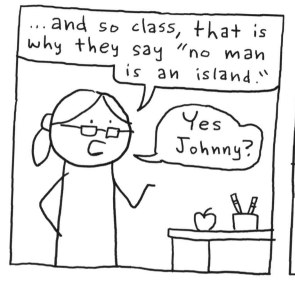

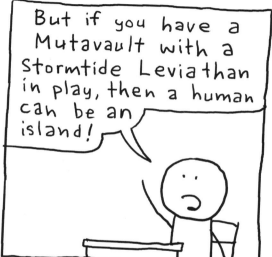

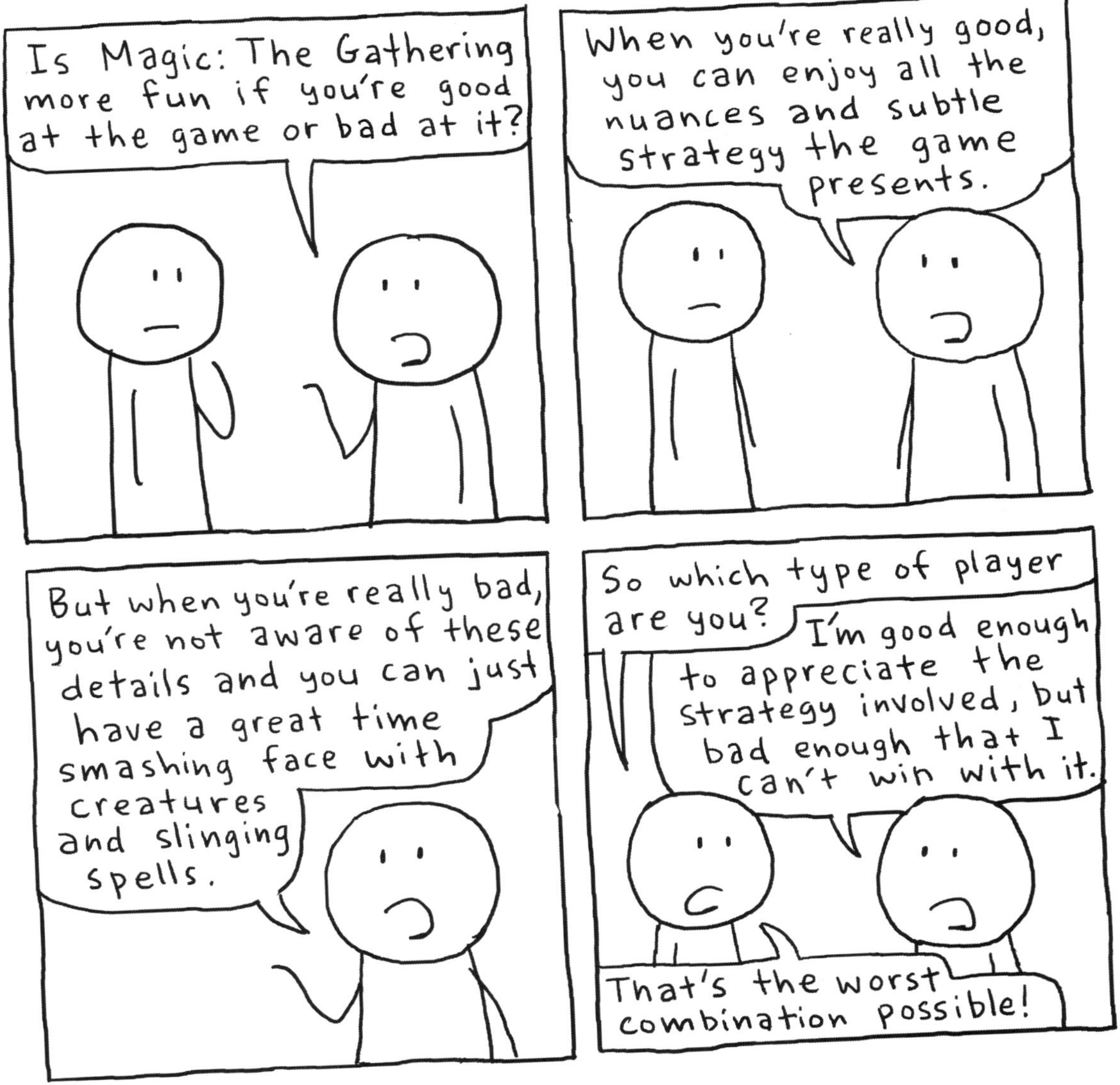
Is Magic: The Gathering more fun if you're good at the game or bad at it?
When you're really good, you can enjoy all the nuances and subtle strategy the game presents.
But when you're really bad, you're not aware of these details and you can just have a great time smashing face with creatures and slinging spells.
So which type of player are you?
I'm good enough to appreciate the strategy involved, but bad enough that I can't win with it.
That's the worst combination possible!

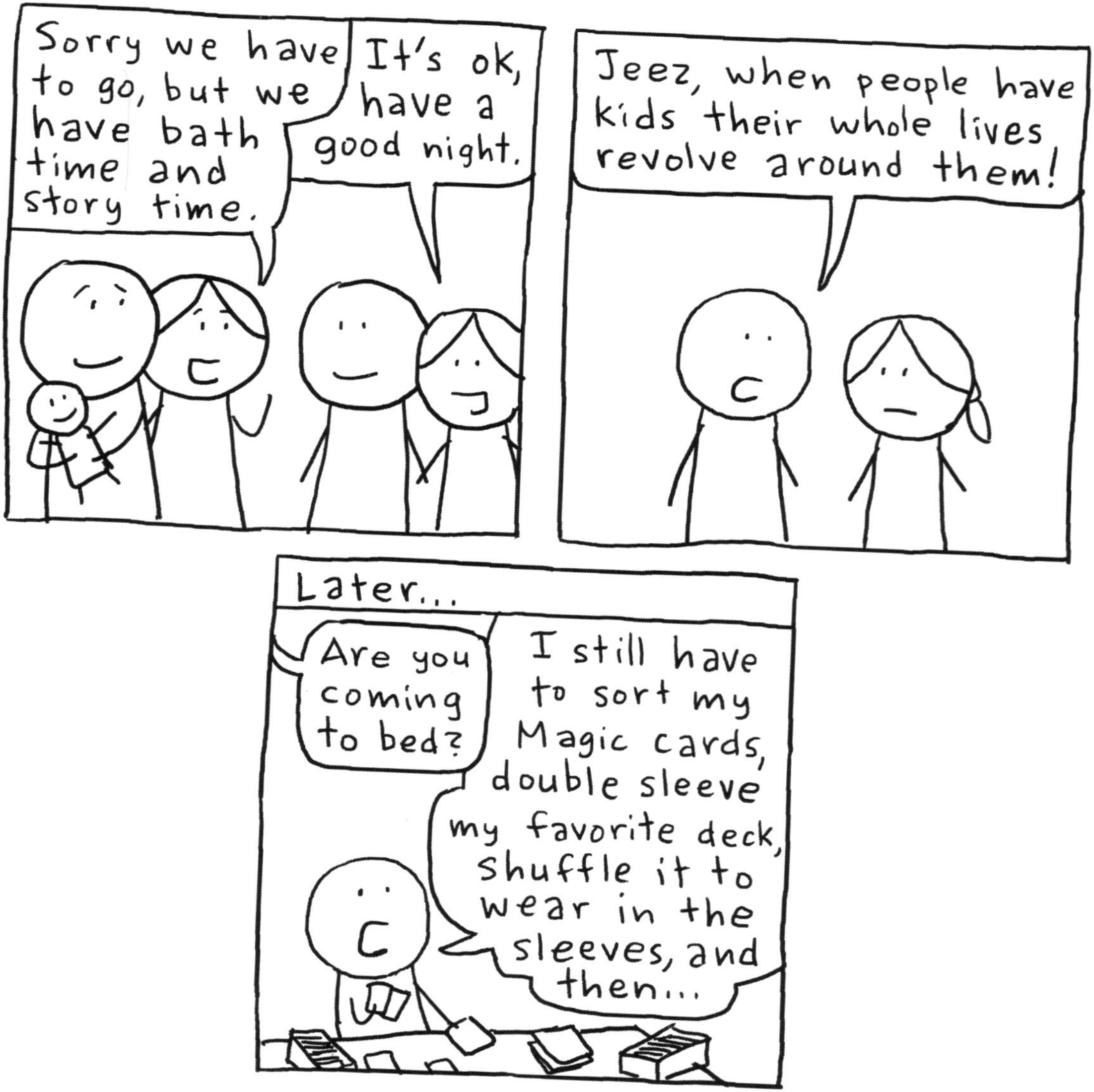
Sorry we have to go, but we have bath time and story time.
It's ok, have a good night.
Jeez, when people have kids their whole lives revolve around them!
Later...
Are you coming to bed?
I still have to sort my Magic cards, double sleeve my favorite deck, shuffle it to wear in the sleeves, and then...

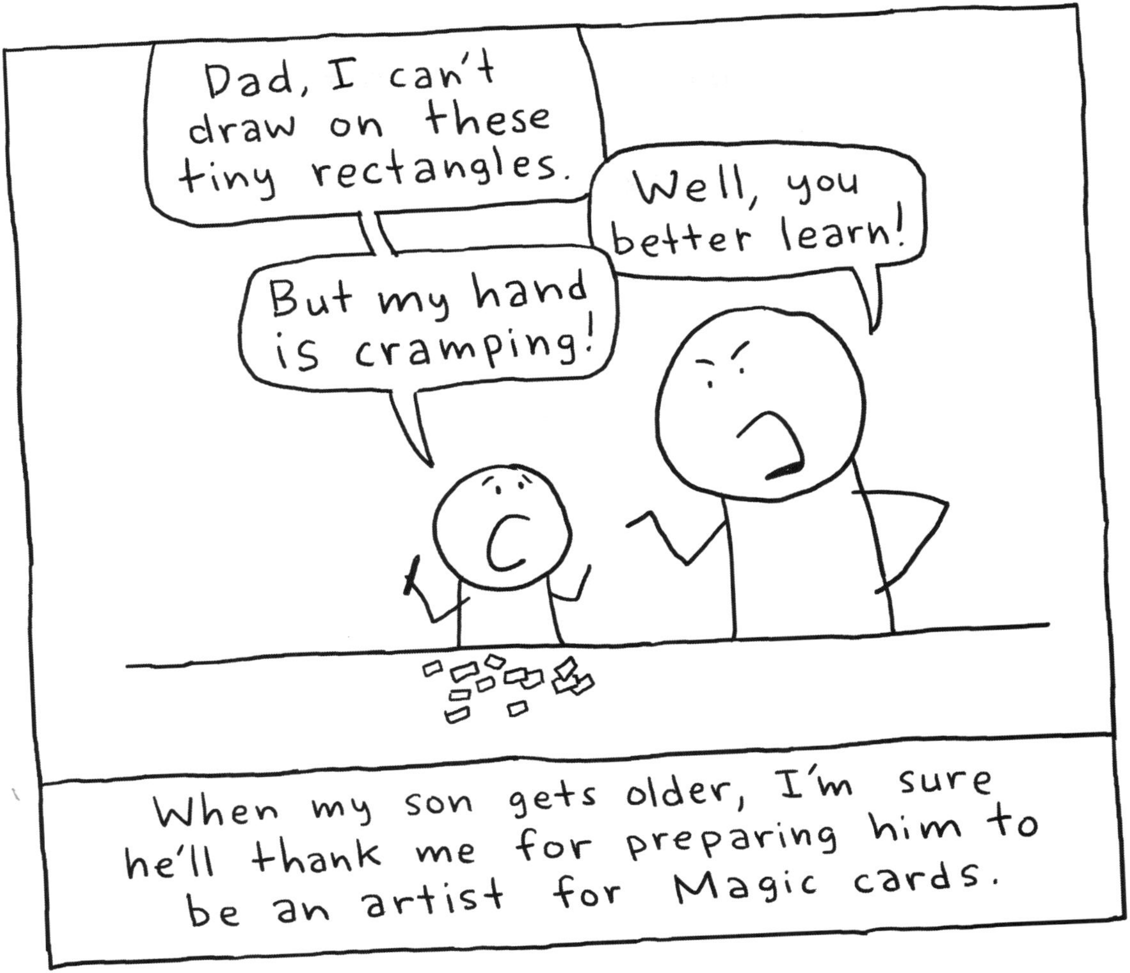
Dad, I can't draw on these tiny rectangles.
But my hand is cramping!
Well, you better learn!
When my son gets older, I'm sure he'll thank me for preparing him to be an artist for Magic cards.

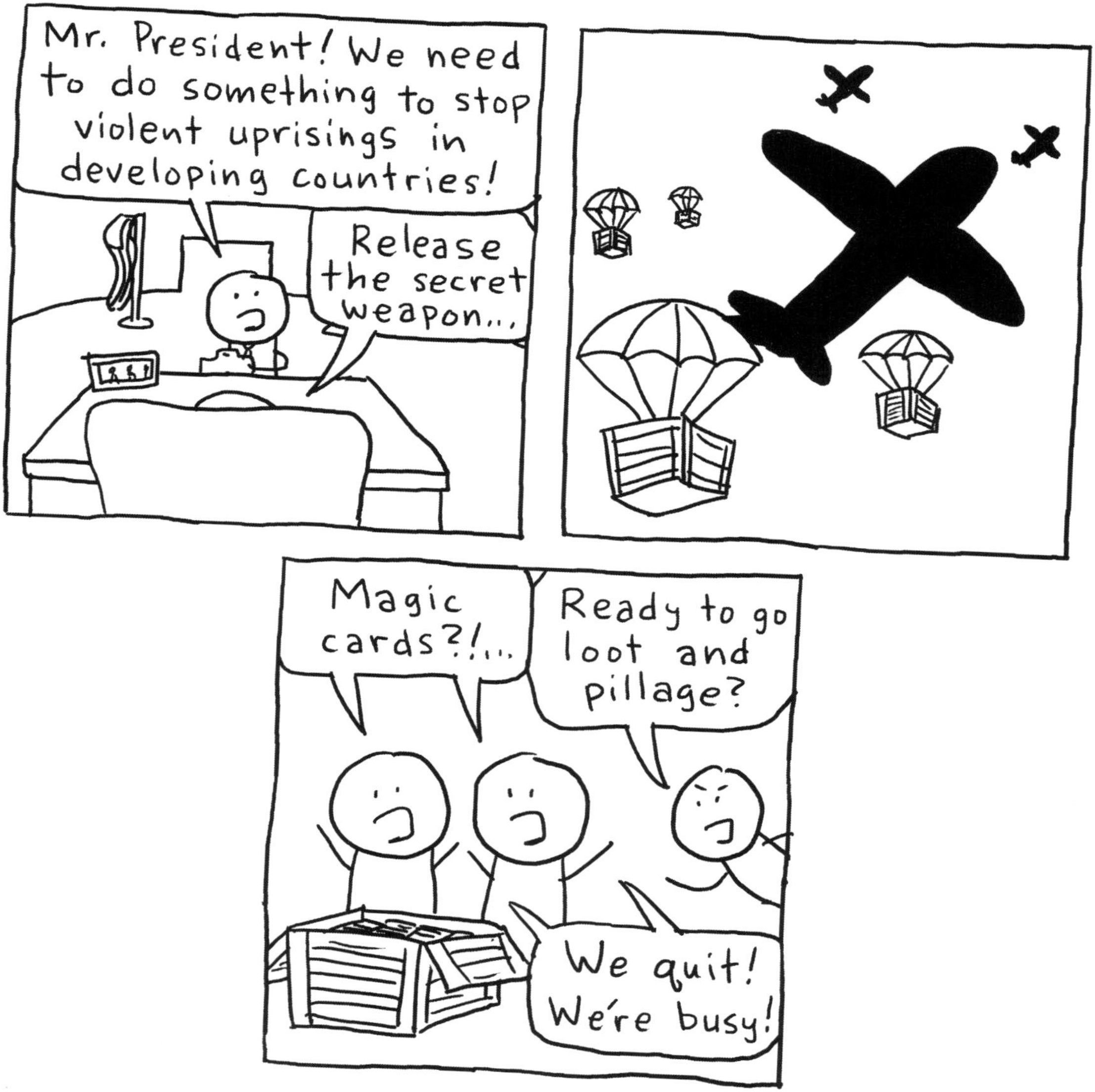
Mr. President! We need to do something to stop violent uprisings in developing countries!
Release the secret weapon...
Magic cards?!...
Ready to go loot and pillage?
We quit! We're busy!

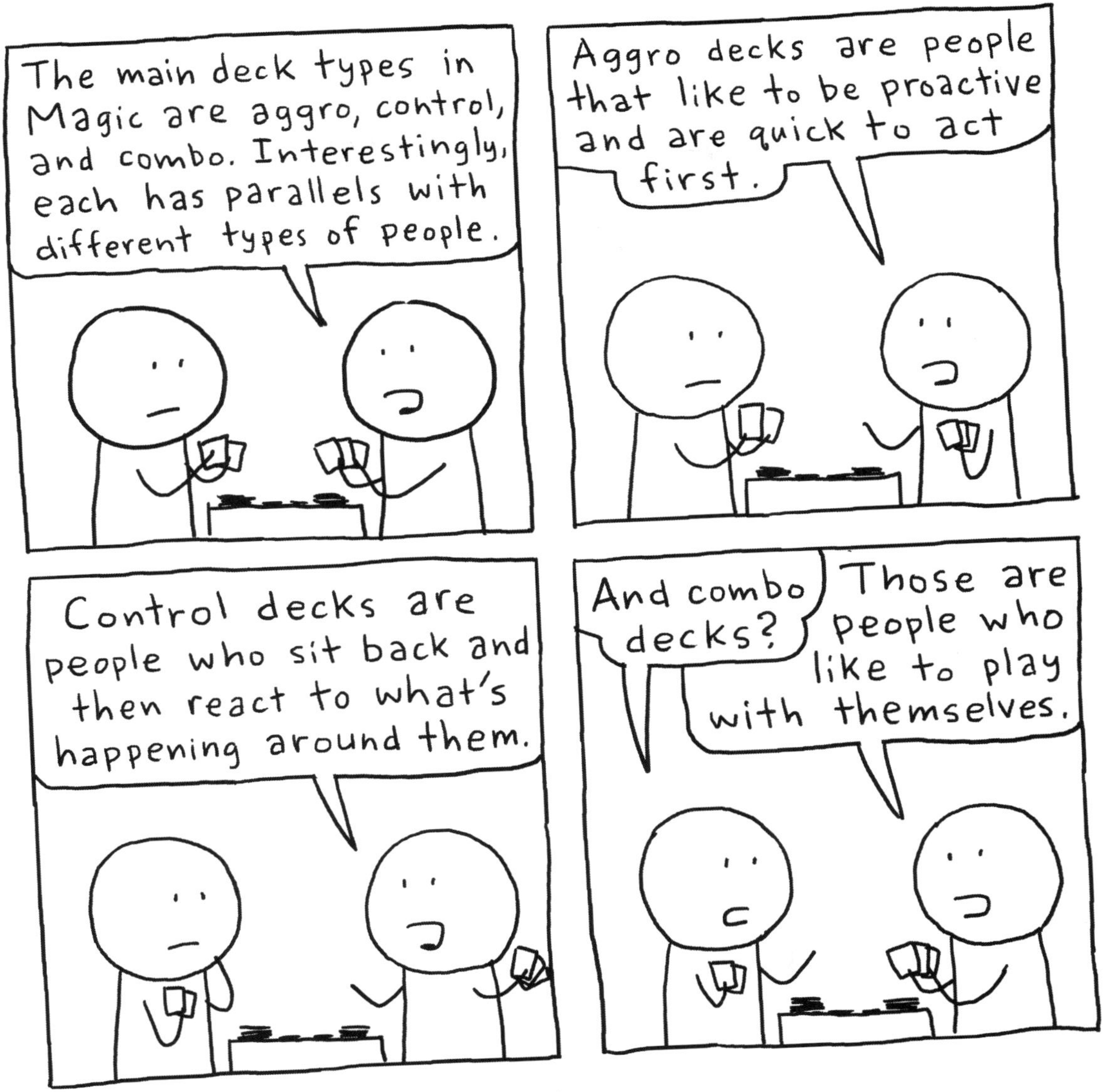
The main deck types in Magic are aggro, control, and combo. Interestingly, each has parallels with different types of people.
Aggro decks are people that like to be proactive and are quick to act first.
Control decks are people who sit back and then react to what's happening around them.
And combo decks?
Those are people who like to play with themselves.

Ten years ago...
I know I spend a lot on Magic cards, but just think of it as an investment.
Now...
What?! You expect me to sell my babies?!

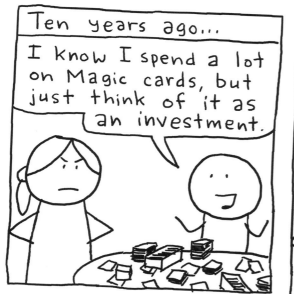

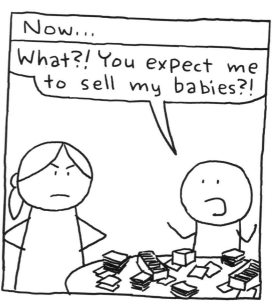

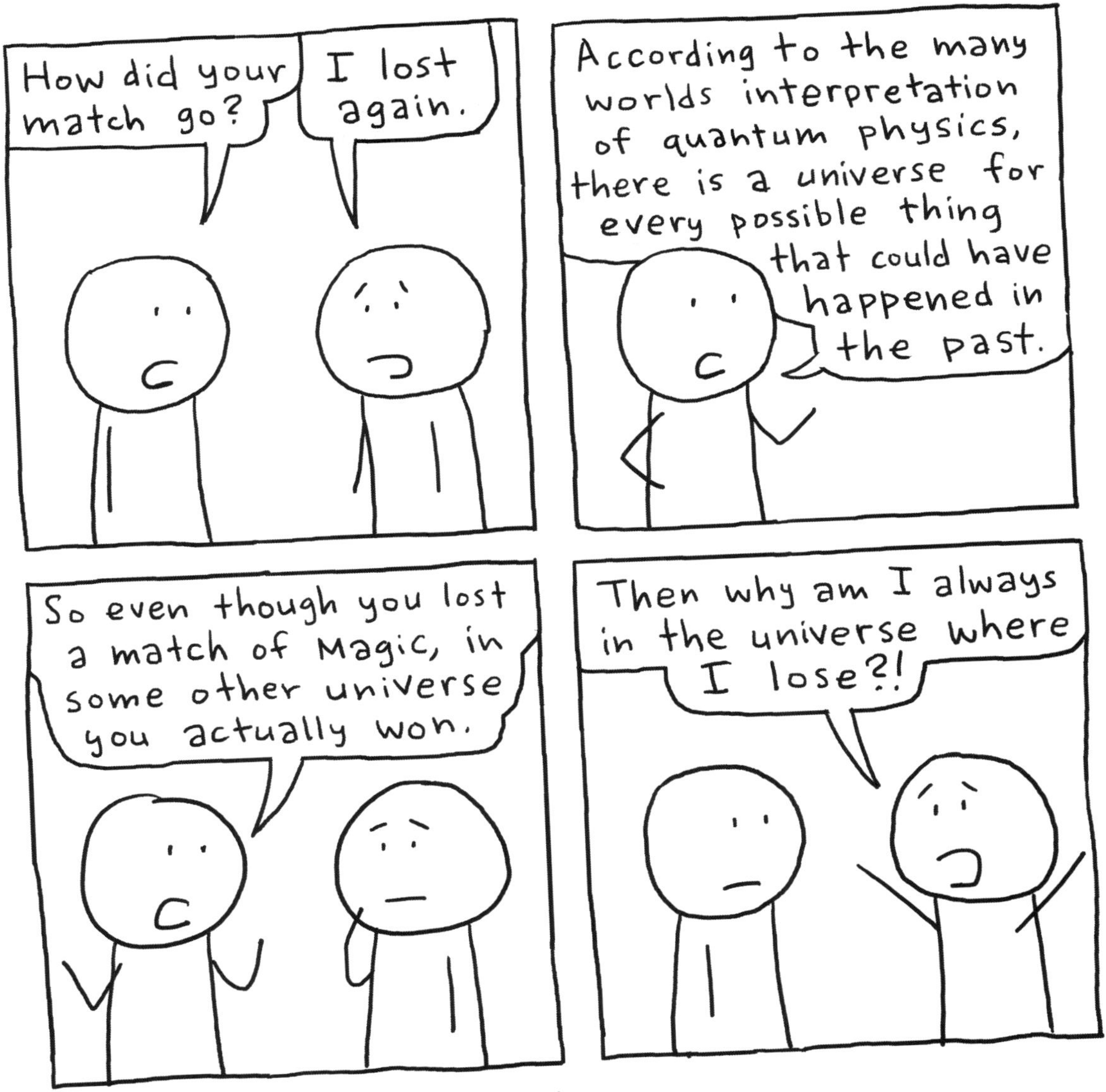
How did your match go?
I lost again.
According to the many worlds interpretation of quantum physics, there is a universe for every possible thing that could have happened in the past.
So even though you lost a match of Magic, in some other universe you actually won.
Then why am I always in the universe where I lose?!

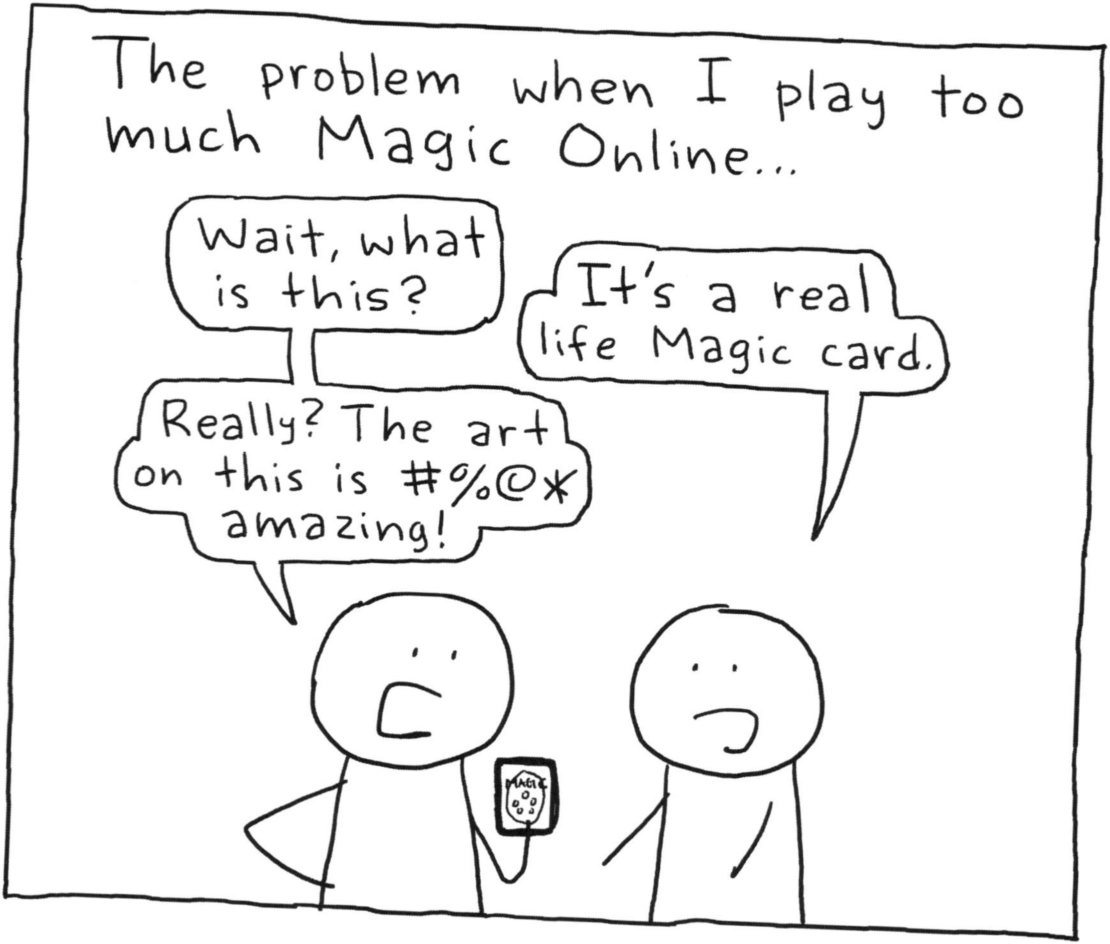
The problem when I play too much Magic Online...
Wait, what is this?
It's a real life Magic card.
Really? The art on this is #%@* amazing!
MAGIC

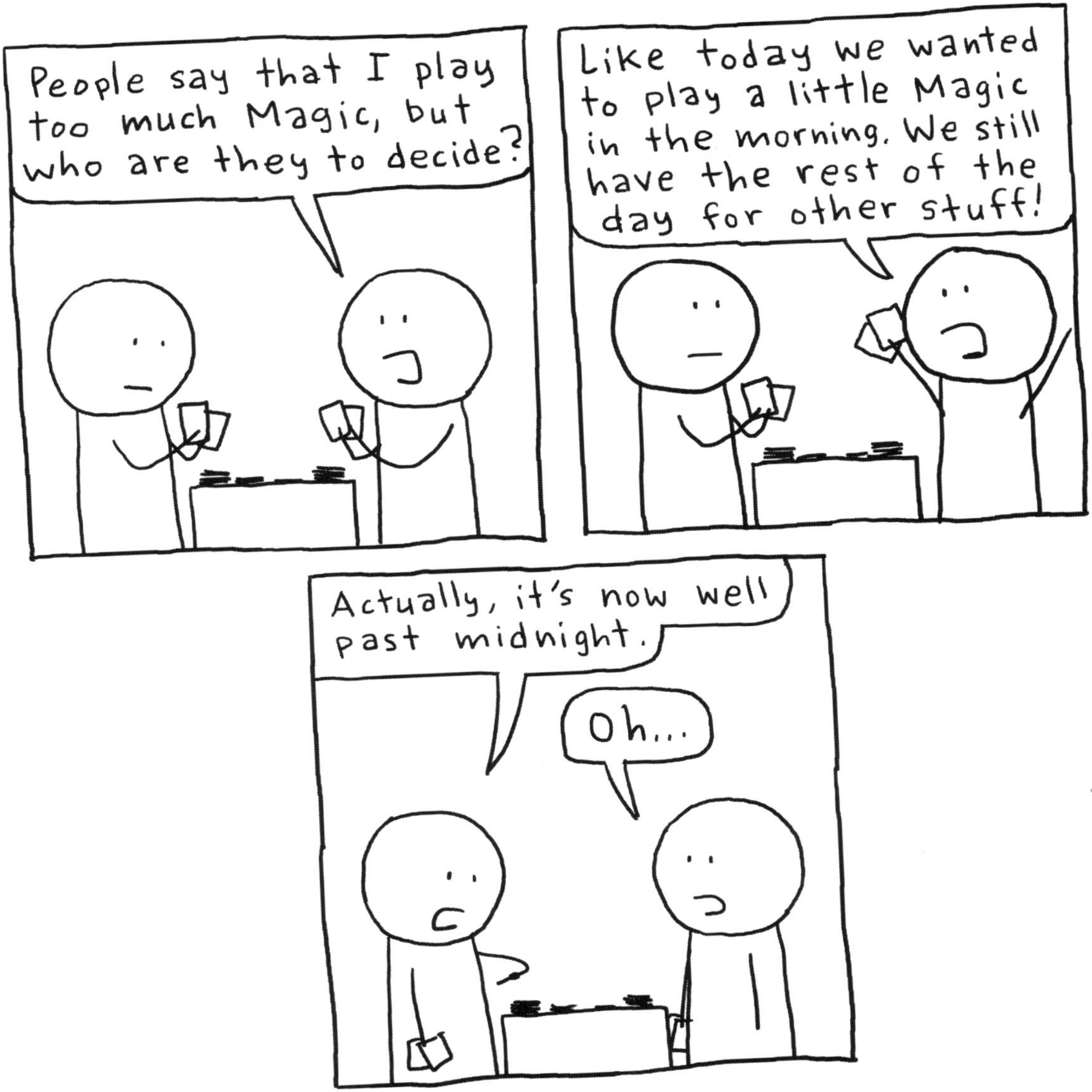
People say that I play too much Magic, but who are they to decide?
Like today we wanted to play a little Magic in the morning. We still have the rest of the day for other stuff!
Actually, it's now well past midnight.
Oh...

Top 5 things overheard when the Jace vs. Vraska Duel Decks were announced...

⑤ "Great, just what everyone wanted -- more Jace-centered products!"

④ "I guess Jace's magical powers don't give him control over his hair."

③ "Is Jace really Christopher Reeve?"

② "Jace, please keep the hood on."

① "Screw it, at least there'll be more copies of Jace, Architect of Thought in circulation."

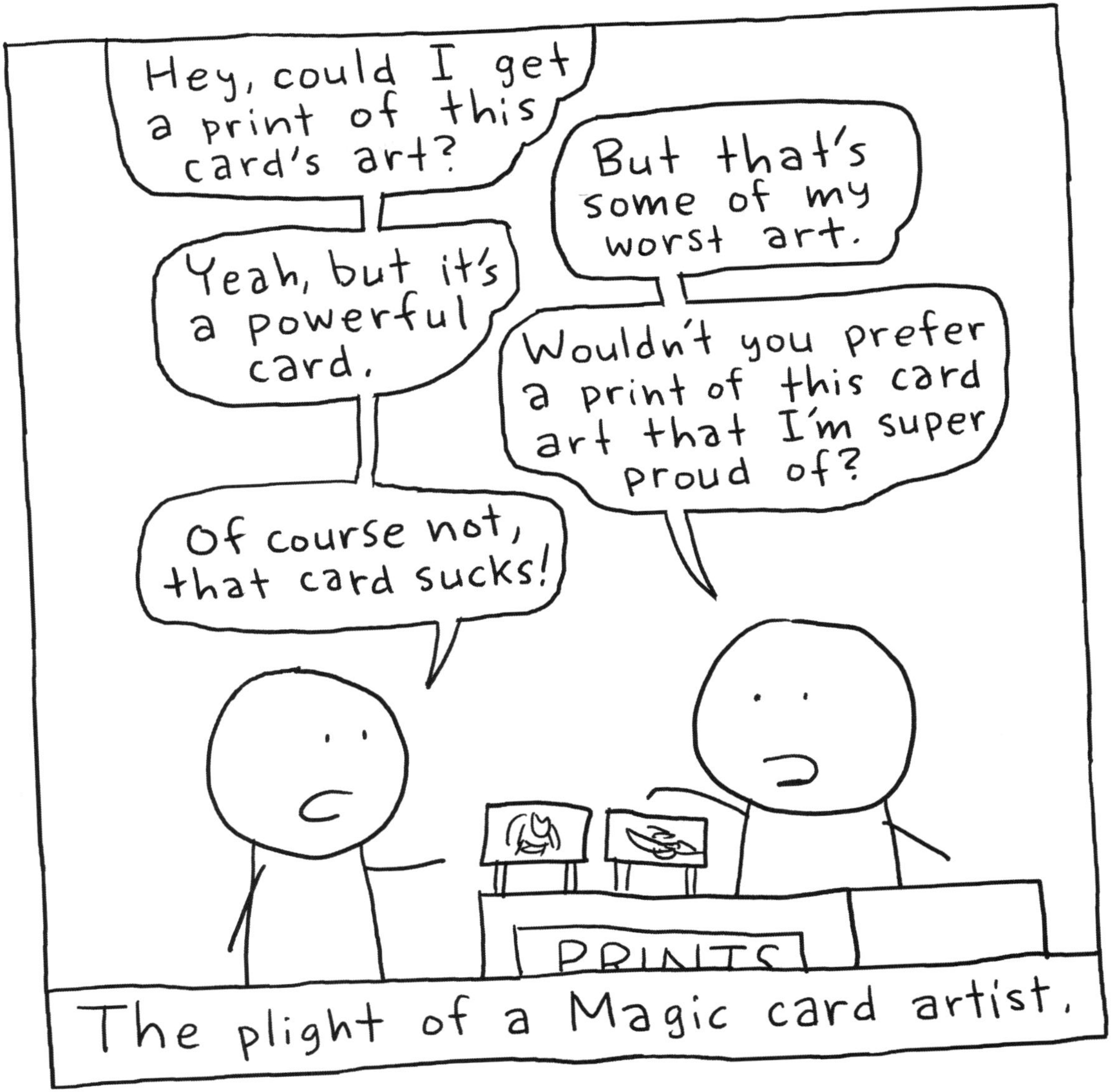
Hey, could I get a print of this card's art?
Yeah, but it's a powerful card.
Of course not, that card sucks!
But that's some of my worst art.
Wouldn't you prefer a print of this card art that I'm super proud of?
PRINTS
The plight of a Magic card artist.

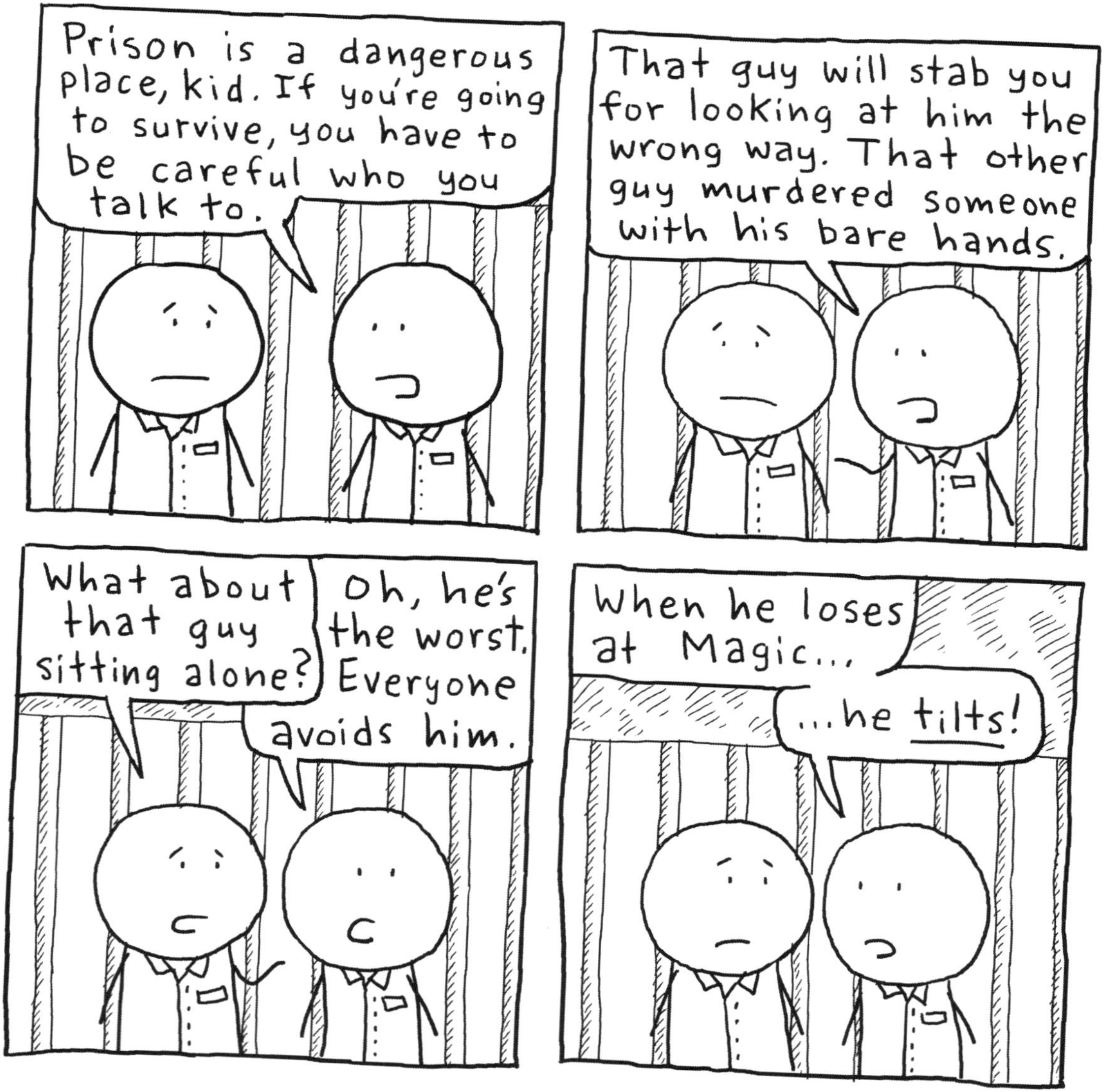
Prison is a dangerous place, kid. If you're going to survive, you have to be careful who you talk to.
That guy will stab you for looking at him the wrong way. That other guy murdered someone with his bare hands.
What about that guy sitting alone?
Oh, he's the worst. Everyone avoids him.
When he loses at Magic...
...he tilts!

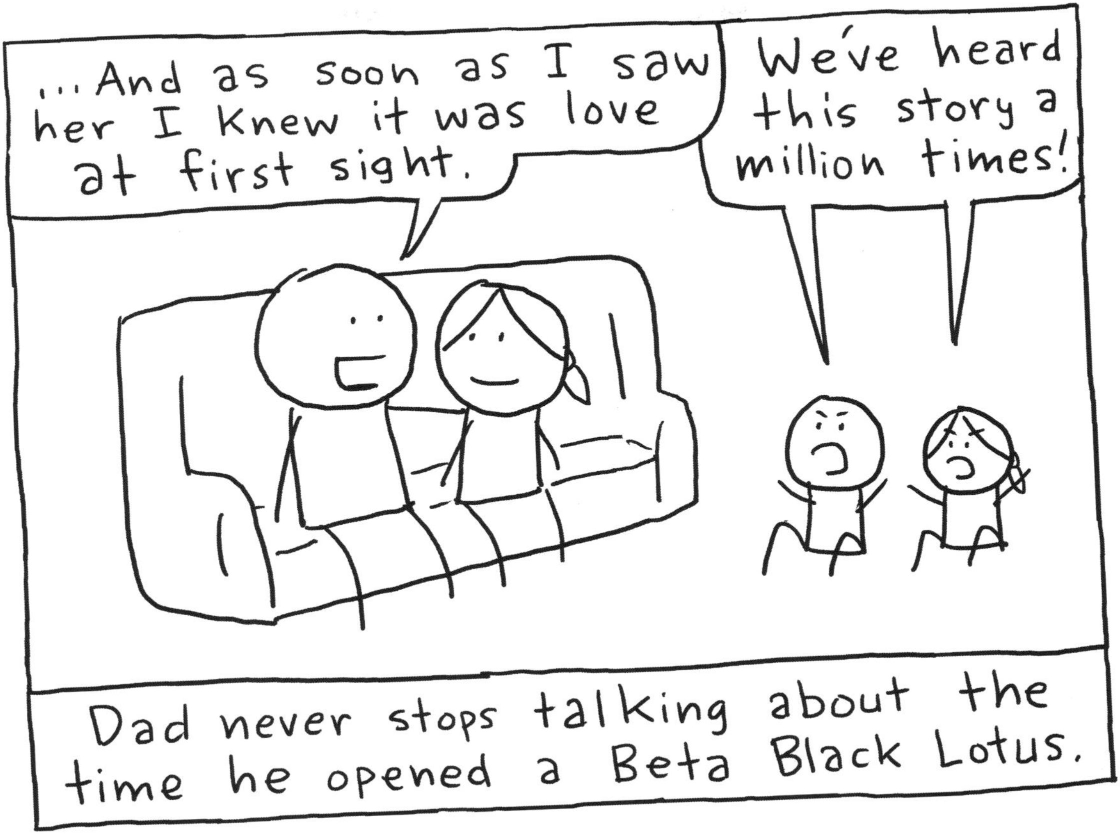
...And as soon as I saw her I knew it was love at first sight.
We've heard this story a million times!
Dad never stops talking about the time he opened a Beta Black Lotus.

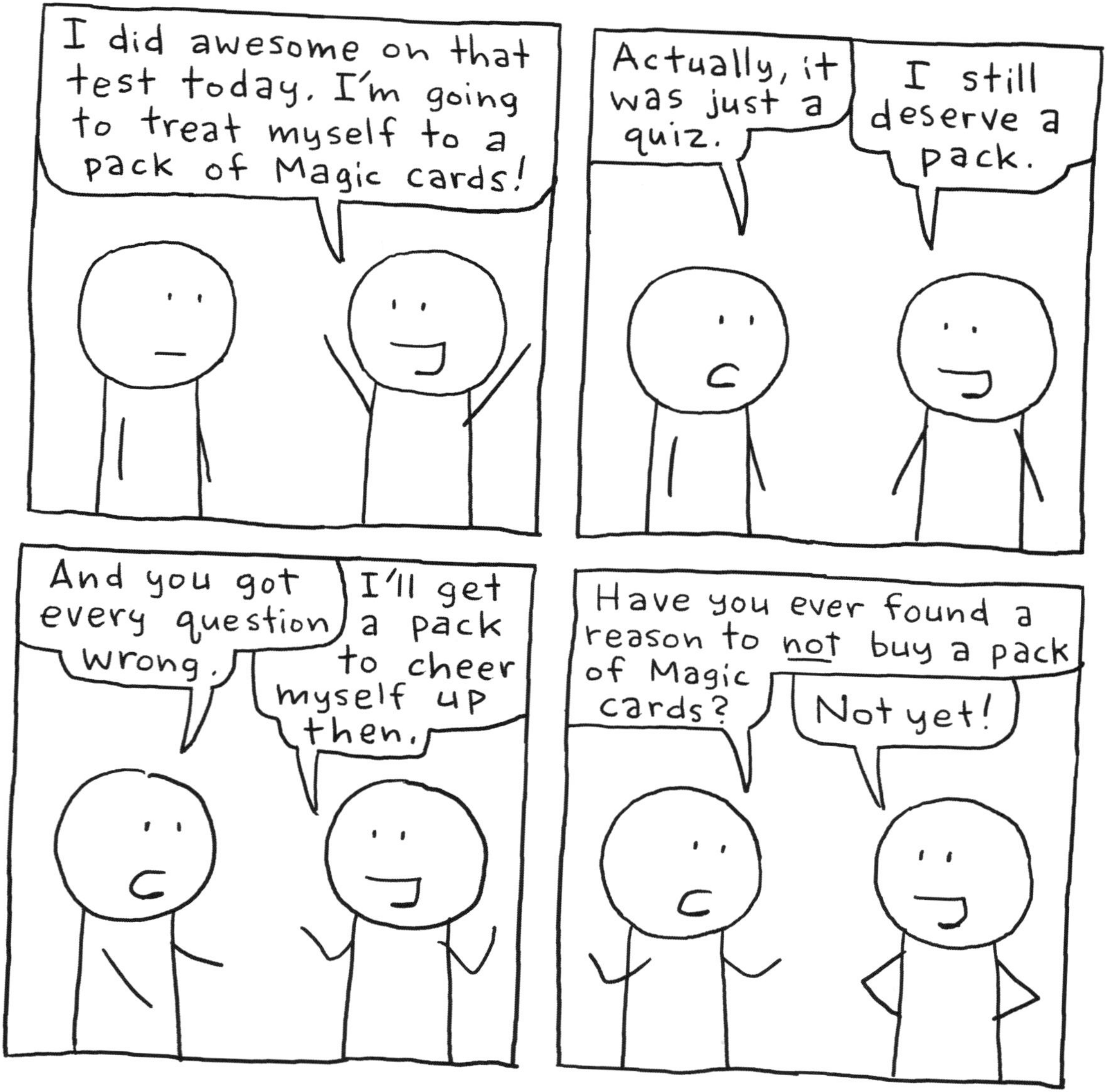
I did awesome on that test today. I'm going to treat myself to a pack of Magic cards!
Actually, it was just a quiz.
I still deserve a pack.
And you got every question wrong.
I'll get a pack to cheer myself up then.
Have you ever found a reason to not buy a pack of Magic cards?
Not yet!

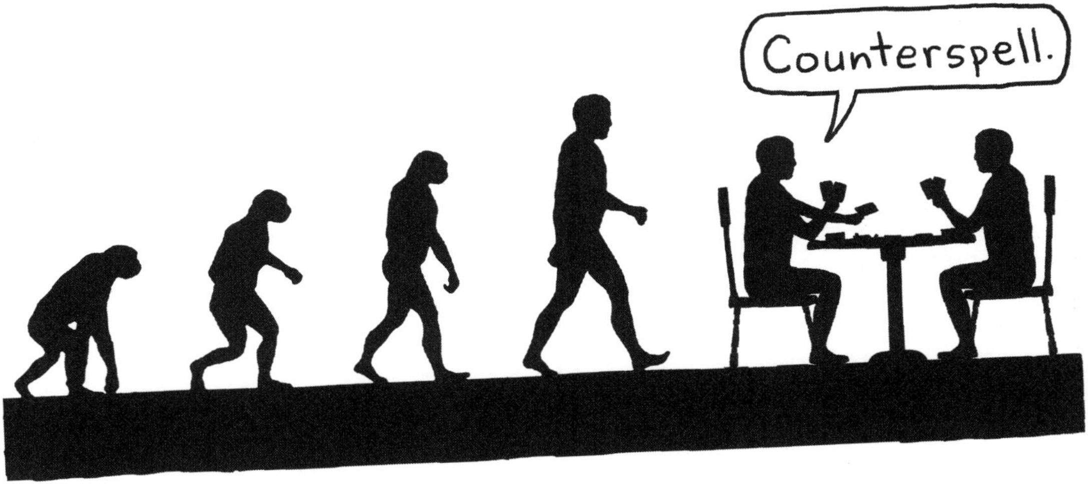
Counterspell.

I'm ready for the Halloween party!
Ahhh! Why aren't you wearing pants?!
No one appreciated my Armada Wurm costume.

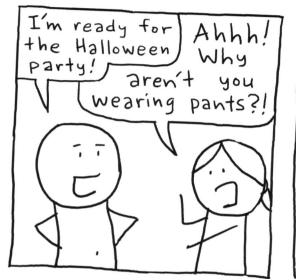

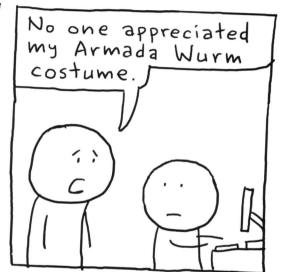

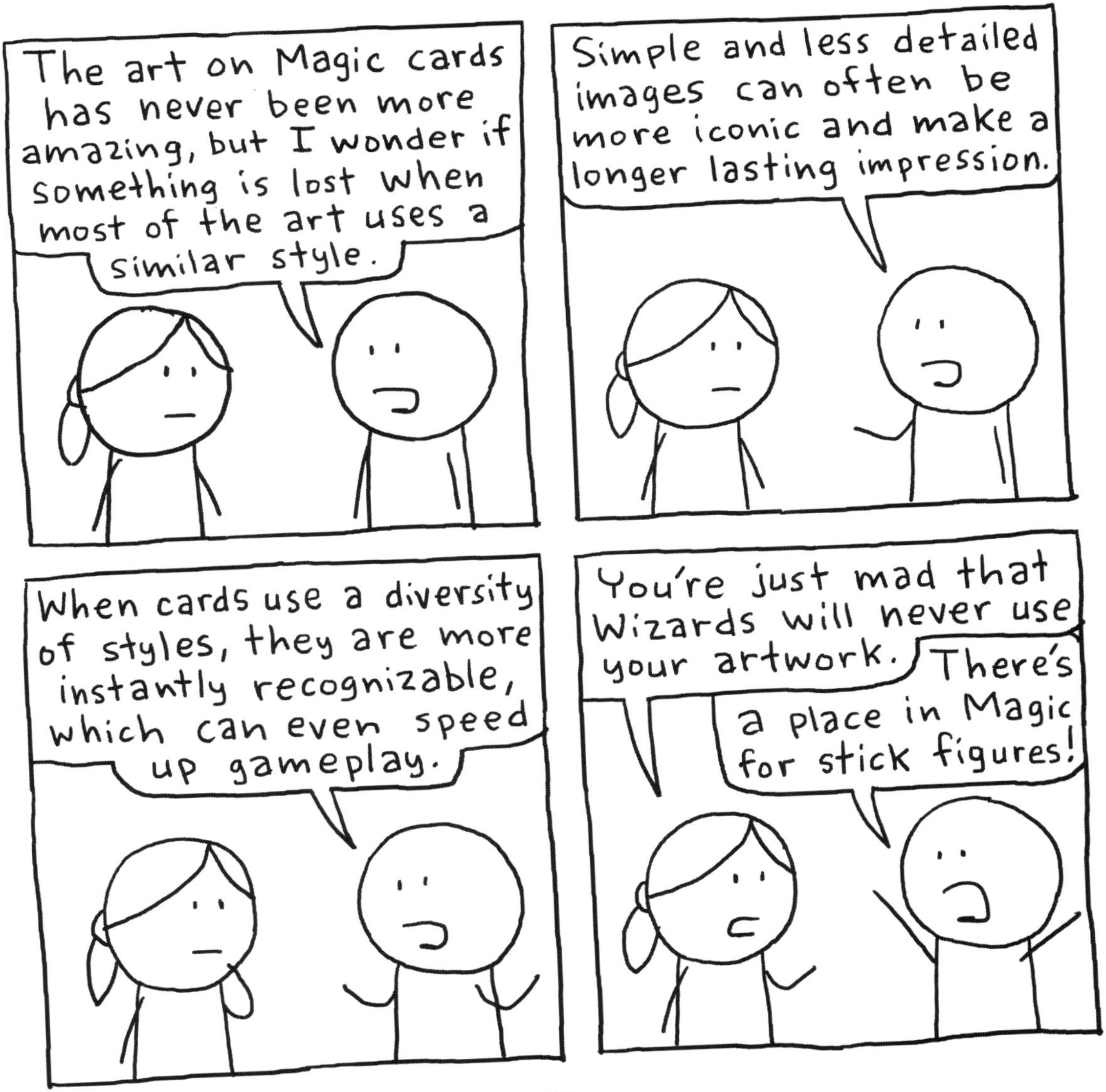
The art on Magic cards has never been more amazing, but I wonder if something is lost when most of the art uses a similar style.
Simple and less detailed images can often be more iconic and make a longer lasting impression.
When cards use a diversity of styles, they are more instantly recognizable, which can even speed up gameplay.
You're just mad that Wizards will never use your artwork.
There's a place in Magic for stick figures!

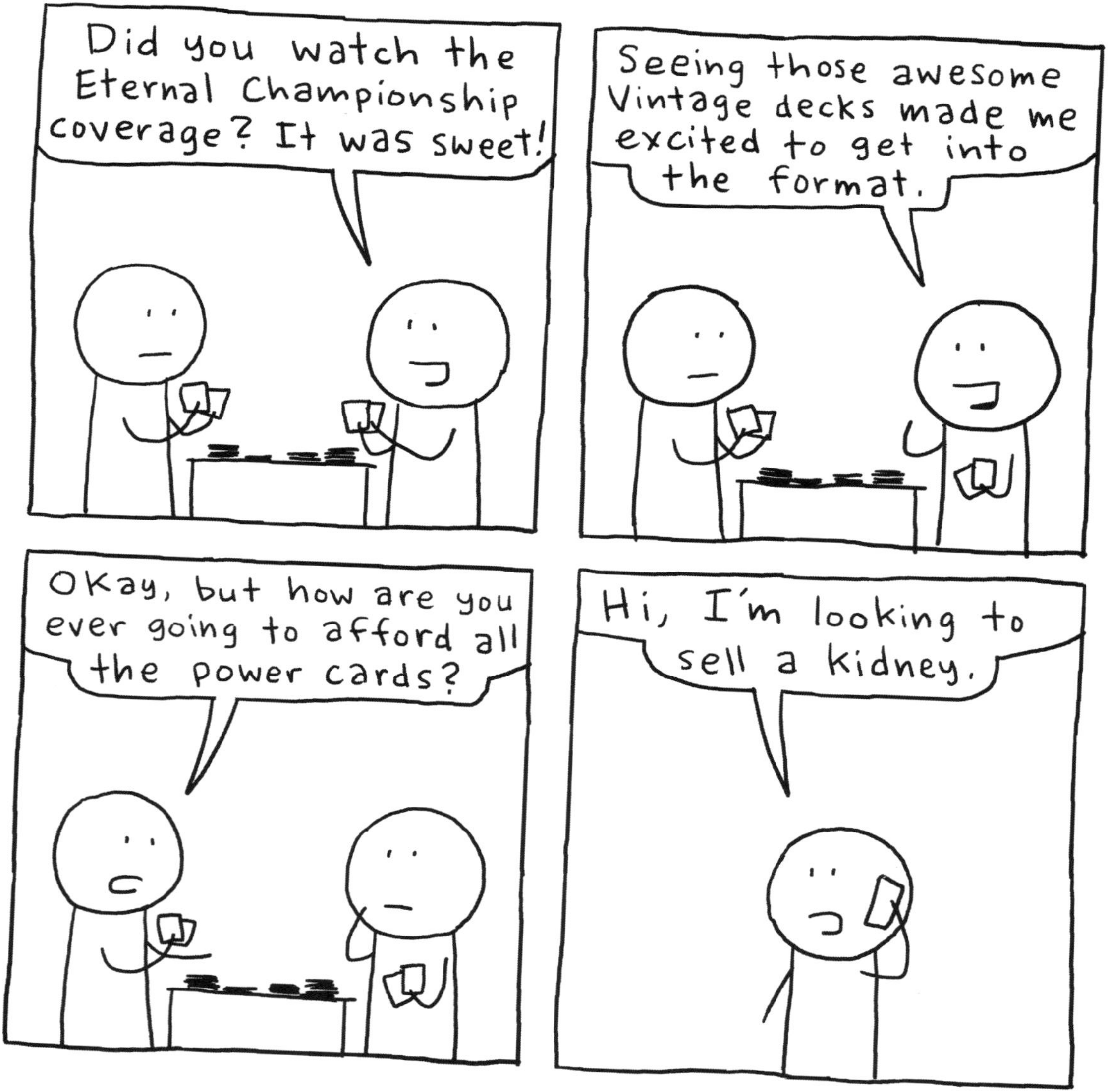
Did you watch the Eternal Championship coverage? It was sweet!
Seeing those awesome Vintage decks made me excited to get into the format.
Okay, but how are you ever going to afford all the power cards?
Hi, I'm looking to sell a kidney.

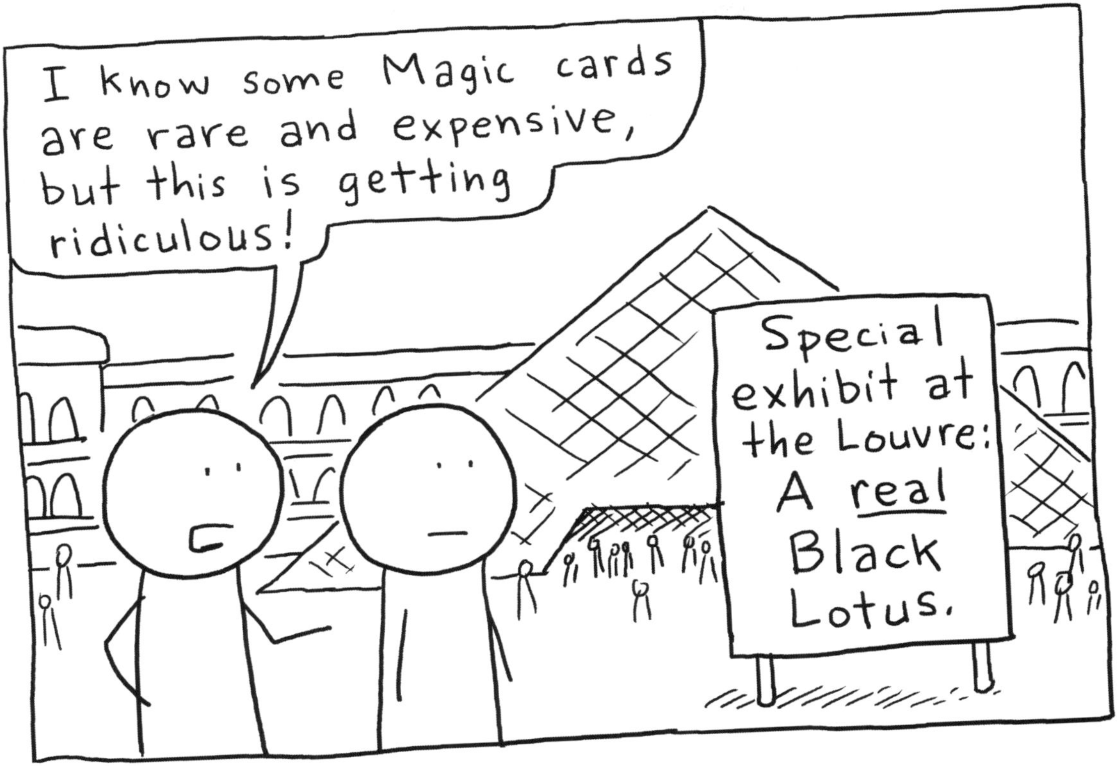
I know some Magic cards are rare and expensive, but this is getting ridiculous!
Special exhibit at the Louvre: A real Black Lotus.

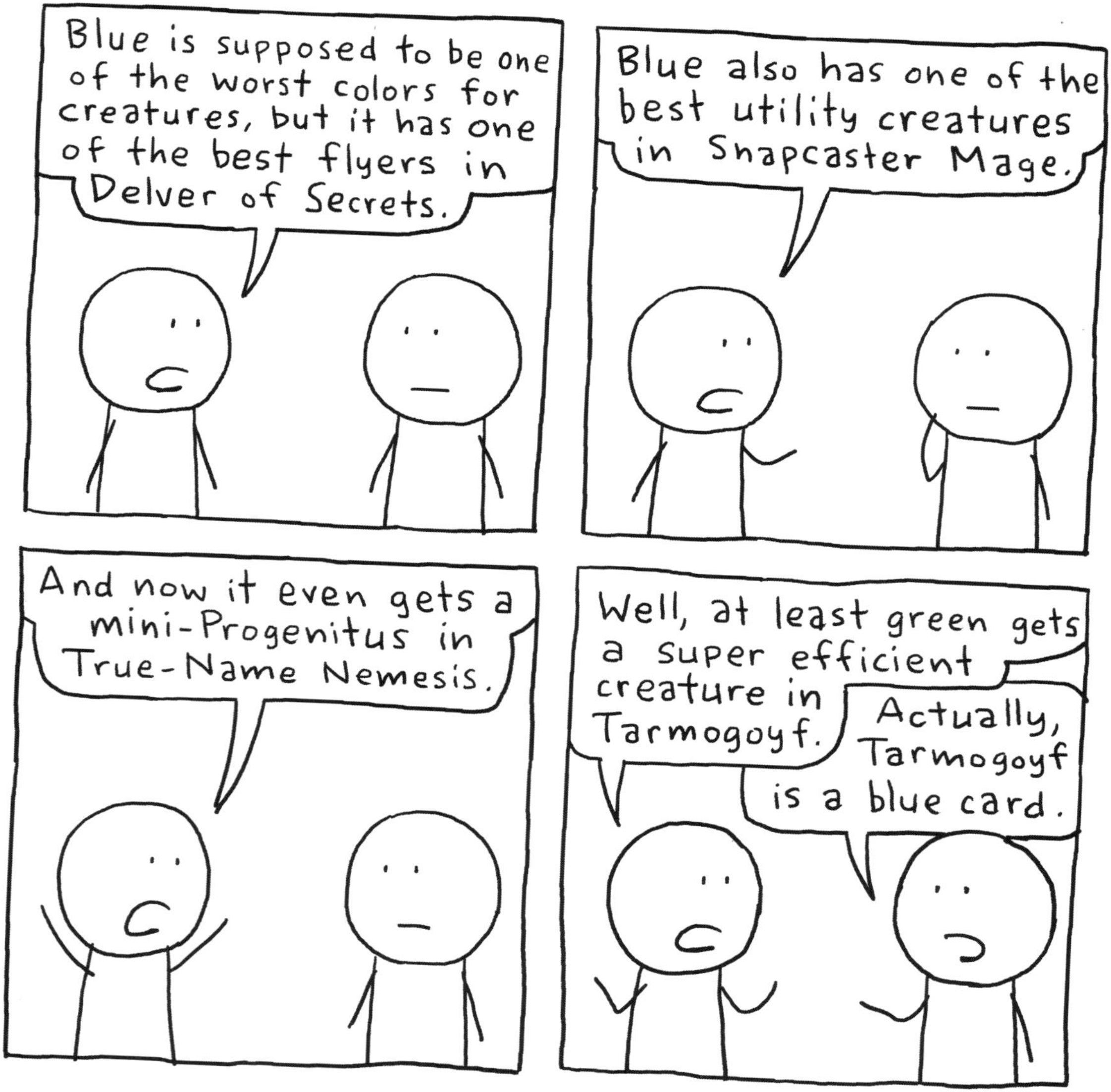
Blue is supposed to be one of the worst colors for creatures, but it has one of the best flyers in Delver of Secrets.
Blue also has one of the best utility creatures in Snapcaster Mage.
And now it even gets a mini-Progenitus in True-Name Nemesis.
Well, at least green gets a super efficient creature in Tarmogoyf.
Actually, Tarmogoyf is a blue card.

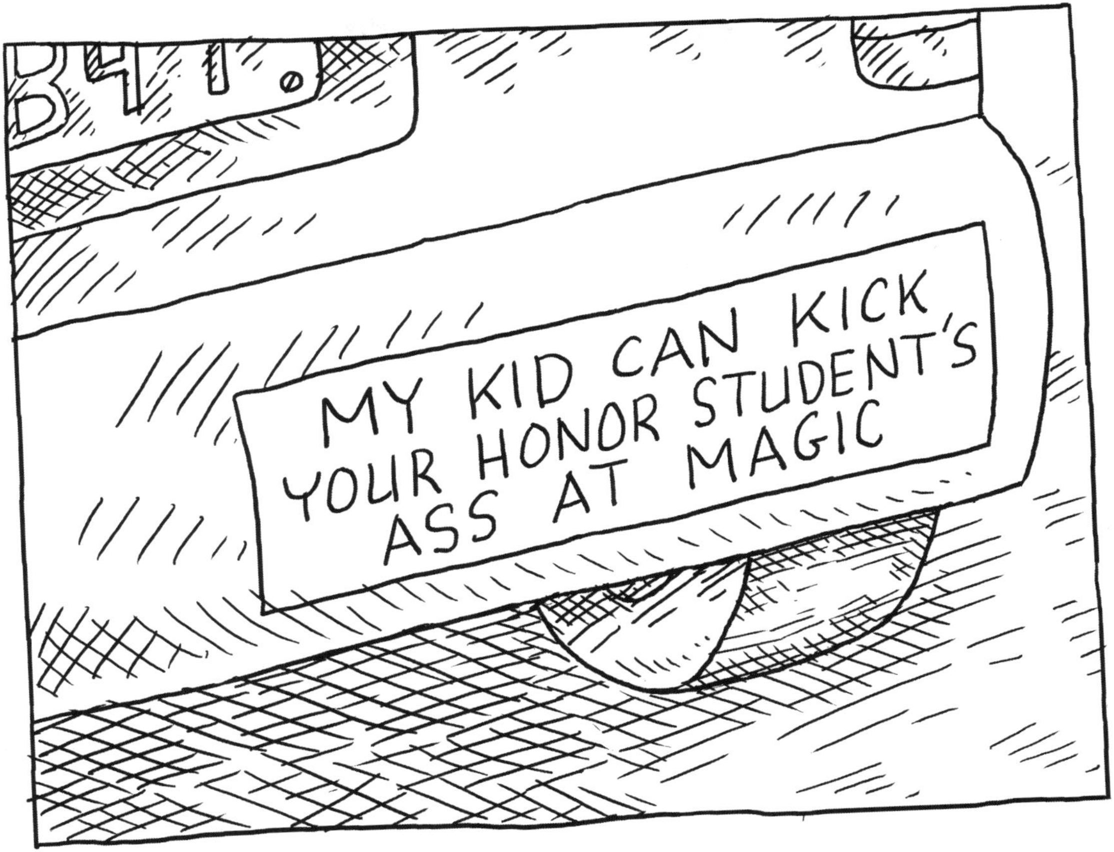
MY KID CAN KICK
YOUR HONOR STUDENT'S
ASS AT MAGIC

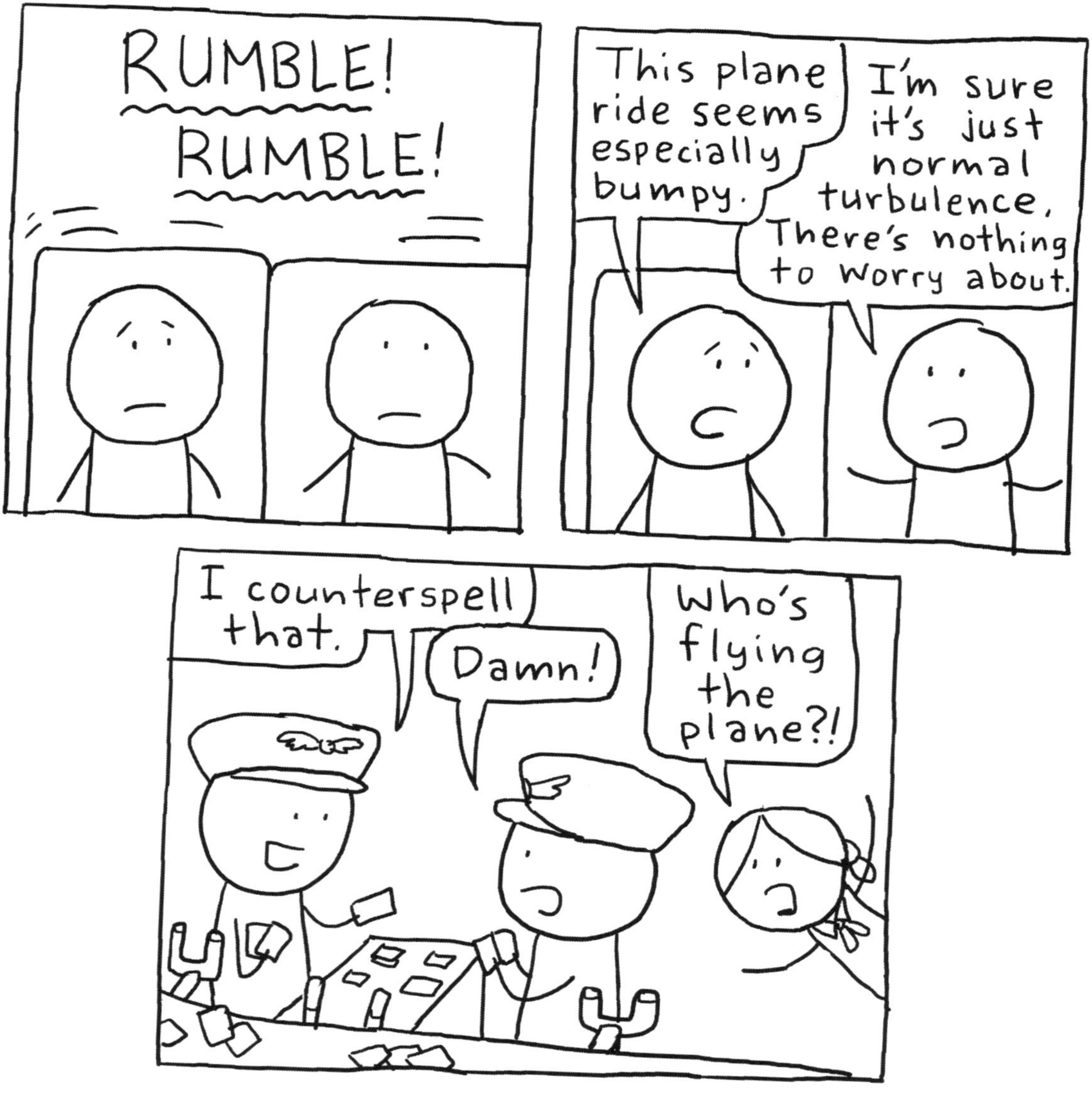
RUMBLE! RUMBLE!
This plane ride seems especially bumpy.
I'm sure it's just normal turbulence. There's nothing to worry about.
I counterspell that.
Damn!
Who's flying the plane?!

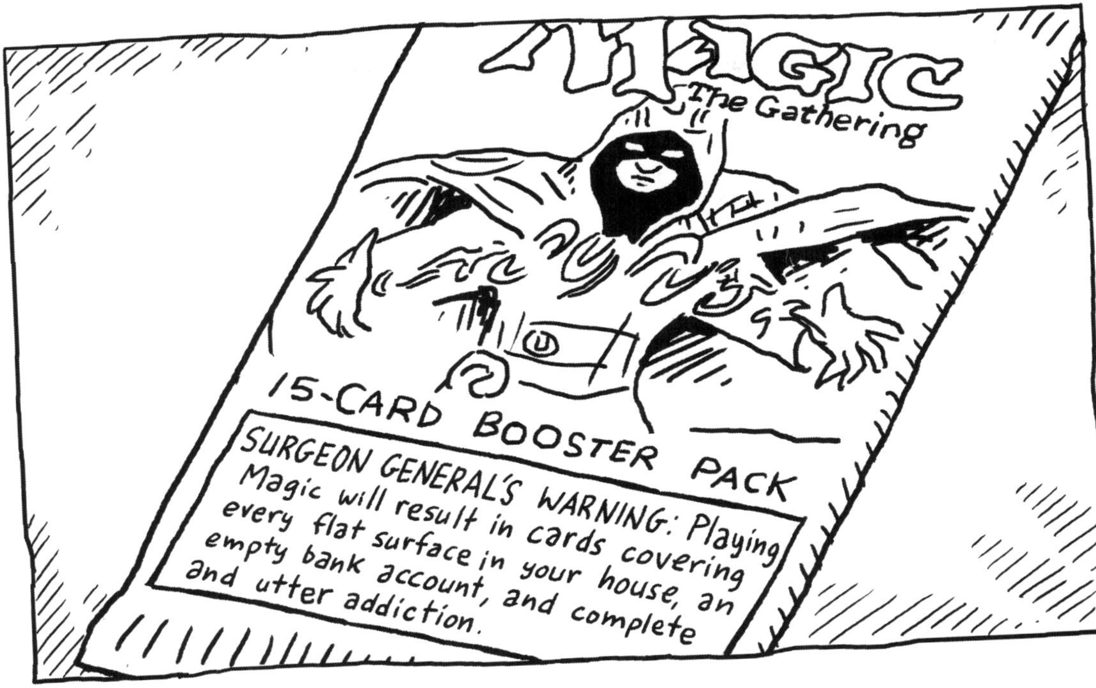
MAGIC
The Gathering
15-CARD BOOSTER PACK
SURGEON GENERAL'S WARNING: Playing Magic will result in cards covering every flat surface in your house, an empty bank account, and complete and utter addiction.

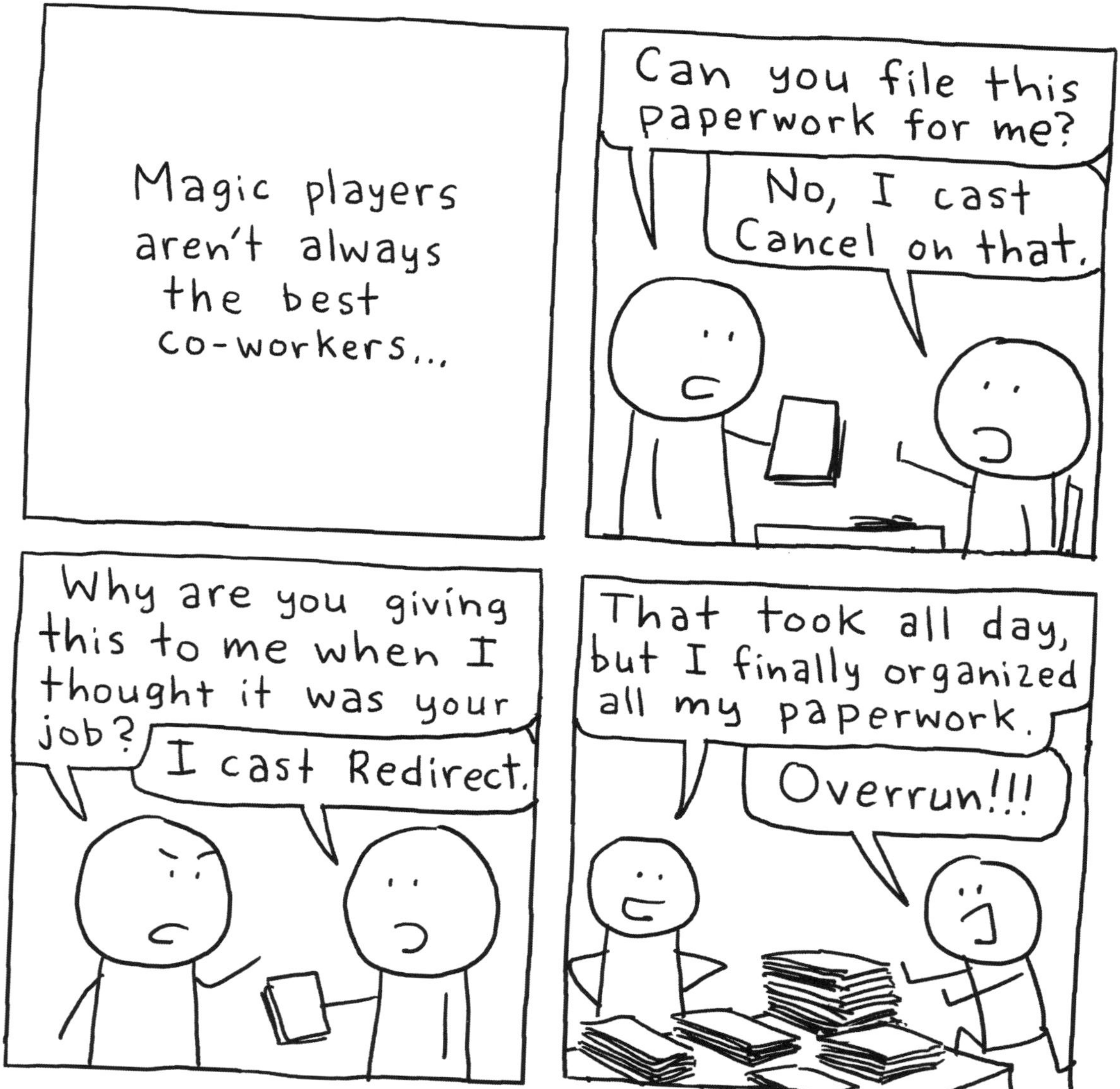
Magic players aren't always the best co-workers...
Can you file this paperwork for me?
No, I cast Cancel on that.
Why are you giving this to me when I thought it was your job?
I cast Redirect.
That took all day, but I finally organized all my paperwork.
Overrun!!!

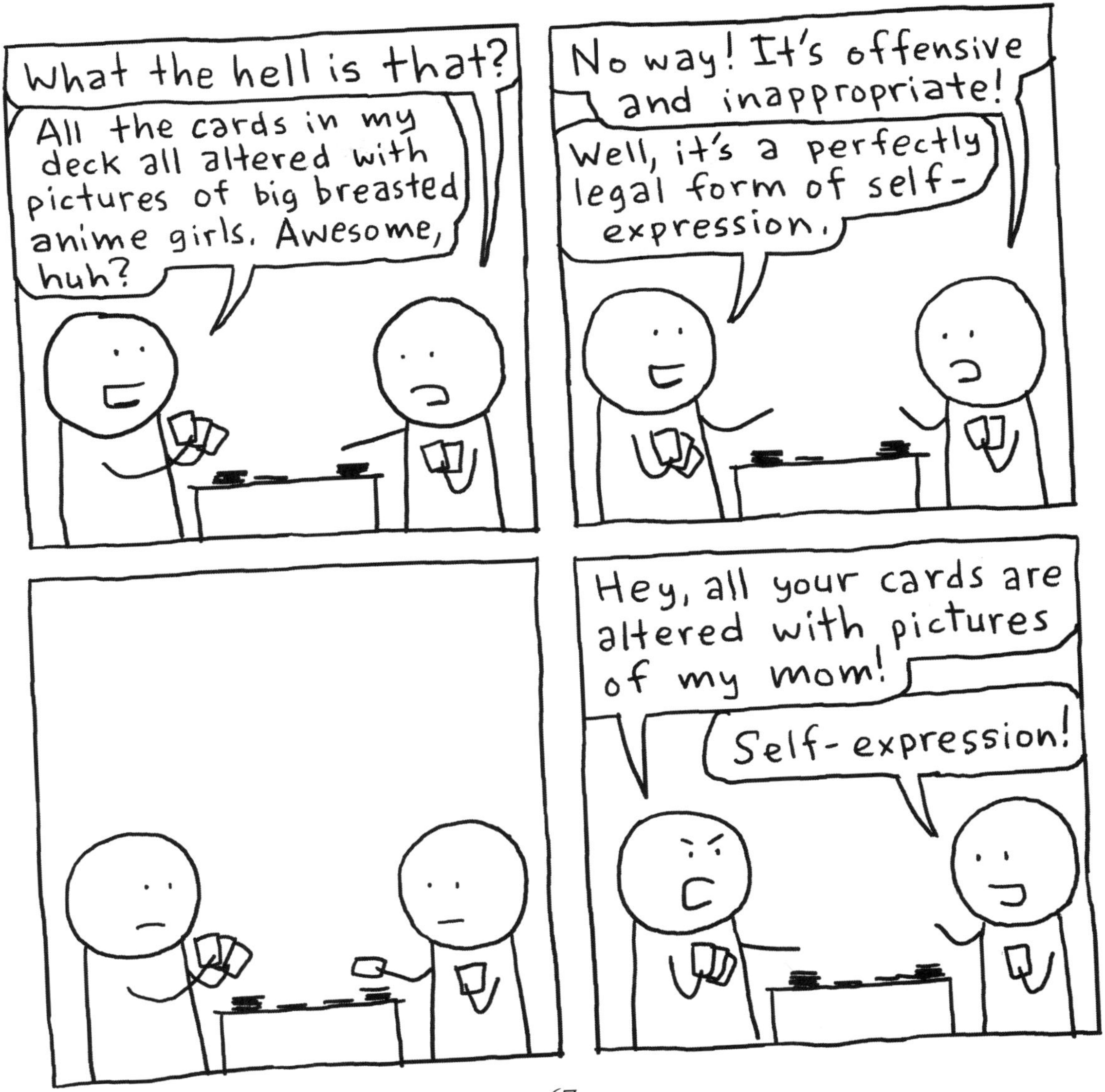
What the hell is that?
All the cards in my deck all altered with pictures of big breasted anime girls. Awesome, huh?
No way! It's offensive and inappropriate!
Well, it's a perfectly legal form of self-expression.
Hey, all your cards are altered with pictures of my mom!
Self-expression!

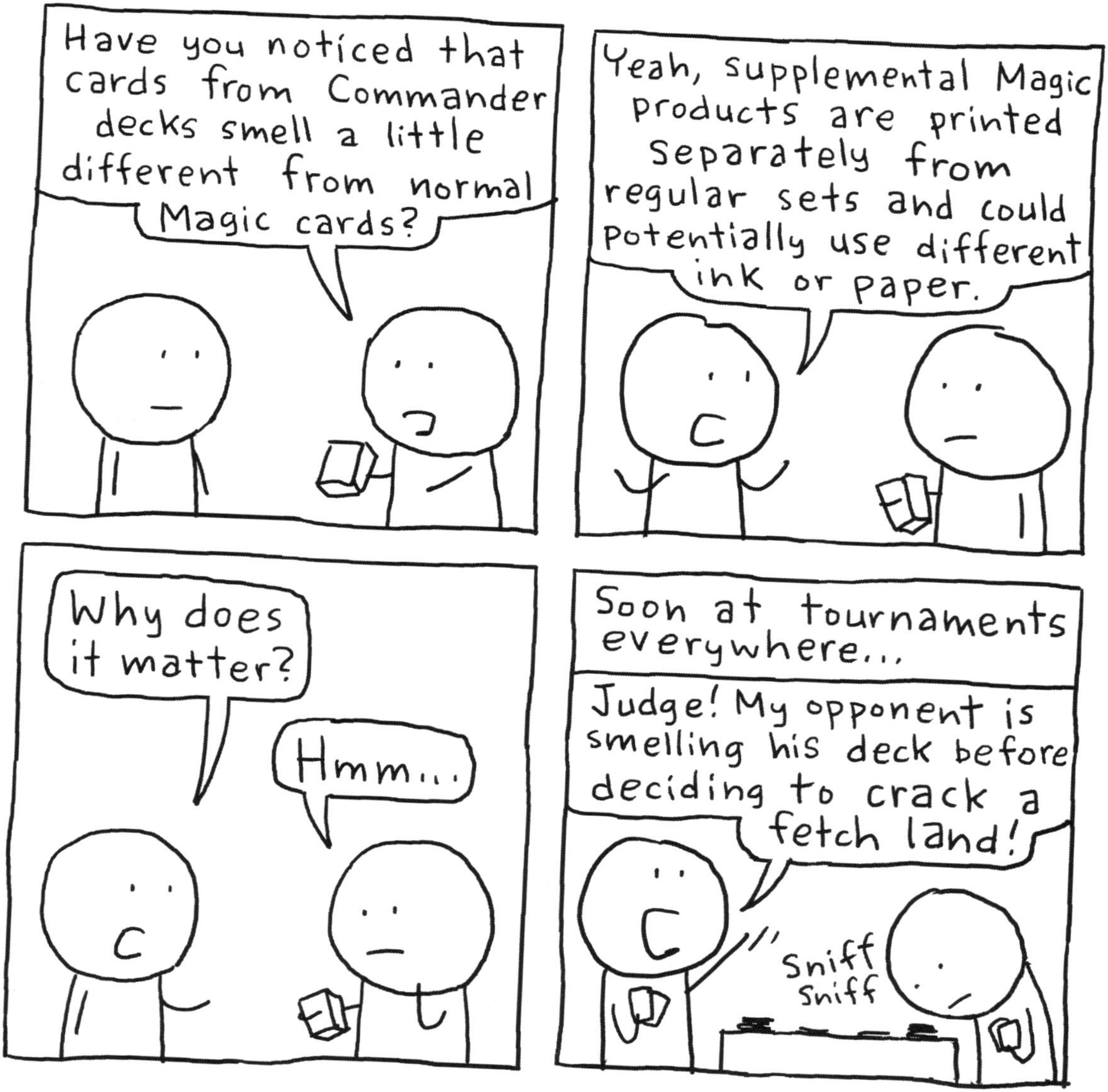

Have you noticed that cards from Commander decks smell a little different from normal Magic cards?
Yeah, supplemental Magic products are printed separately from regular sets and could potentially use different ink or paper.
Why does it matter?
Hmm...
Soon at tournaments everywhere...
Judge! My opponent is smelling his deck before deciding to crack a fetch land!
Sniff Sniff

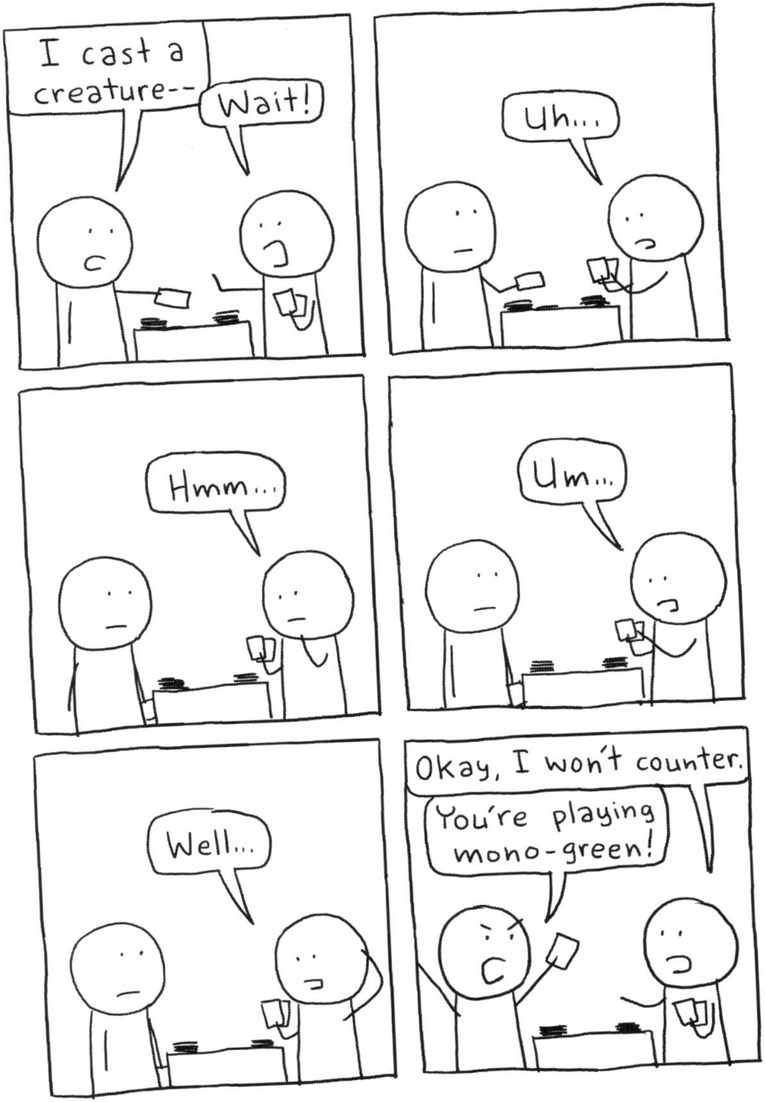
I cast a creature--
Wait!
Uh...
Hmm...
Um...
Well...
Okay, I won't counter.
You're playing mono-green!

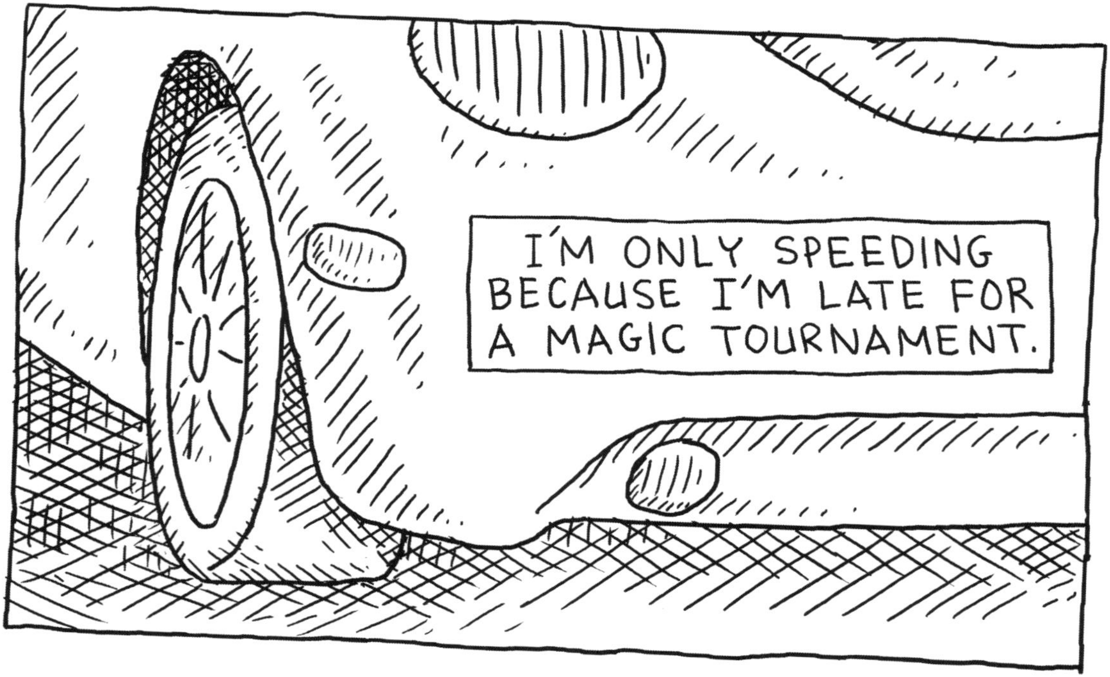
I'M ONLY SPEEDING BECAUSE I'M LATE FOR A MAGIC TOURNAMENT.

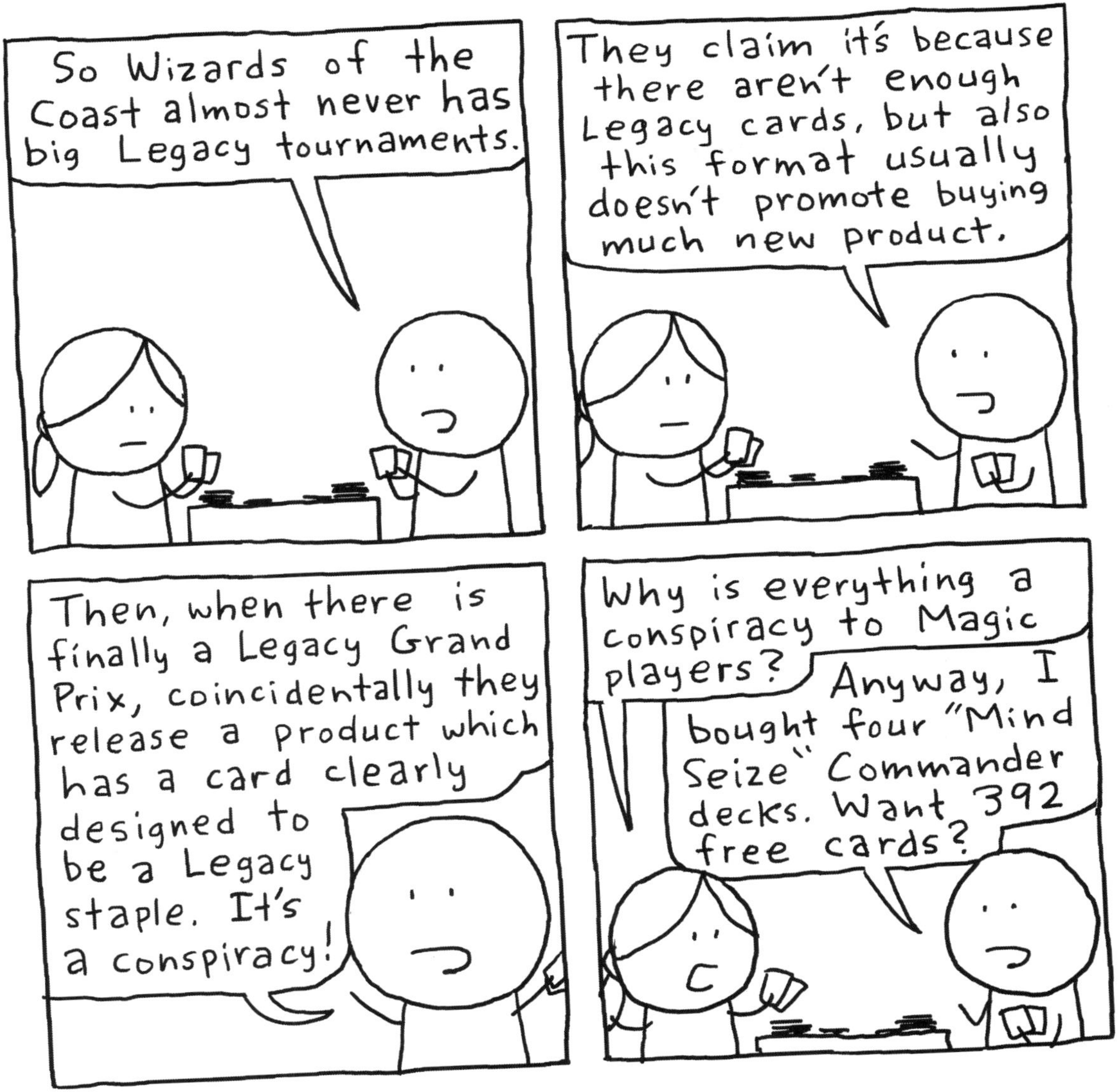

So Wizards of the Coast almost never has big Legacy tournaments.
They claim it's because there aren't enough Legacy cards, but also this format usually doesn't promote buying much new product.
Then, when there is finally a Legacy Grand Prix, coincidentally they release a product which has a card clearly designed to be a Legacy staple. It's a conspiracy!
Why is everything a conspiracy to Magic players?
Anyway, I bought four "Mind Seize" Commander decks. Want 392 free cards?

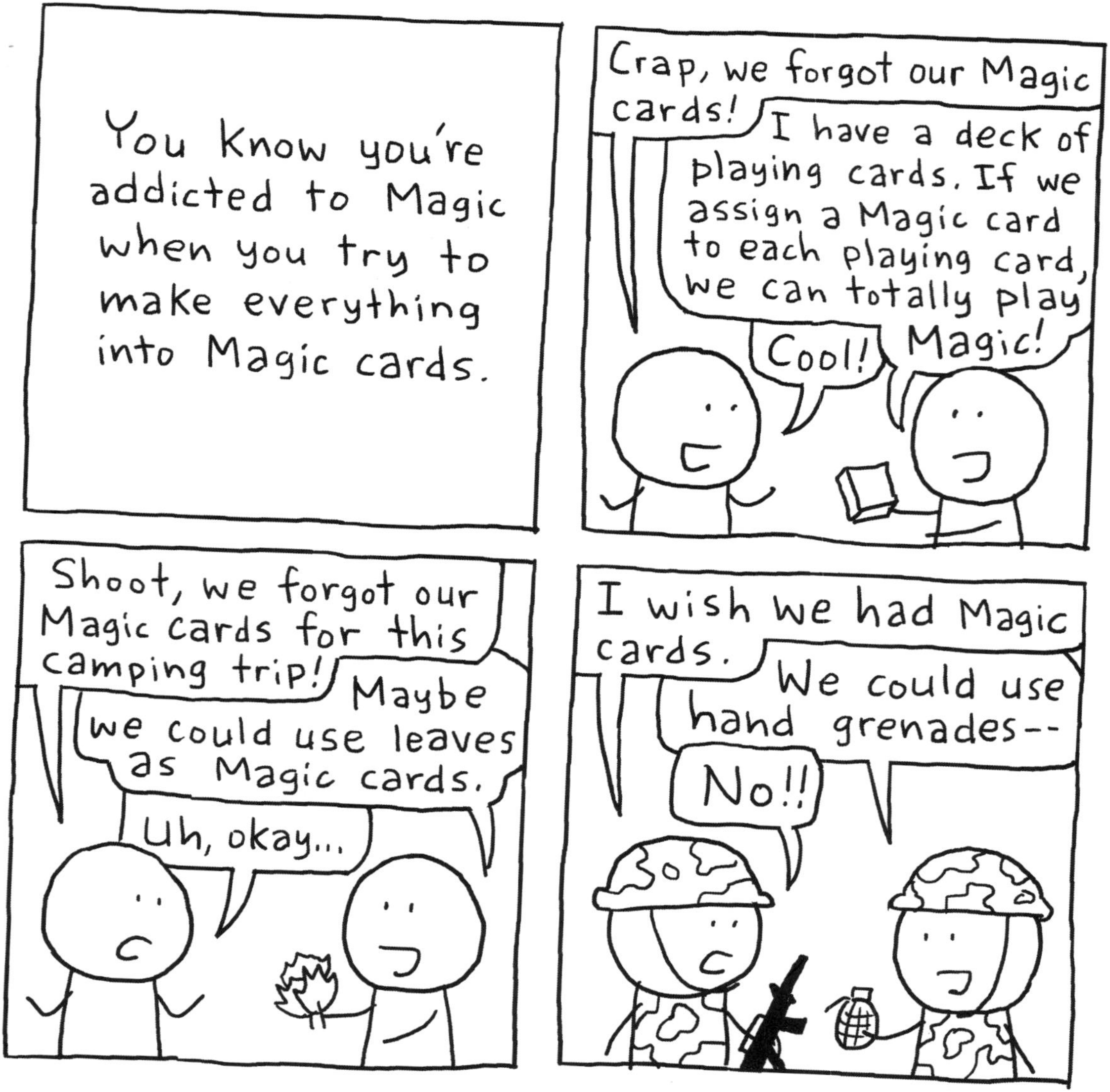
You know you're addicted to Magic when you try to make everything into Magic cards.
Crap, we forgot our Magic cards!
I have a deck of playing cards. If we assign a Magic card to each playing card, we can totally play Magic!
Cool!
Shoot, we forgot our Magic cards for this camping trip!
Maybe we could use leaves as Magic cards.
Uh, okay...
I wish we had Magic cards.
We could use hand grenades--
No!!

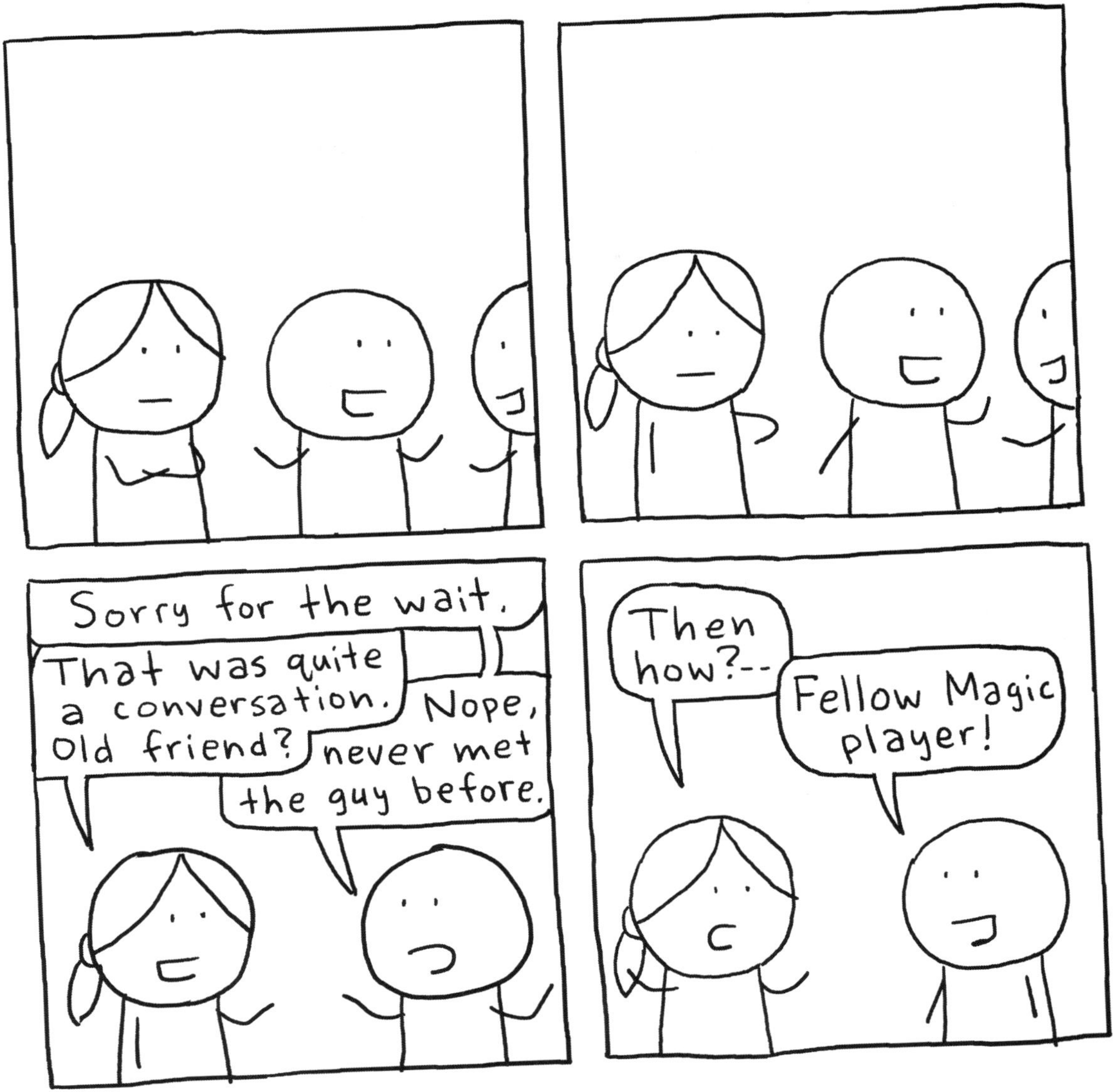
Sorry for the wait.
That was quite a conversation. Old friend?
Nope, never met the guy before.
Then how?--
Fellow Magic player!

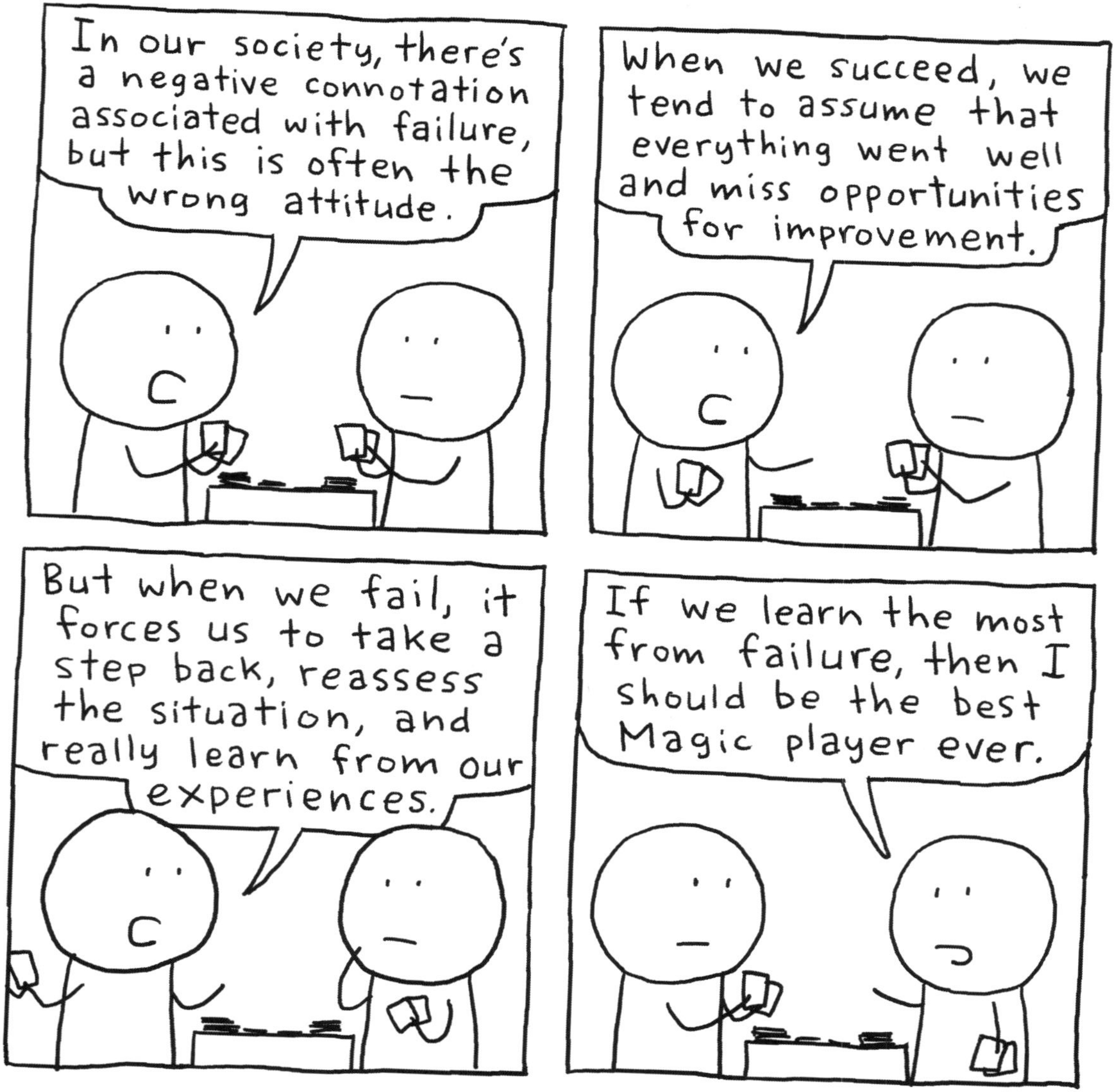
In our society, there's a negative connotation associated with failure, but this is often the wrong attitude.
When we succeed, we tend to assume that everything went well and miss opportunities for improvement.
But when we fail, it forces us to take a step back, reassess the situation, and really learn from our experiences.
If we learn the most from failure, then I should be the best Magic player ever.

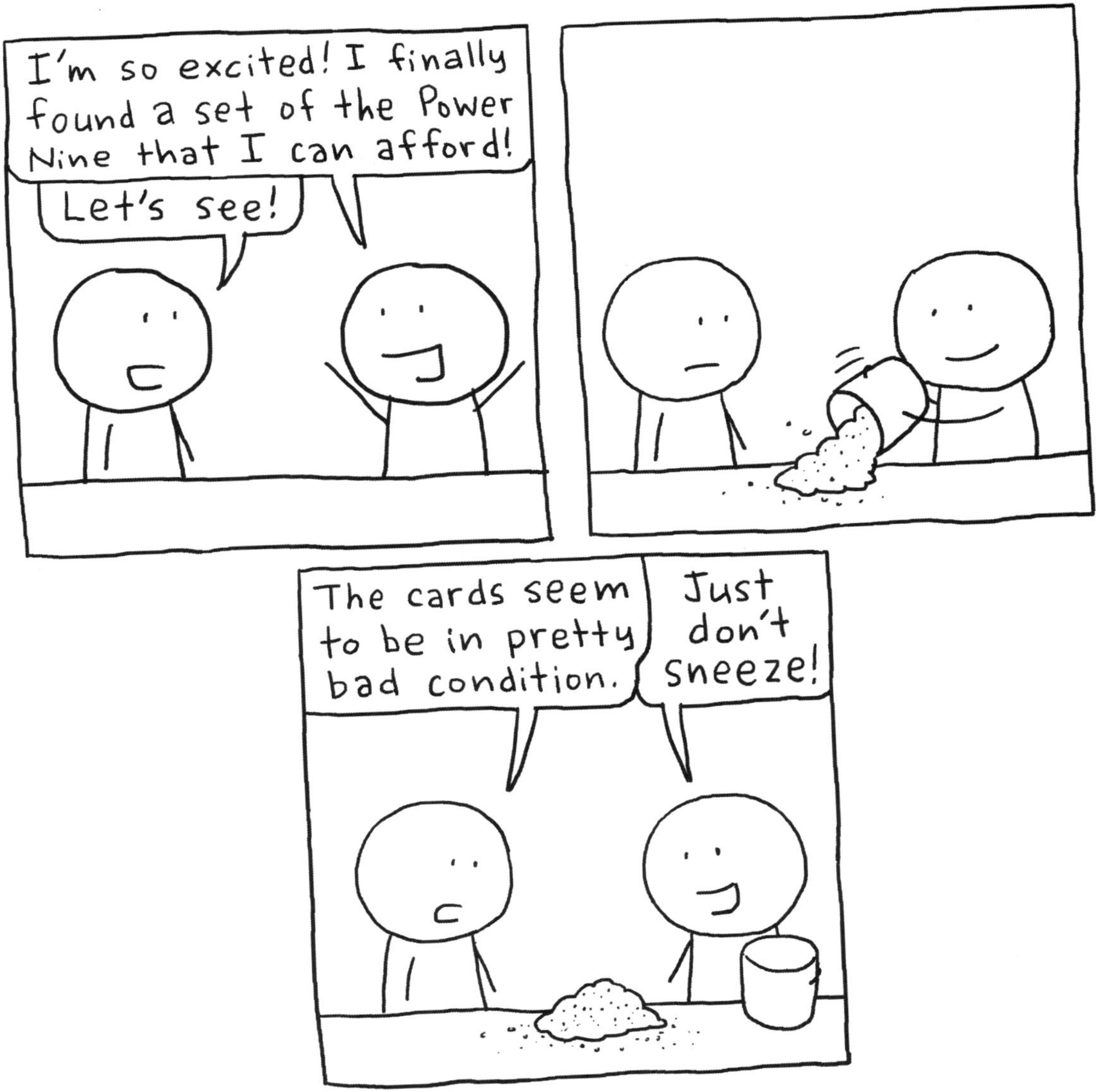
I'm so excited! I finally found a set of the Power Nine that I can afford!
Let's see!
The cards seem to be in pretty bad condition.
Just don't sneeze!

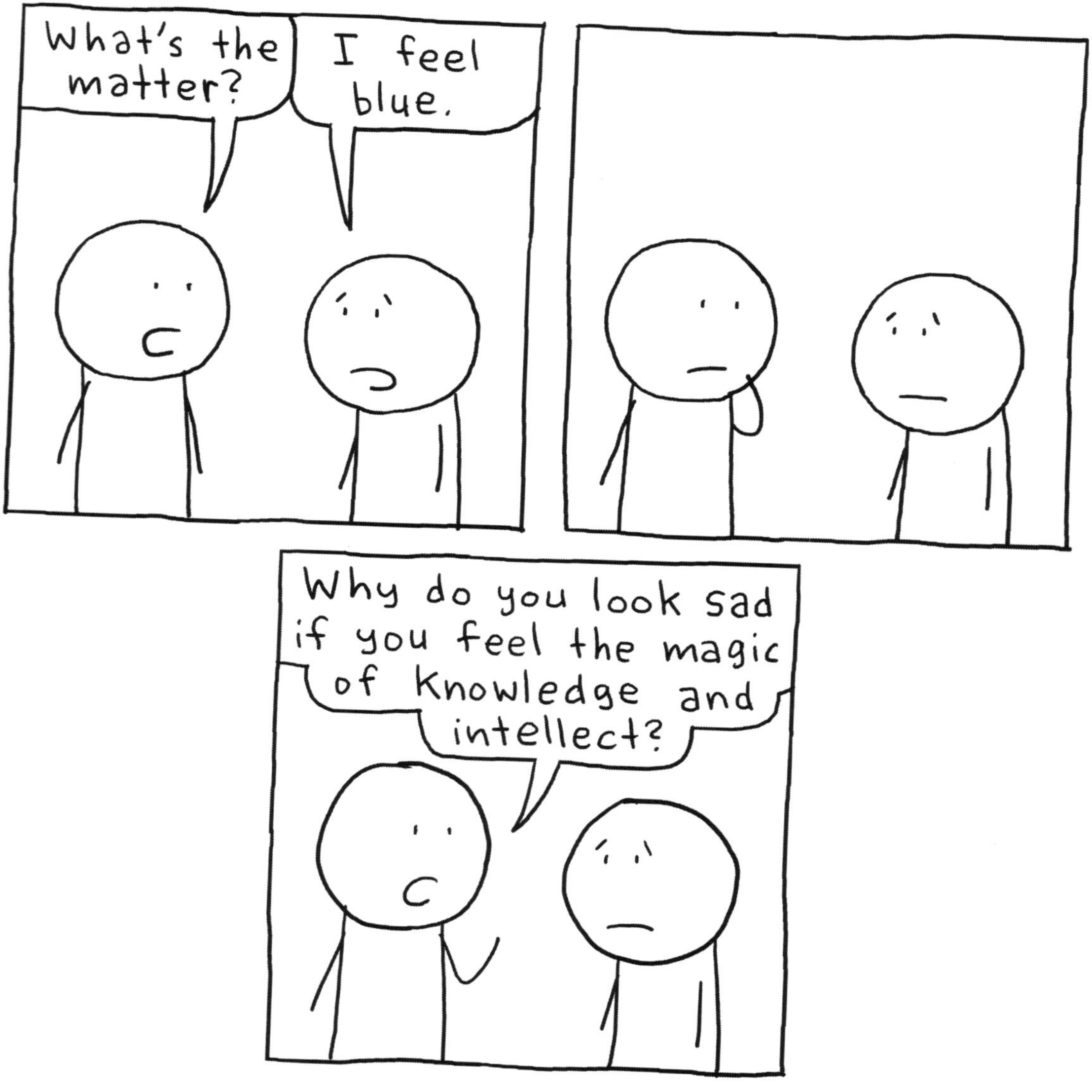
What's the matter?
I feel blue.
Why do you look sad if you feel the magic of knowledge and intellect?

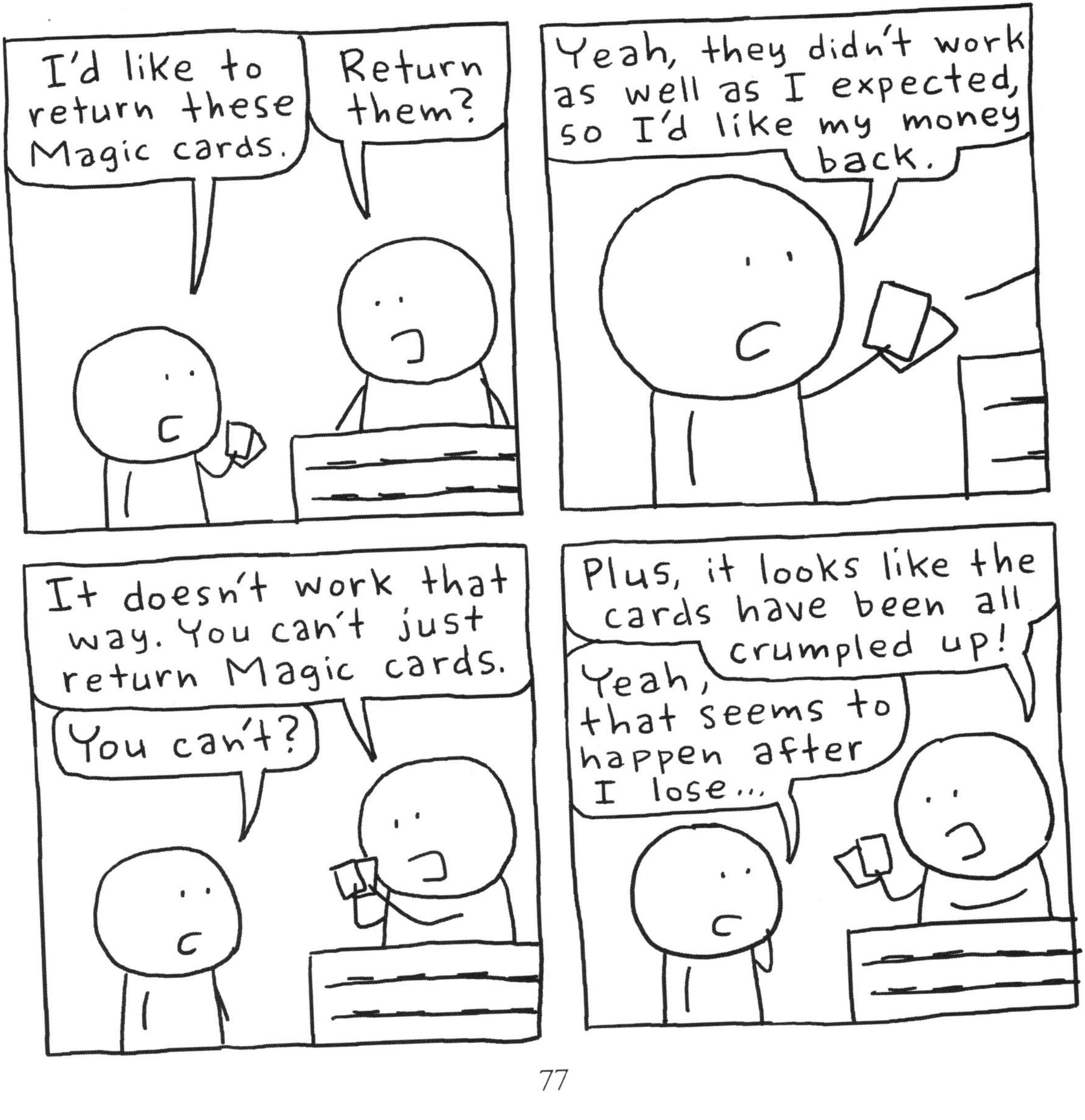
I'd like to return these Magic cards.
Return them?
Yeah, they didn't work as well as I expected, so I'd like my money back.
It doesn't work that way. You can't just return Magic cards.
You can't?
Plus, it looks like the cards have been all crumpled up!
Yeah, that seems to happen after I lose...

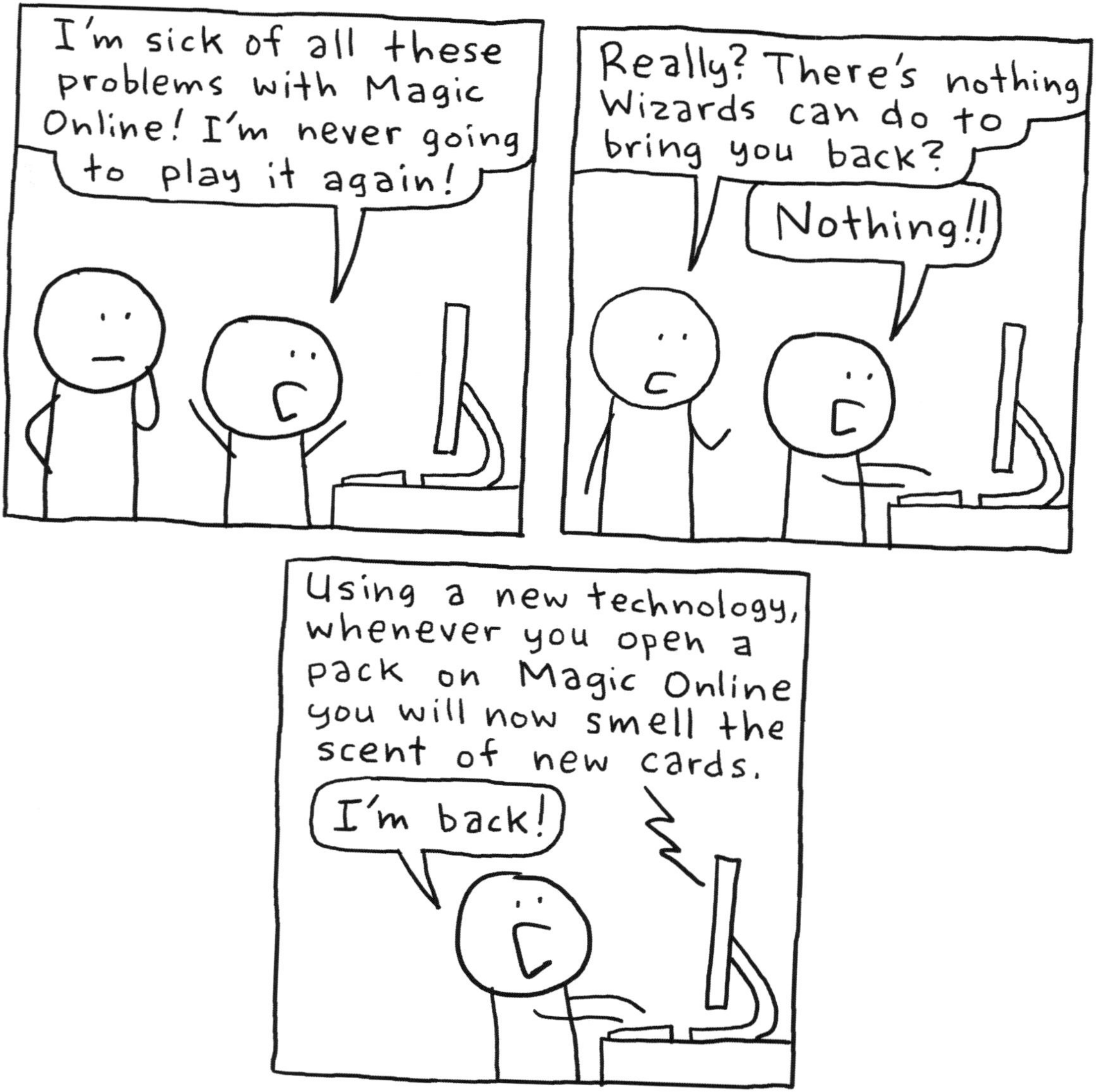
I'm sick of all these problems with Magic Online! I'm never going to play it again!
Really? There's nothing Wizards can do to bring you back?
Nothing!!
Using a new technology, whenever you open a pack on Magic Online you will now smell the scent of new cards.
I'm back!

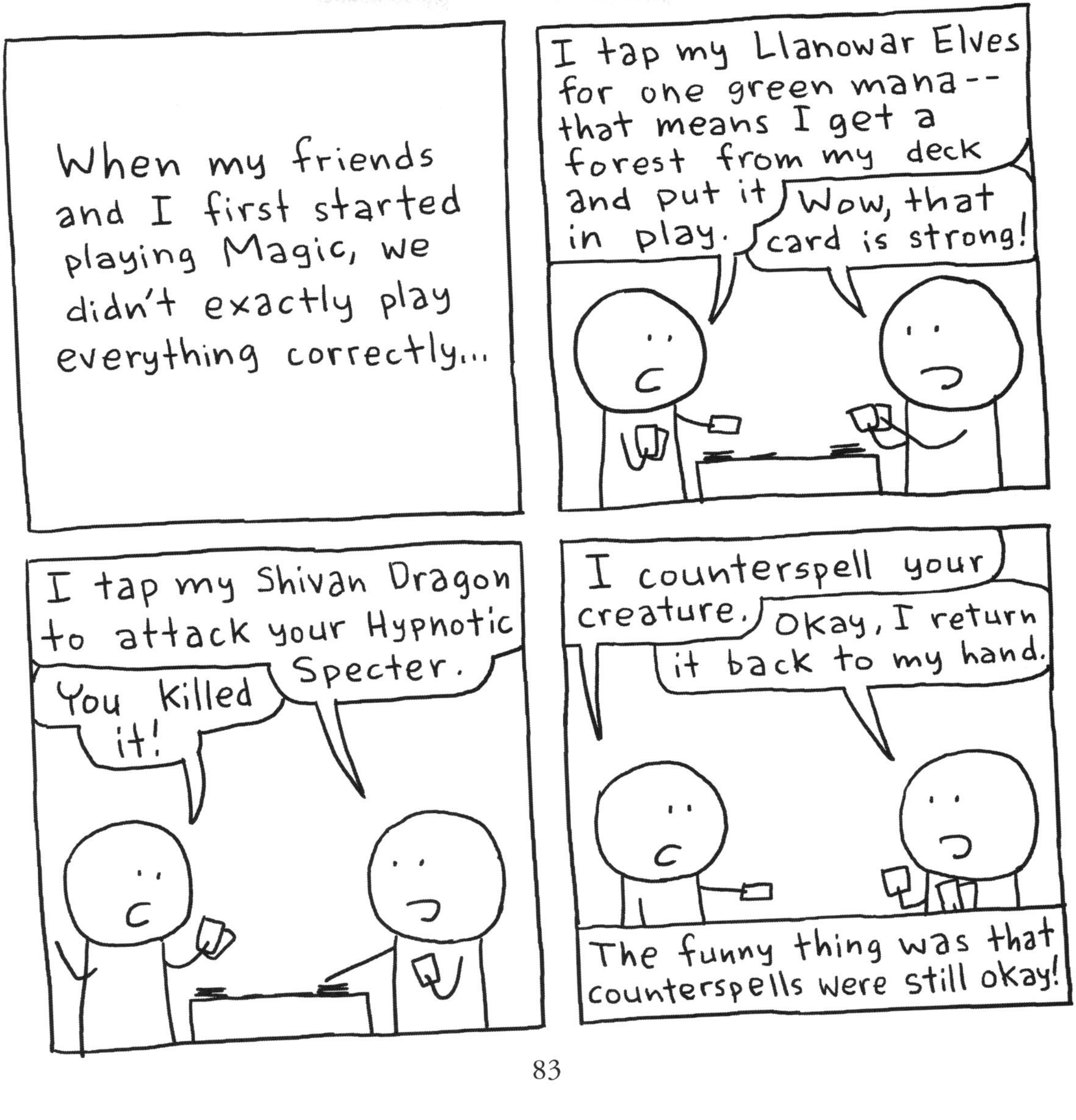
When my friends and I first started playing Magic, we didn't exactly play everything correctly...
I tap my Llanowar Elves for one green mana-- that means I get a forest from my deck and put it in play.
Wow, that card is strong!
I tap my Shivan Dragon to attack your Hypnotic Specter.
You killed it!
I counterspell your creature.
Okay, I return it back to my hand.
The funny thing was that counterspells were still okay!

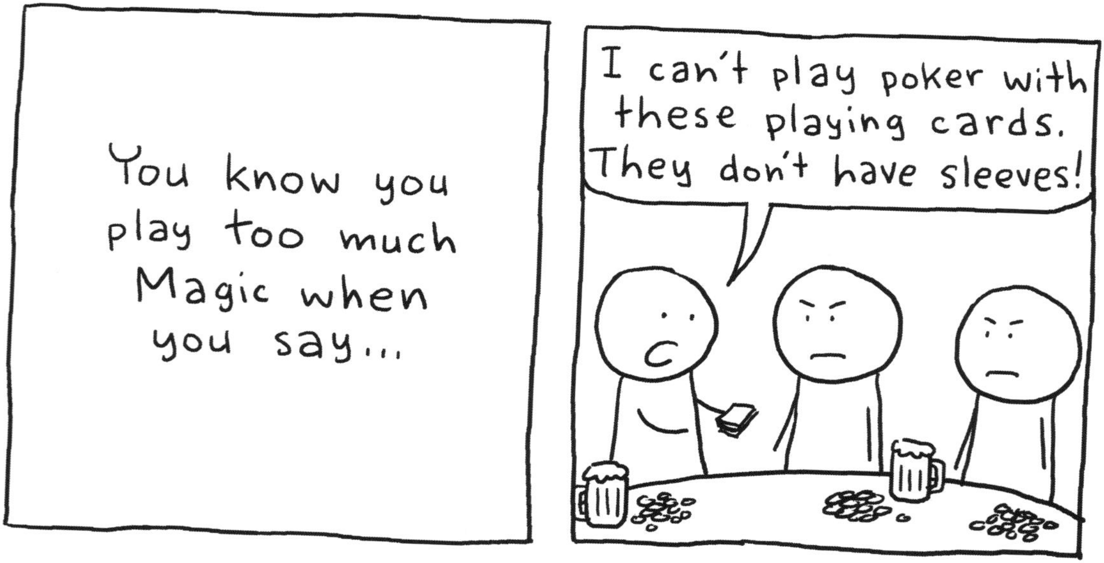
You know you play too much Magic when you say...
I can't play poker with these playing cards. They don't have sleeves!

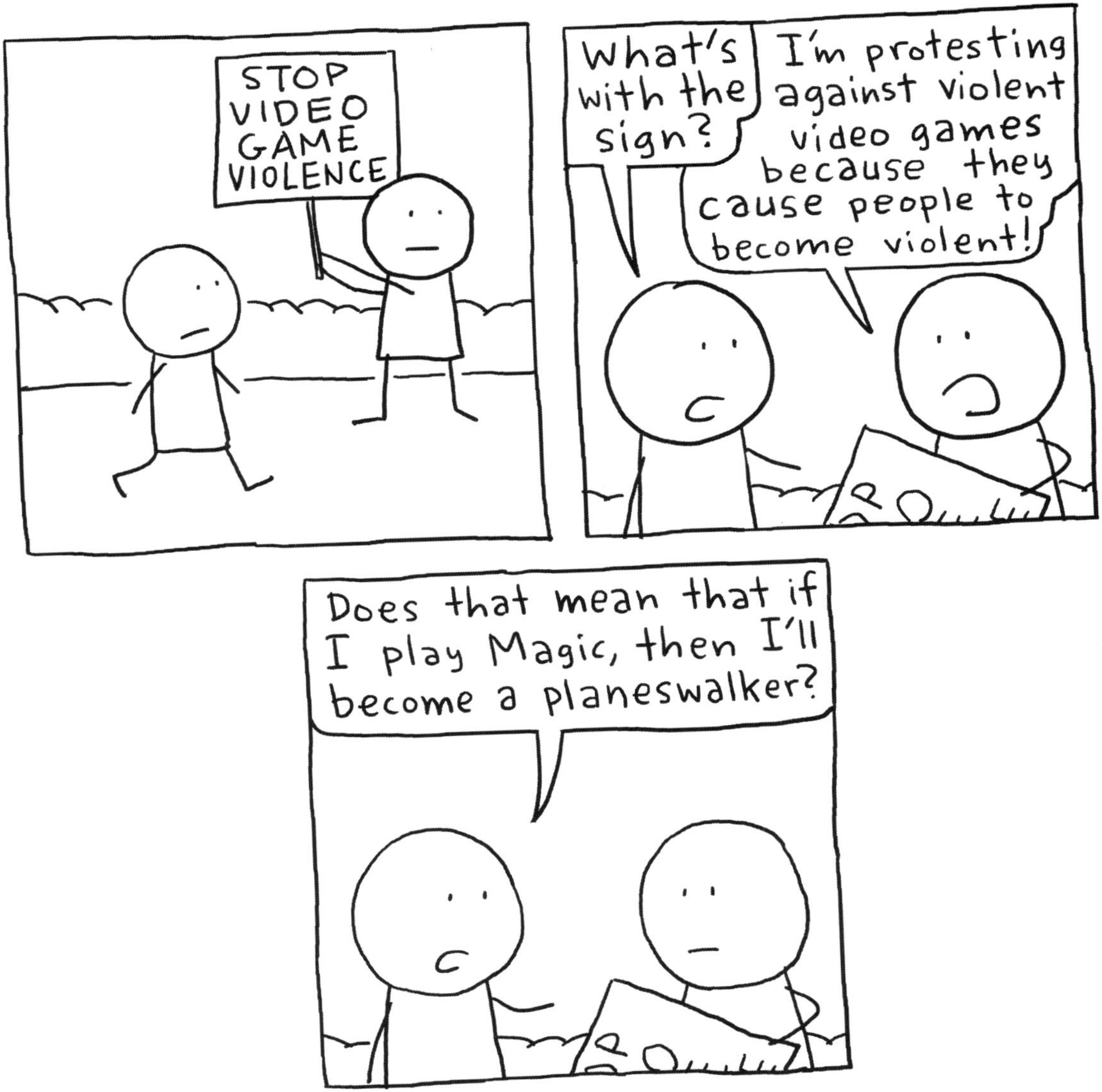
STOP VIDEO GAME VIOLENCE
What's with the sign?
I'm protesting against violent video games because they cause people to become violent!
Does that mean that if I play Magic, then I'll become a planeswalker?

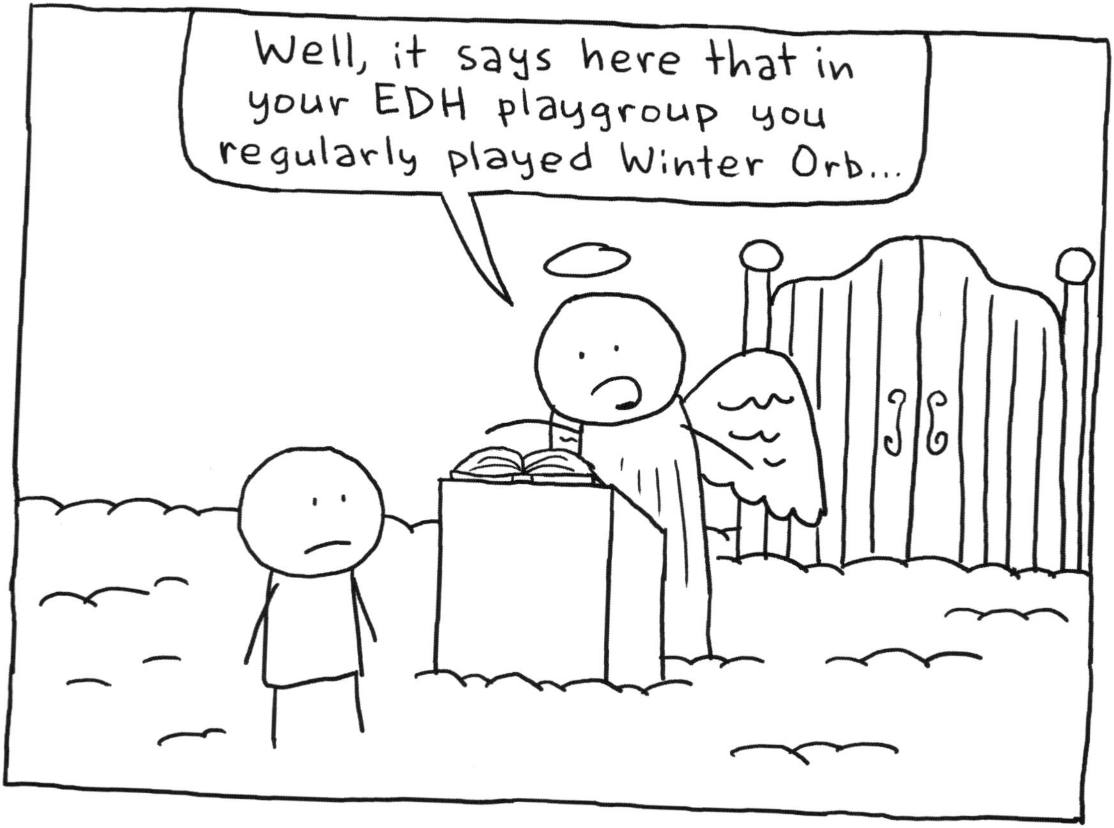
Well, it says here that in your EDH playgroup you regularly played Winter Orb...

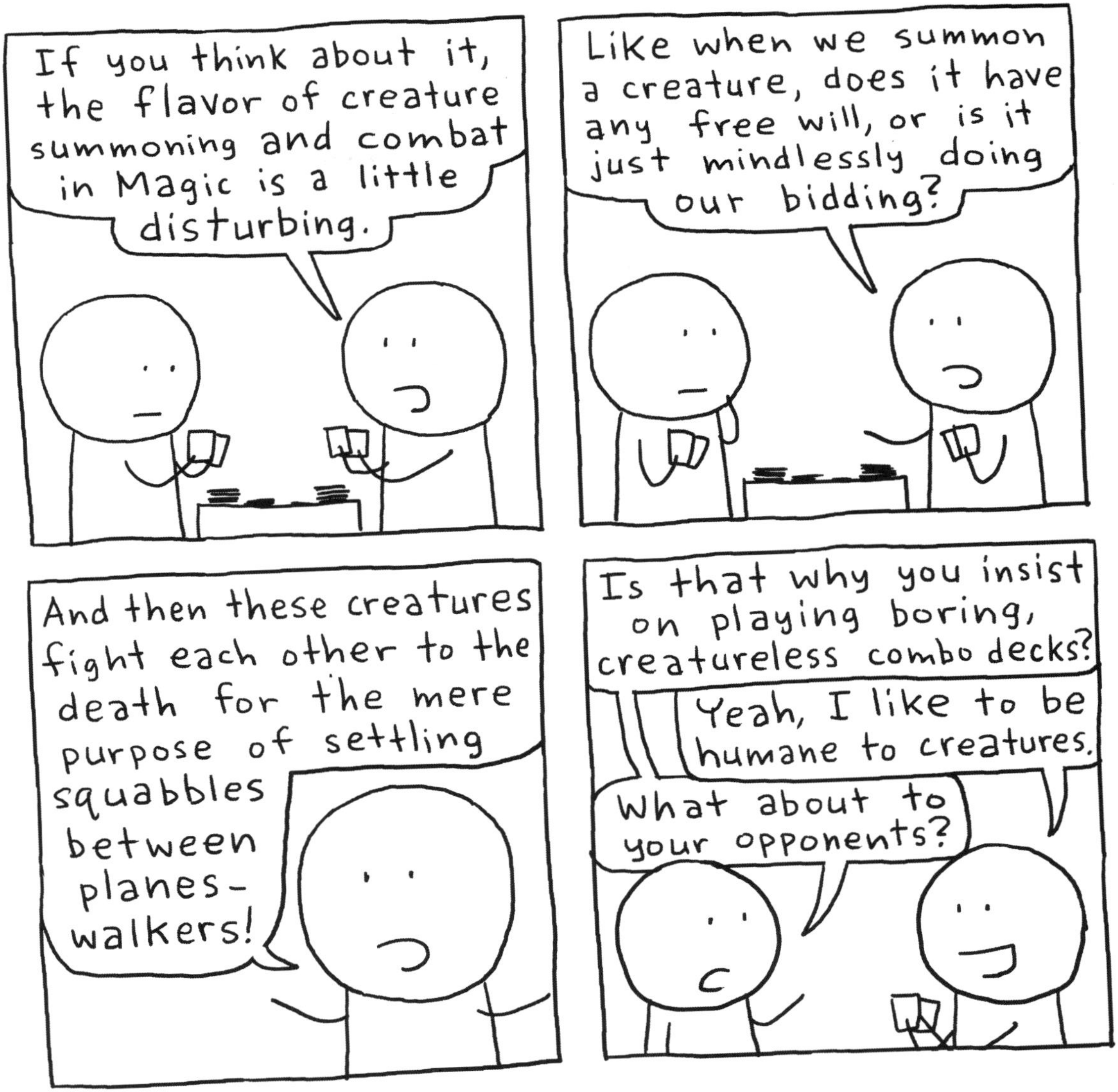
If you think about it, the flavor of creature summoning and combat in Magic is a little disturbing.
Like when we summon a creature, does it have any free will, or is it just mindlessly doing our bidding?
And then these creatures fight each other to the death for the mere purpose of settling squabbles between planes-walkers!
Is that why you insist on playing boring, creatureless combo decks?
Yeah, I like to be humane to creatures.
What about to your opponents?

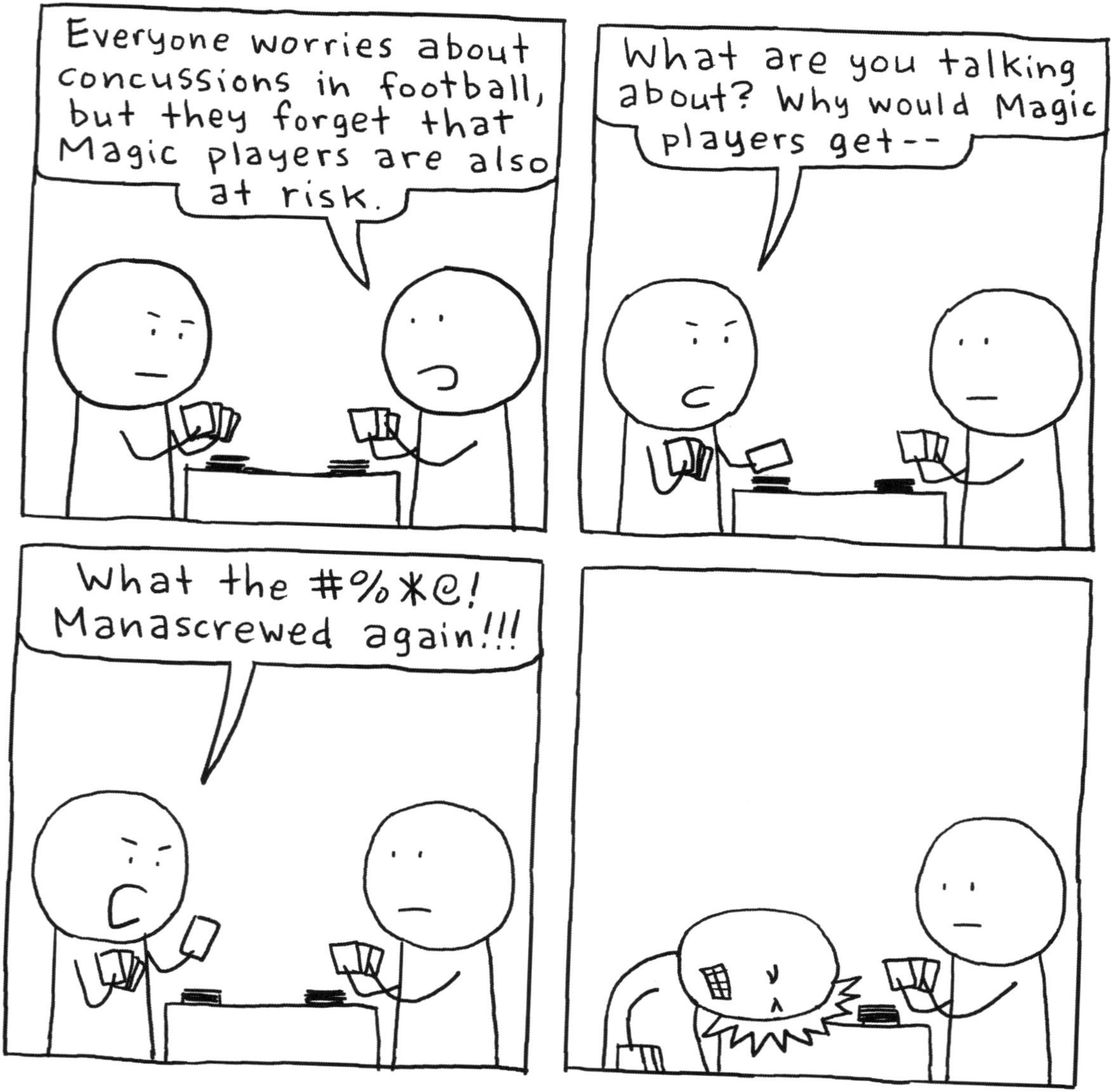
Everyone worries about concussions in football, but they forget that Magic players are also at risk.
What are you talking about? Why would Magic players get--
What the #%*@! Manascrewed again!!!

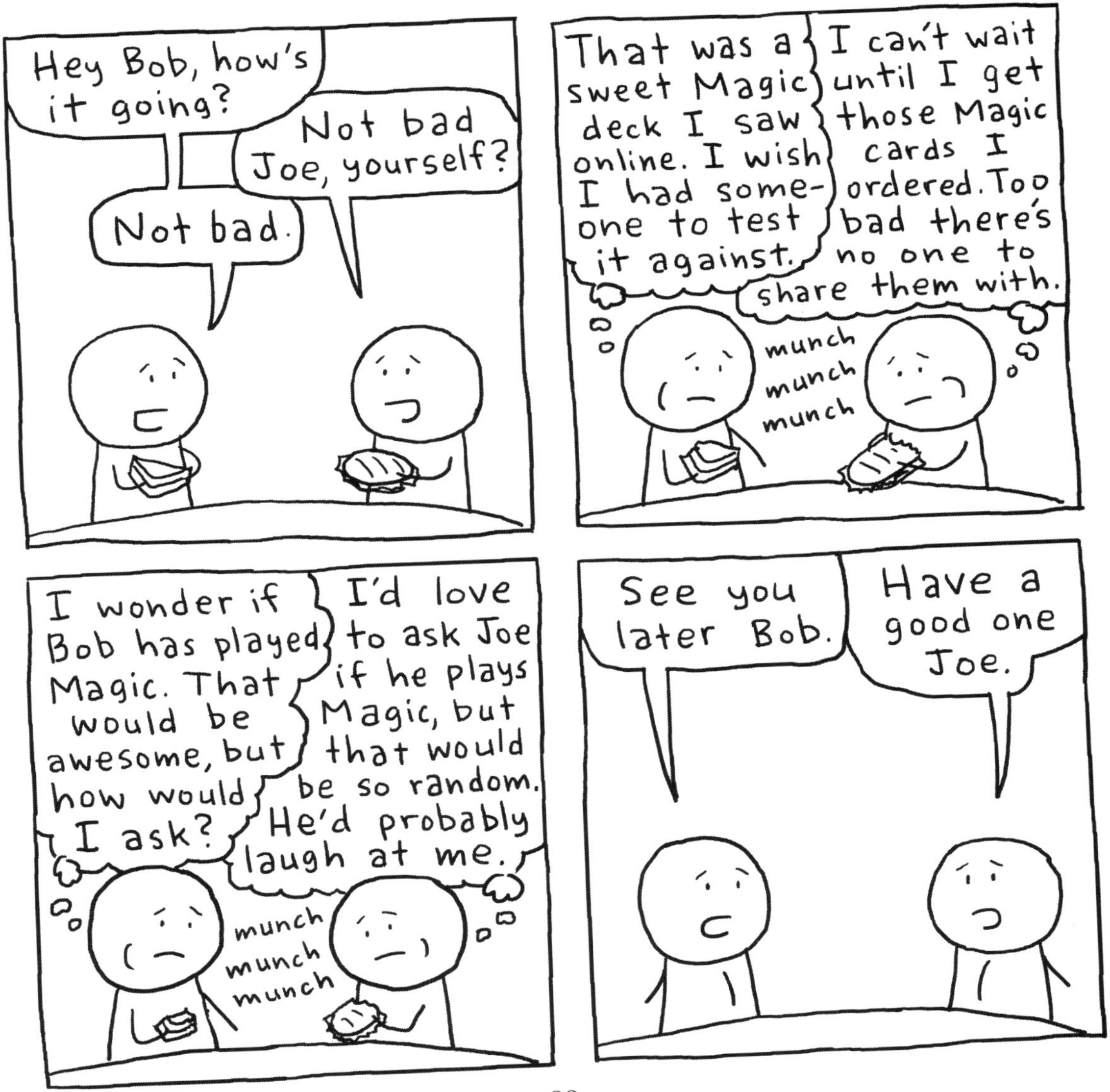
Hey Bob, how's it going?
Not bad Joe, yourself?
Not bad.
That was a sweet Magic deck I saw online. I wish I had some-one to test it against.
I can't wait until I get those Magic cards I ordered. Too bad there's no one to share them with.
munch munch munch
I wonder if Bob has played Magic. That would be awesome, but how would I ask?
I'd love to ask Joe if he plays Magic, but that would be so random. He'd probably laugh at me.
munch munch munch
See you later Bob.
Have a good one Joe.

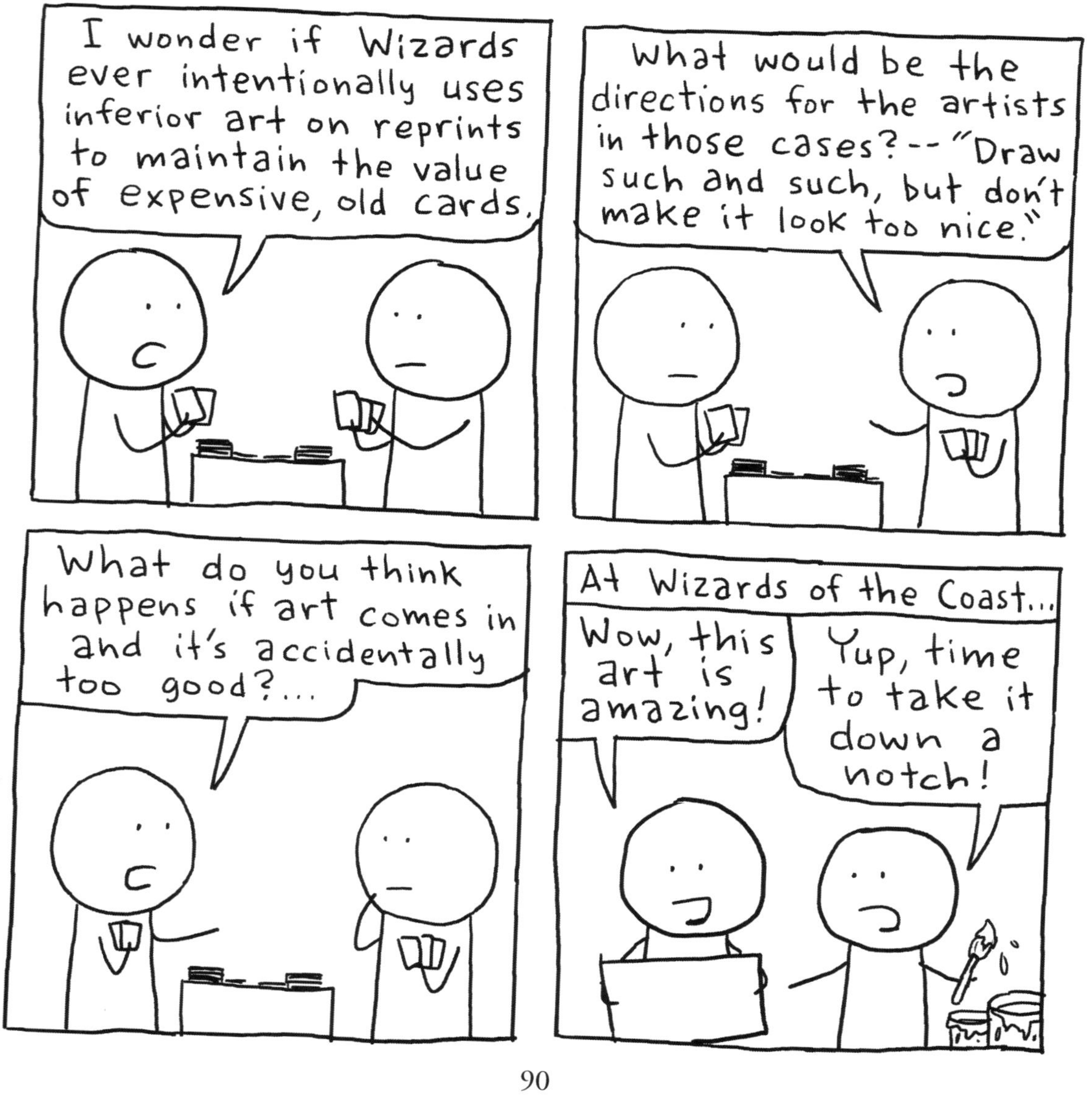

I wonder if Wizards ever intentionally uses inferior art on reprints to maintain the value of expensive, old cards.
What would be the directions for the artists in those cases?--"Draw such and such, but don't make it look too nice."
What do you think happens if art comes in and it's accidentally too good?...
At Wizards of the Coast...
Wow, this art is amazing!
Yup, time to take it down a notch!

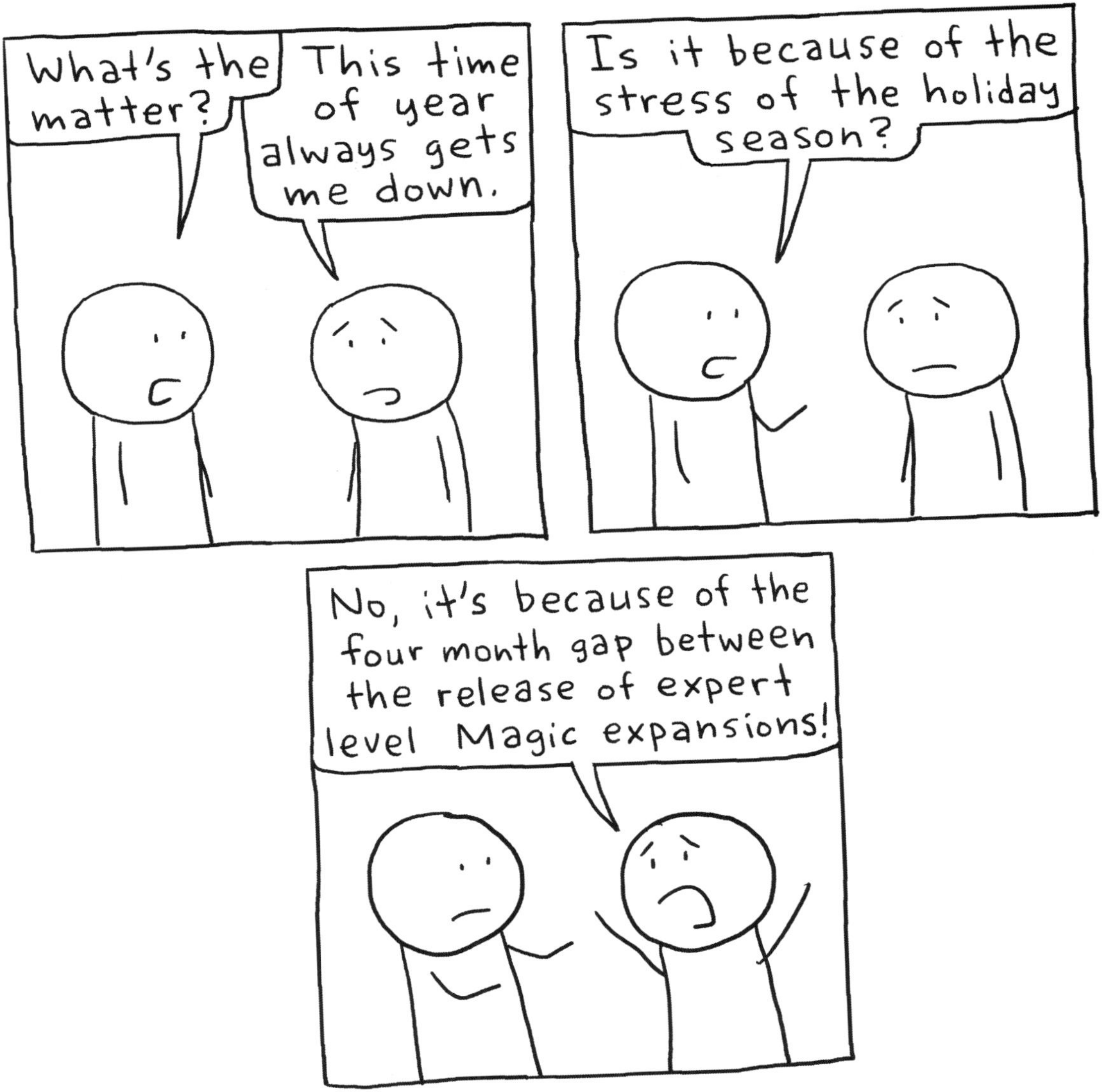
What's the matter?
This time of year always gets me down.
Is it because of the stress of the holiday season?
No, it's because of the four month gap between the release of expert level Magic expansions!

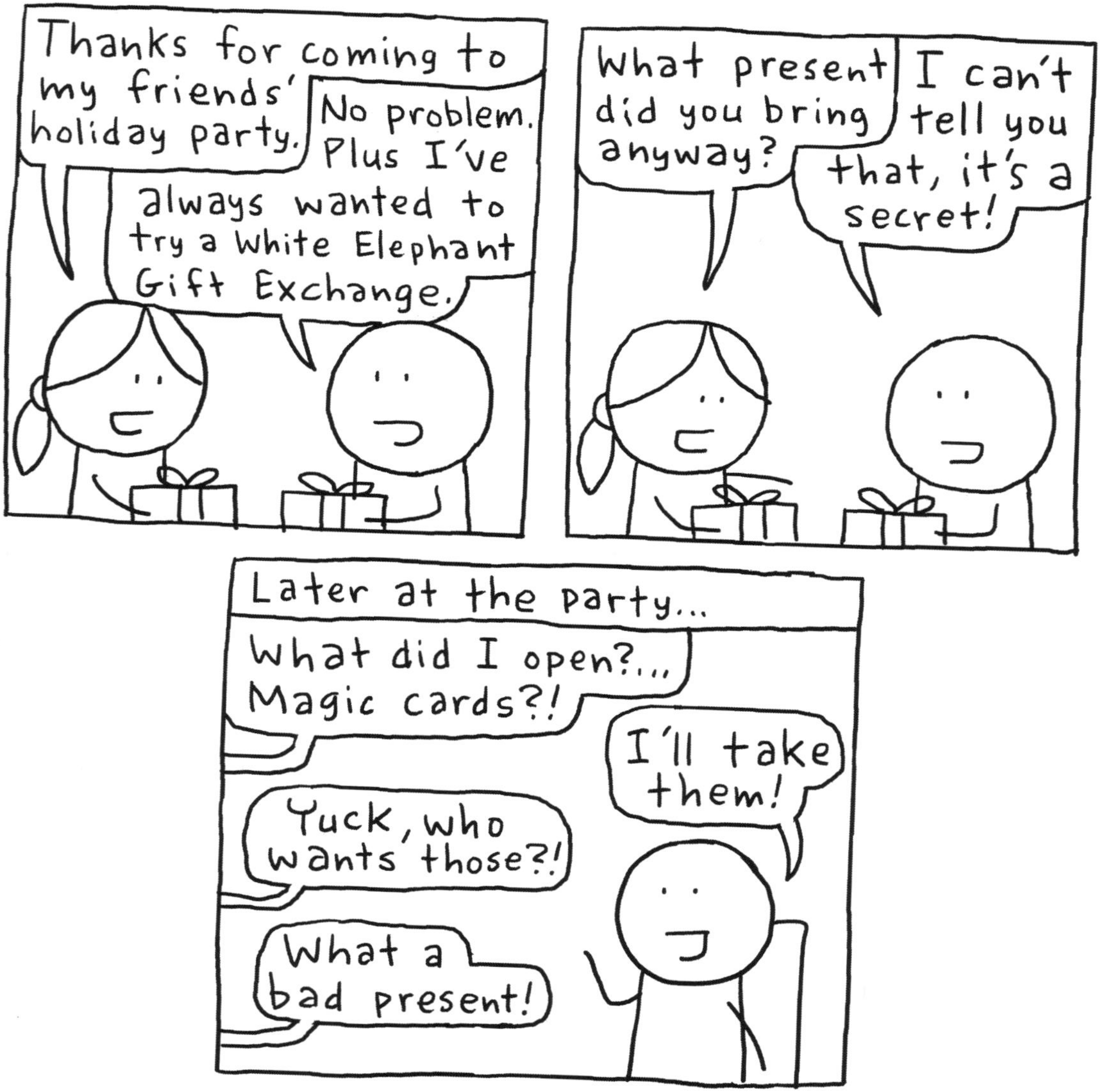
Thanks for coming to my friends' holiday party.
No problem. Plus I've always wanted to try a White Elephant Gift Exchange.
What present did you bring anyway?
I can't tell you that, it's a secret!
Later at the party...
What did I open?... Magic cards?!
I'll take them!
Yuck, who wants those?!
What a bad present!

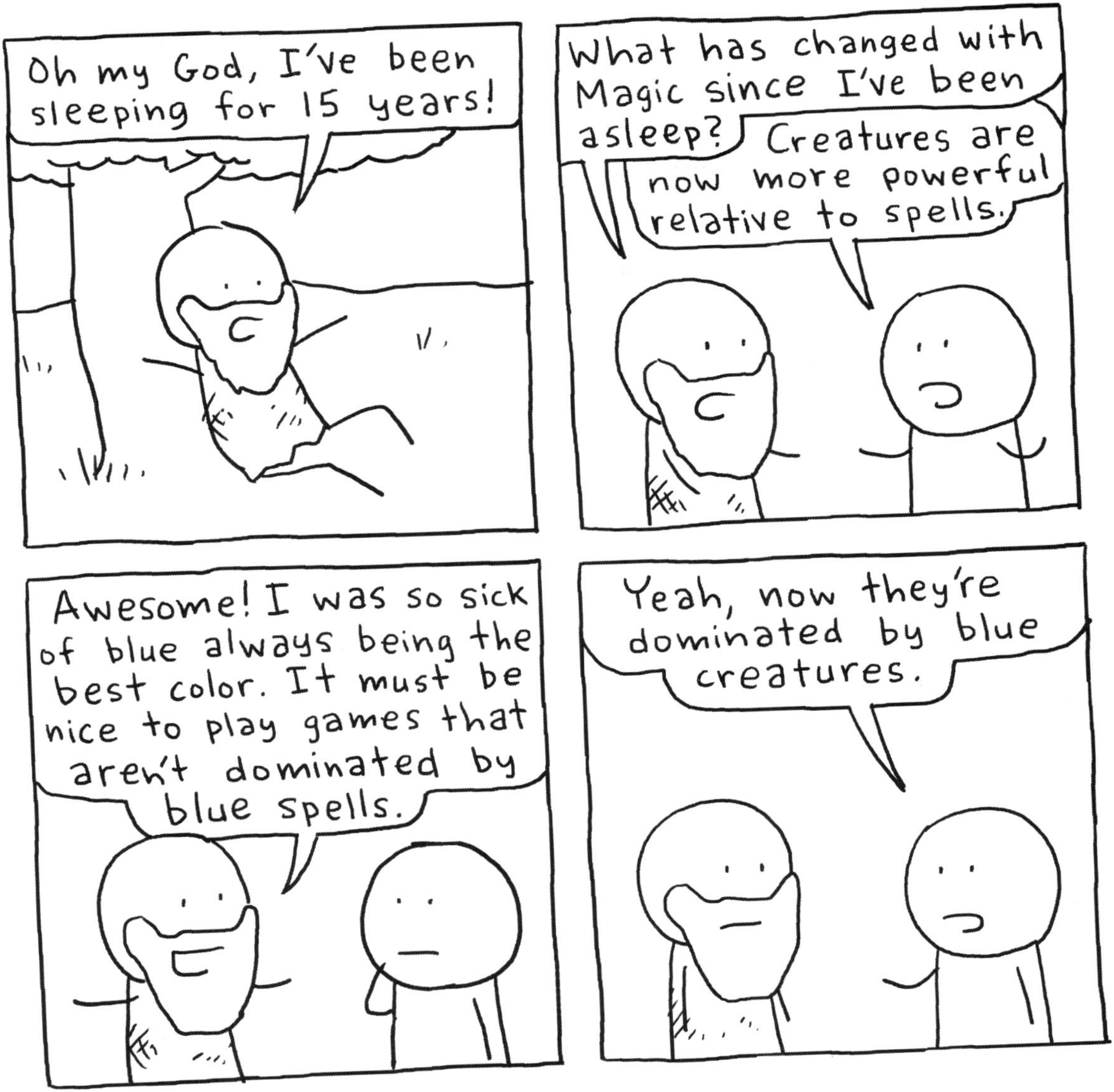
Oh my God, I've been sleeping for 15 years!
What has changed with Magic since I've been asleep?
Creatures are now more powerful relative to spells.
Awesome! I was so sick of blue always being the best color. It must be nice to play games that aren't dominated by blue spells.
Yeah, now they're dominated by blue creatures.

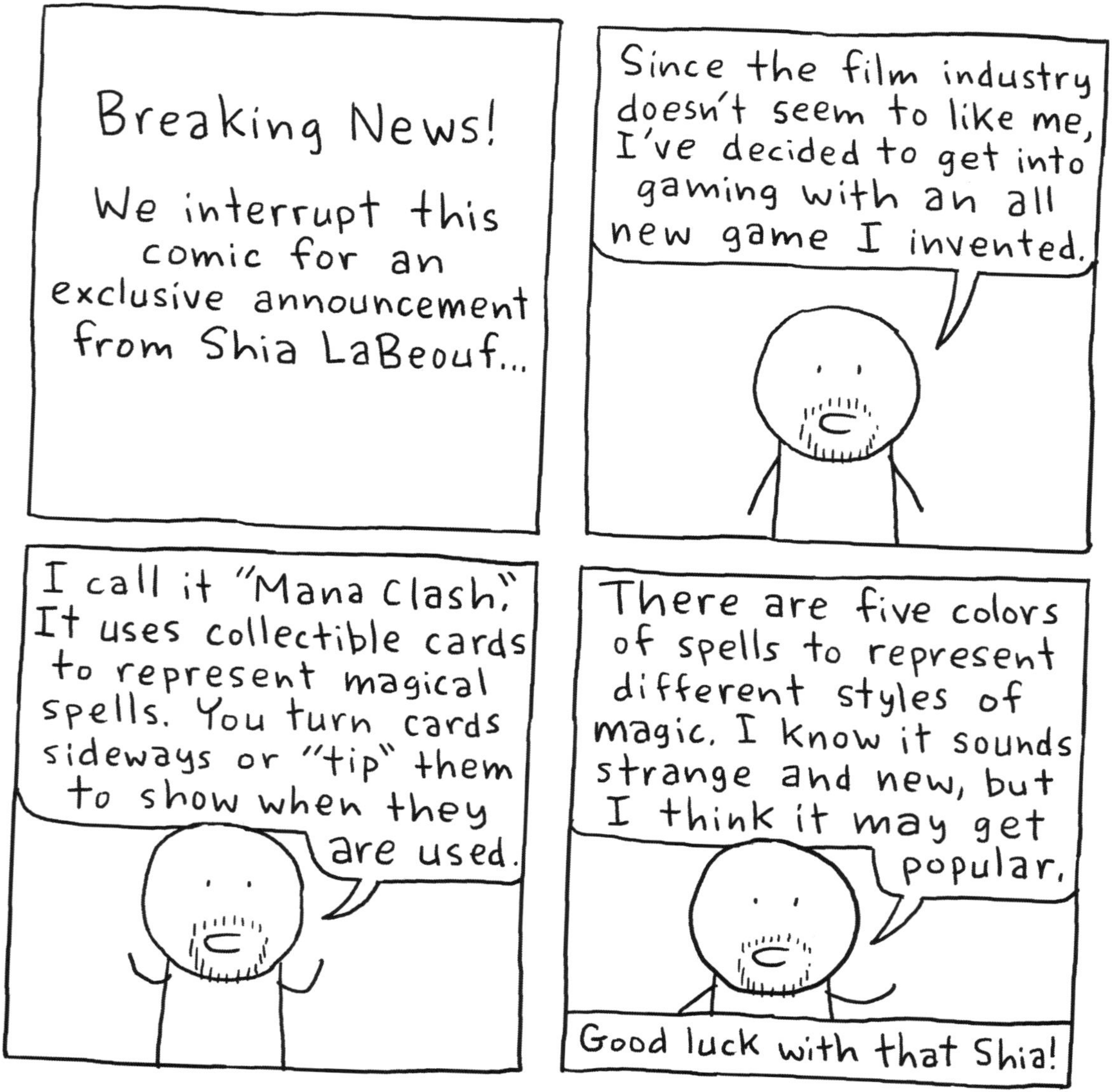
Breaking News!
We interrupt this comic for an exclusive announcement from Shia LaBeouf...
Since the film industry doesn't seem to like me, I've decided to get into gaming with an all new game I invented.
I call it "Mana Clash." It uses collectible cards to represent magical spells. You turn cards sideways or "tip" them to show when they are used.
There are five colors of spells to represent different styles of magic. I know it sounds strange and new, but I think it may get popular.
Good luck with that Shia!

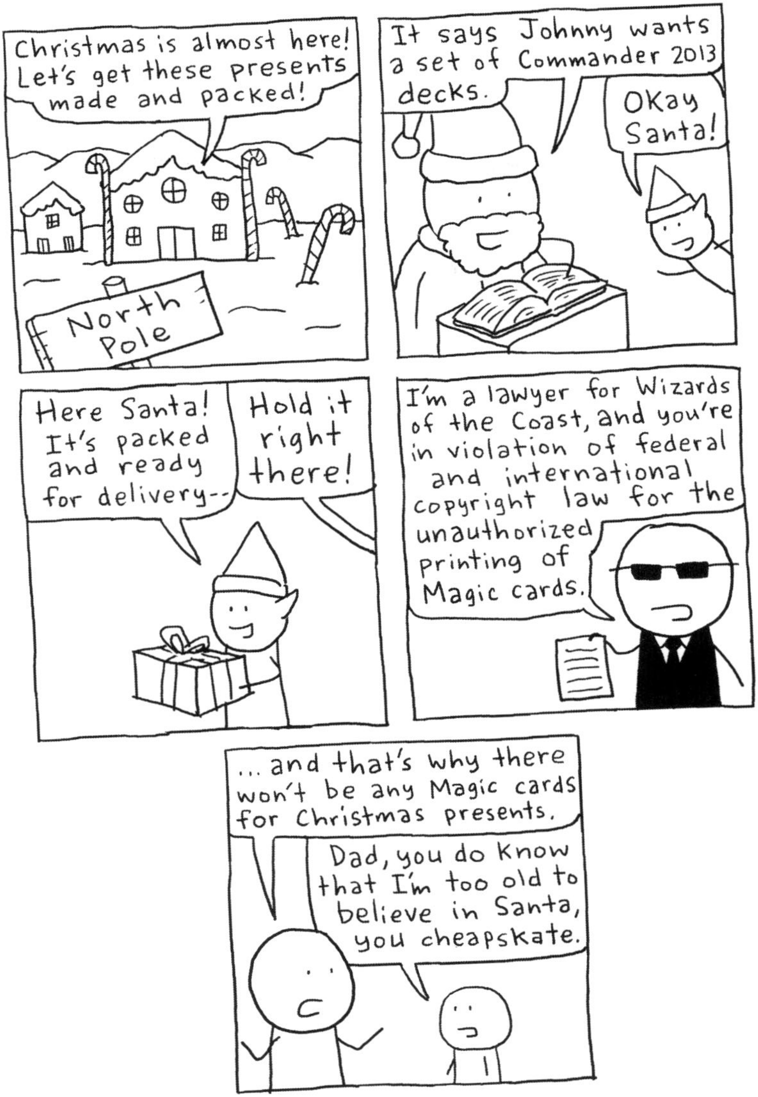
Christmas is almost here! Let's get these presents made and packed!
North Pole
It says Johnny wants a set of Commander 2013 decks.
OKay Santa!
Here Santa! It's packed and ready for delivery--
Hold it right there!
I'm a lawyer for Wizards of the Coast, and you're in violation of federal and international copyright law for the unauthorized printing of Magic cards.
...and that's why there won't be any Magic cards for Christmas presents.
Dad, you do Know that I'm too old to believe in Santa, you cheapskate.

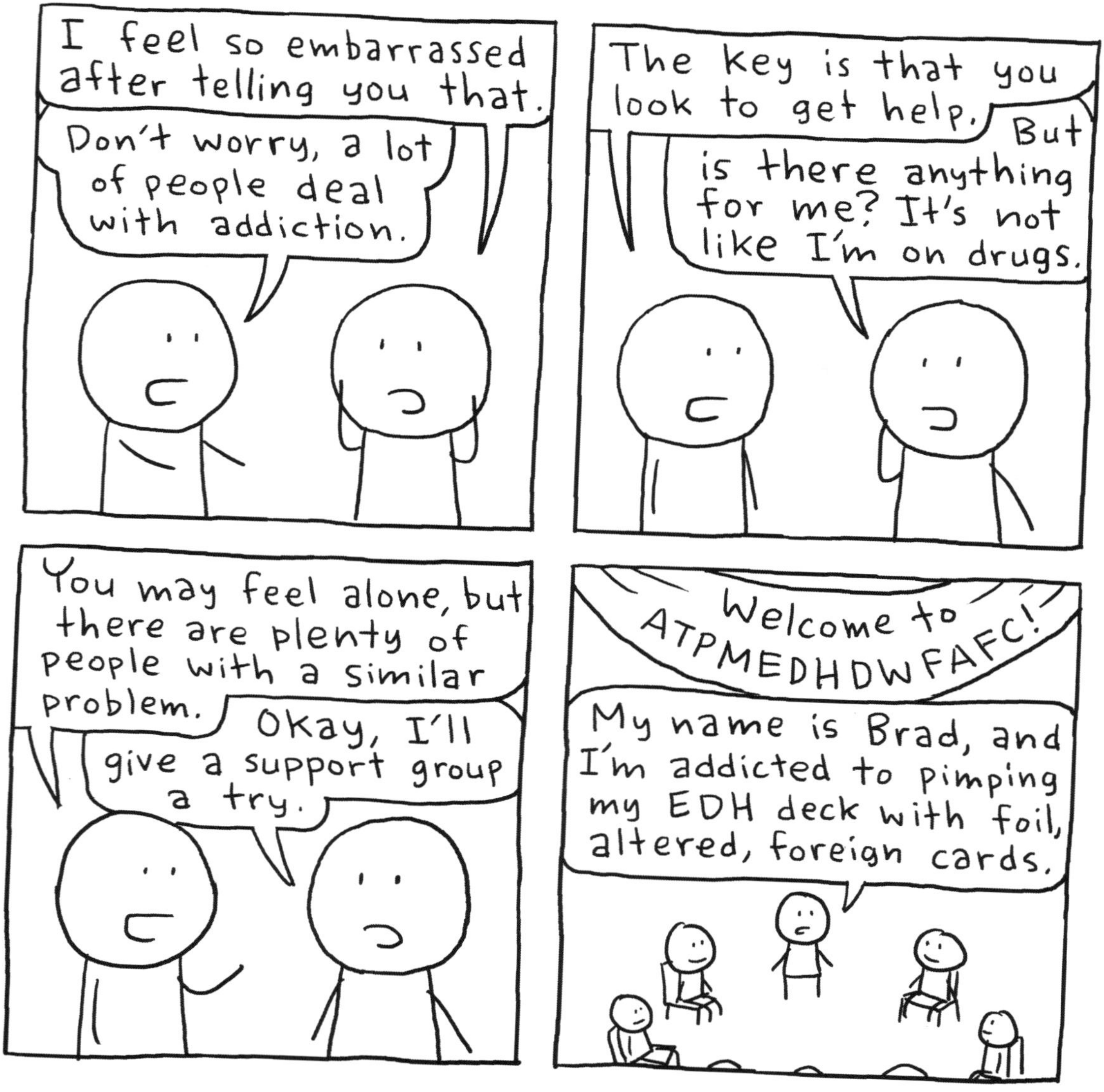
I feel so embarrassed after telling you that.
Don't worry, a lot of people deal with addiction.
The key is that you look to get help.
But is there anything for me? It's not like I'm on drugs.
You may feel alone, but there are plenty of people with a similar problem.
Okay, I'll give a support group a try.
Welcome to ATPMEDHDWFAFC!
My name is Brad, and I'm addicted to pimping my EDH deck with foil, altered, foreign cards.

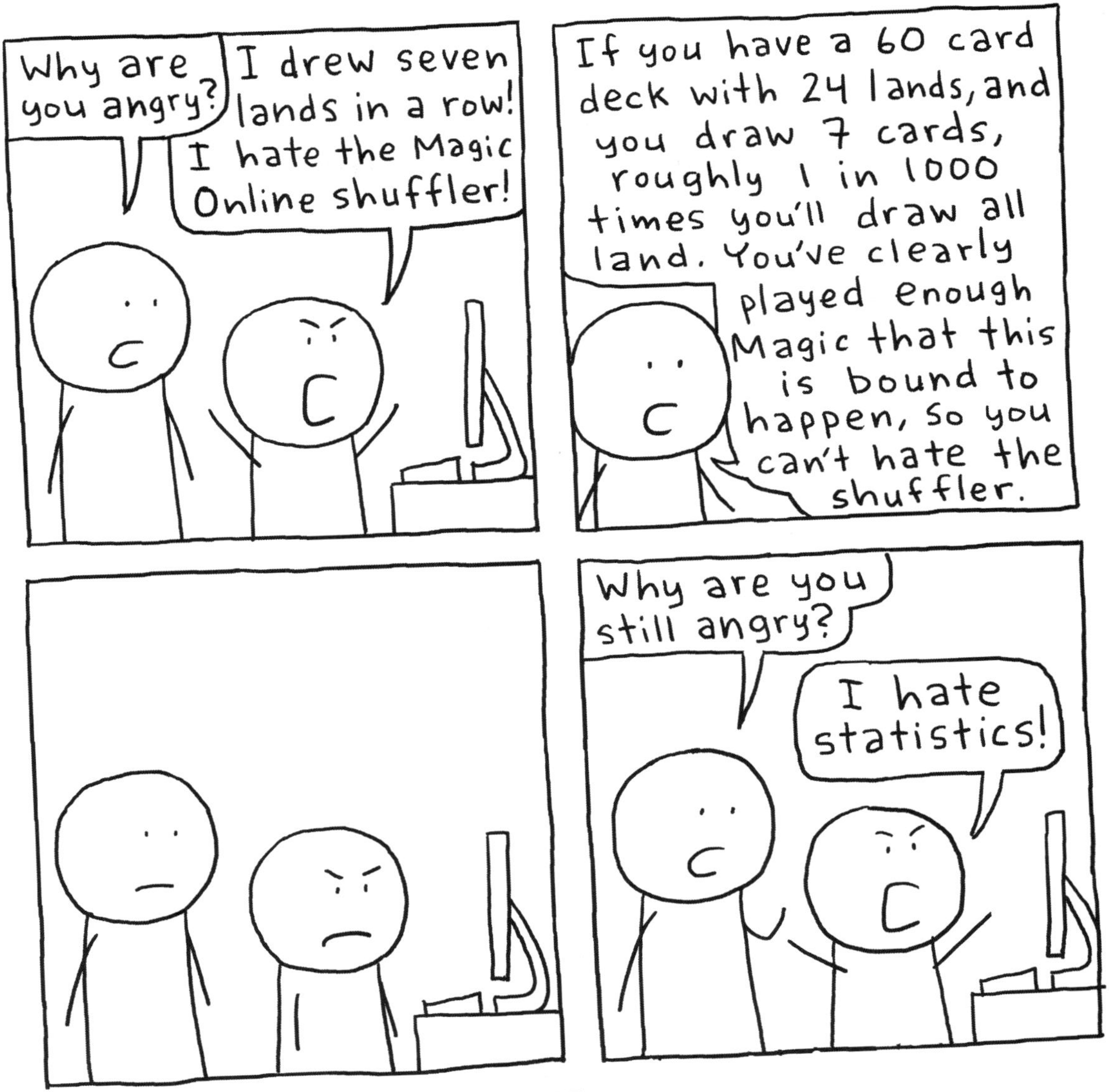
Why are you angry?
I drew seven lands in a row! I hate the Magic Online shuffler!
If you have a 60 card deck with 24 lands, and you draw 7 cards, roughly 1 in 1000 times you'll draw all land. You've clearly played enough Magic that this is bound to happen, so you can't hate the shuffler.
Why are you still angry?
I hate statistics!

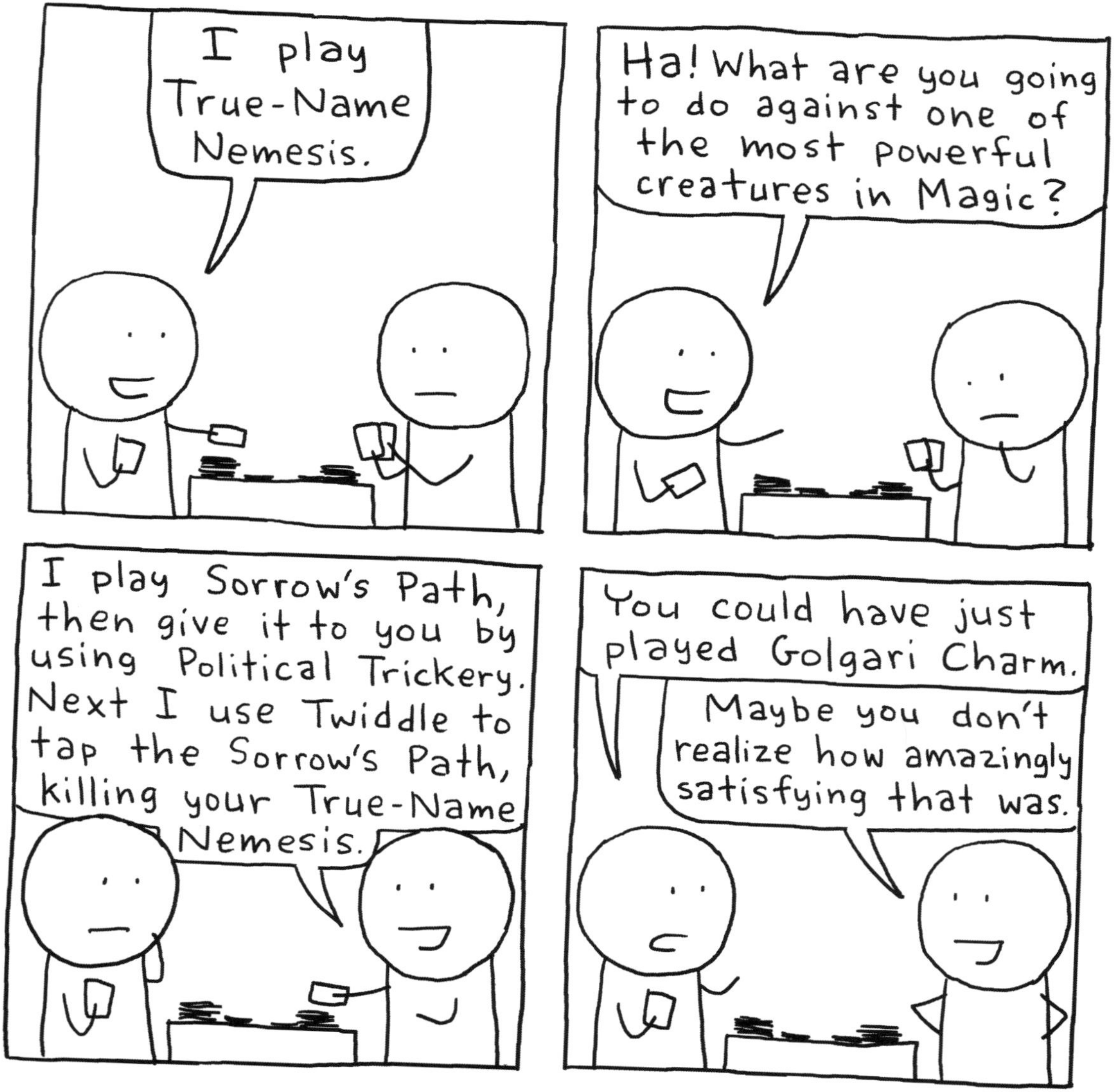
I play True-Name Nemesis.
Ha! What are you going to do against one of the most powerful creatures in Magic?
I play Sorrow's Path, then give it to you by using Political Trickery. Next I use Twiddle to tap the Sorrow's Path, killing your True-Name Nemesis.
You could have just played Golgari Charm.
Maybe you don't realize how amazingly satisfying that was.

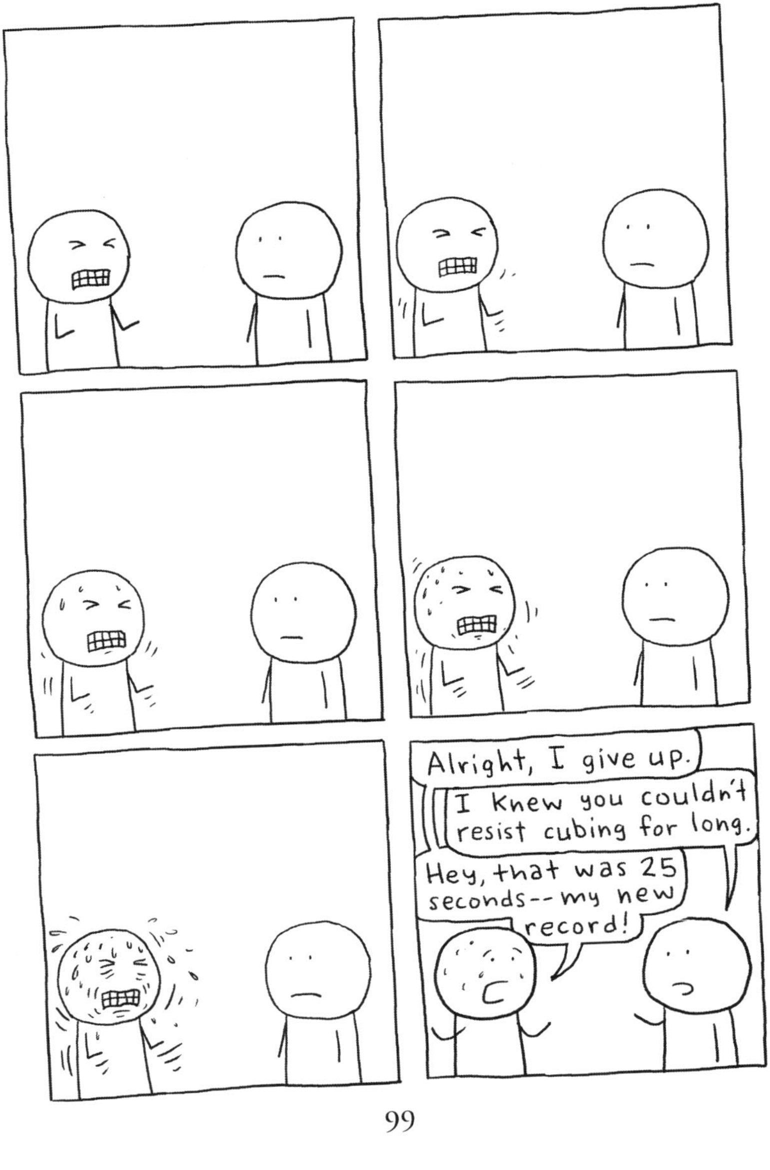
Alright, I give up.
I knew you couldn't resist cubing for long.
Hey, that was 25 seconds--my new record!

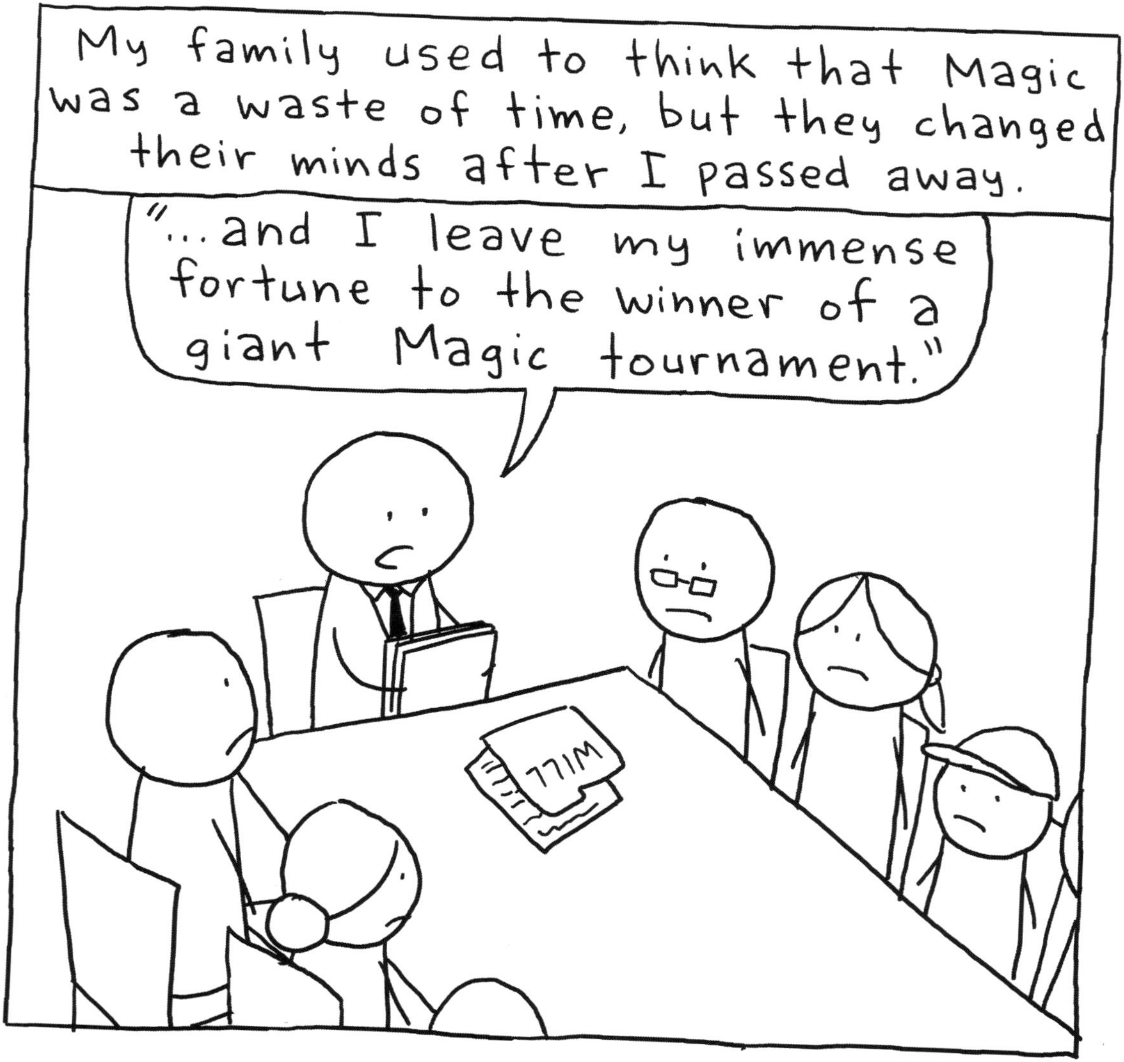
My family used to think that Magic was a waste of time, but they changed their minds after I passed away.
"...and I leave my immense fortune to the winner of a giant Magic tournament."
WILL

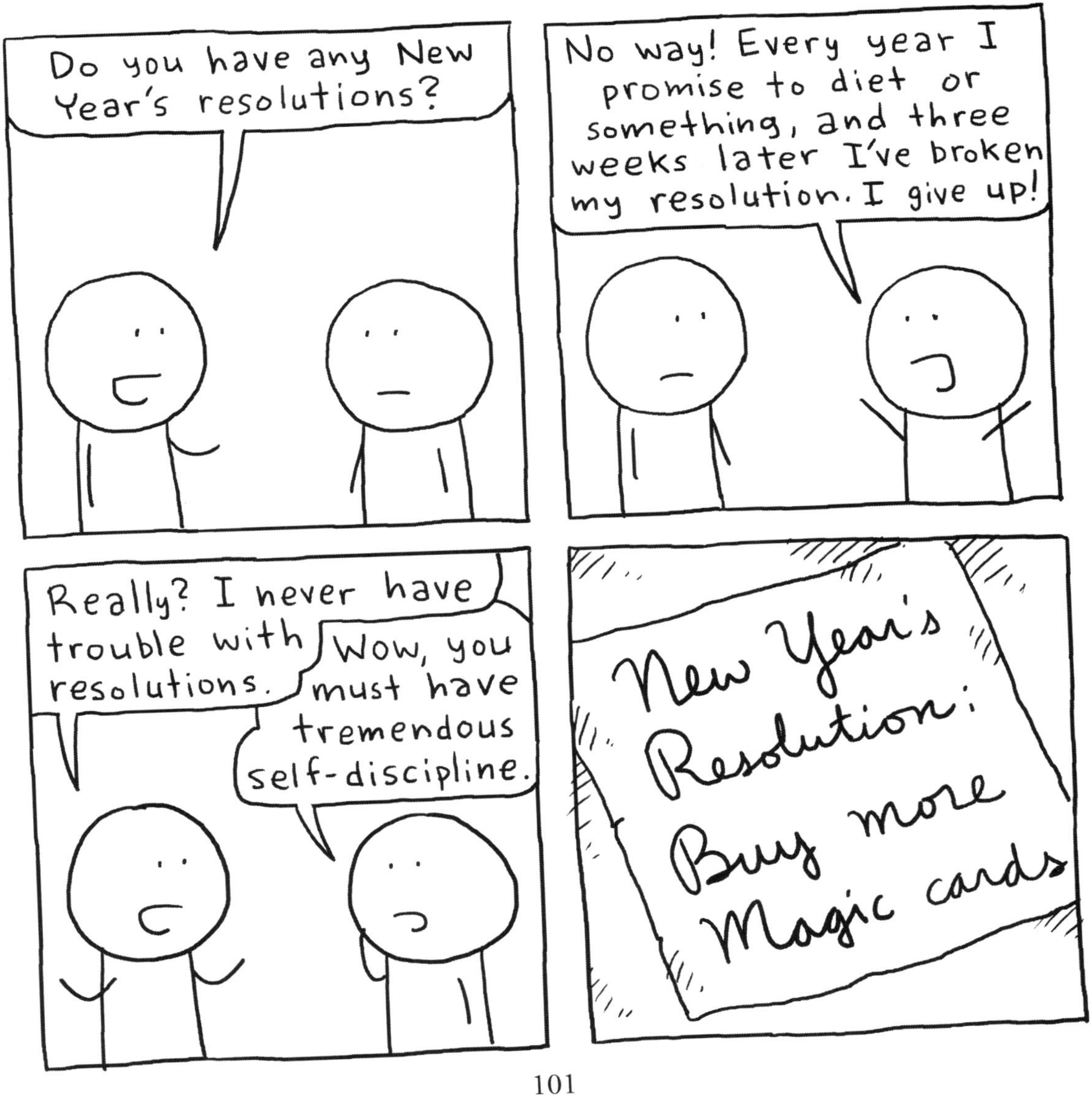
Do you have any New Year's resolutions?
No way! Every year I promise to diet or something, and three weeks later I've broken my resolution. I give up!
Really? I never have trouble with resolutions.
Wow, you must have tremendous self-discipline.
New Year's Resolution: Buy more Magic cards

Alright, ready to go to the strip club?
And no bringing any Magic cards for tips.
But I made sure they're each worth about a dollar!

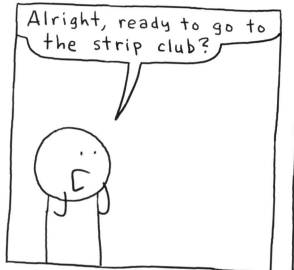

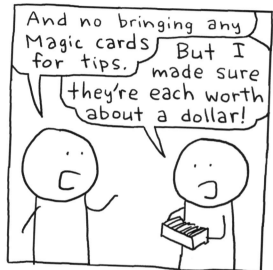

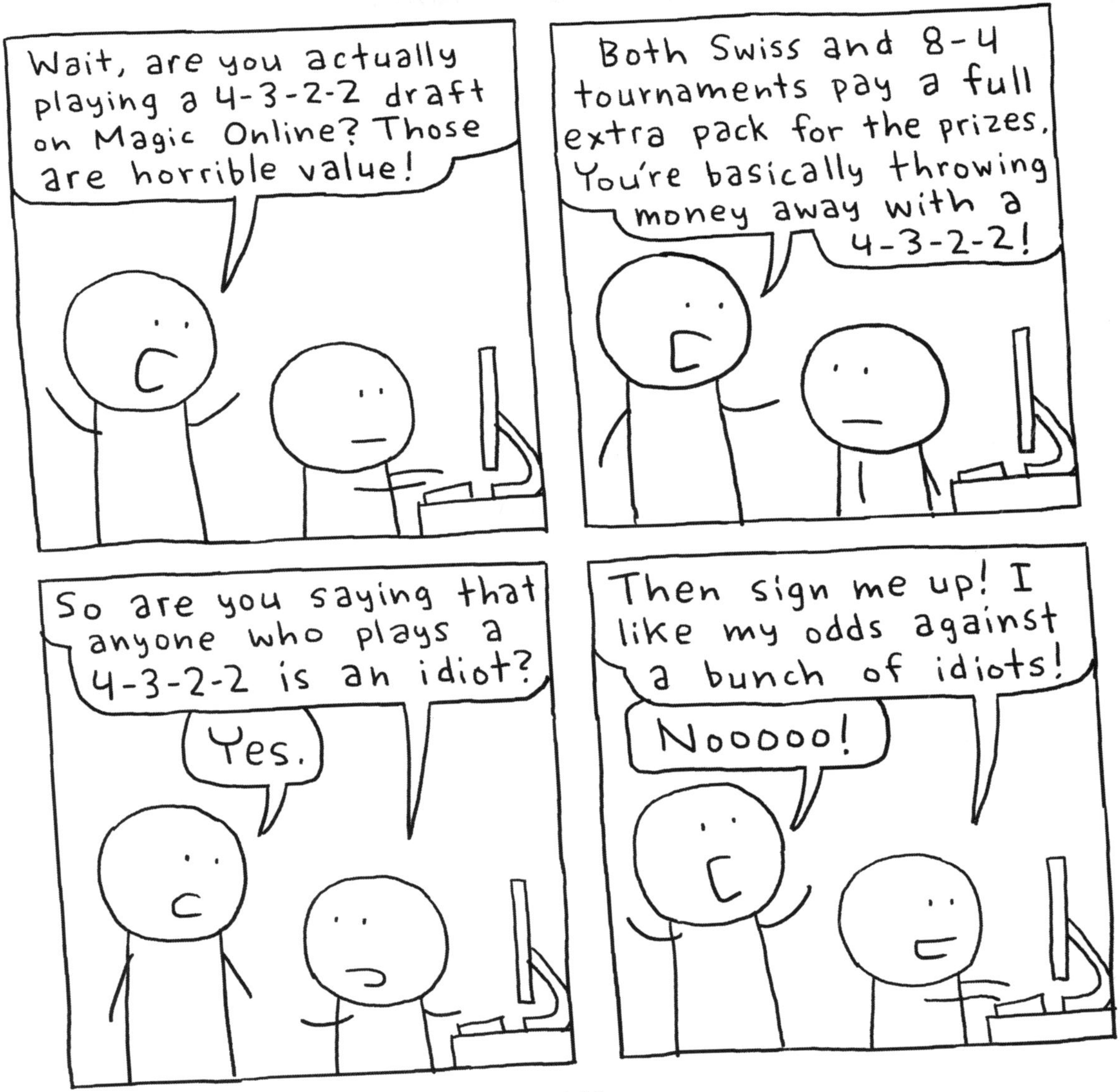
Wait, are you actually playing a 4-3-2-2 draft on Magic Online? Those are horrible value!
Both Swiss and 8-4 tournaments pay a full extra pack for the prizes. You're basically throwing money away with a 4-3-2-2!
So are you saying that anyone who plays a 4-3-2-2 is an idiot?
Yes.
Then sign me up! I like my odds against a bunch of idiots!
Nooooo!

Nine months ago...
I am so sick of multi-color decks in Stardard! Some decks don't even bother with basic lands. It's ridiculous!
Now...
If I have to play against another devotion deck, I'm going to shoot myself in the head!

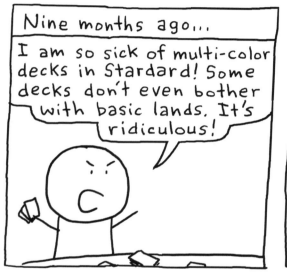

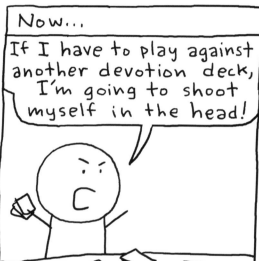

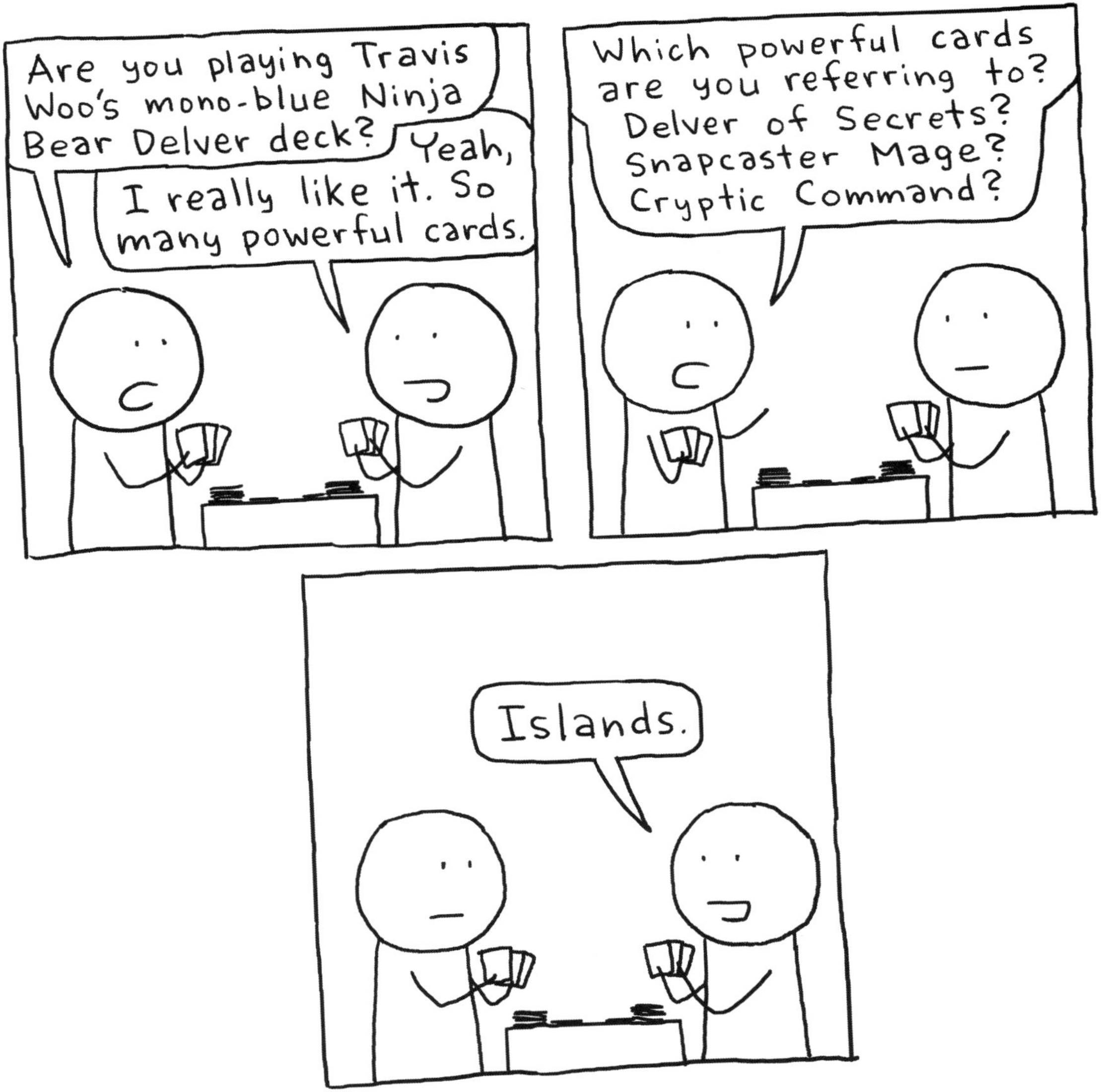
Are you playing Travis Woo's mono-blue Ninja Bear Delver deck?
Yeah, I really like it. So many powerful cards.
Which powerful cards are you referring to? Delver of Secrets? Snapcaster Mage? Cryptic Command?
Islands.

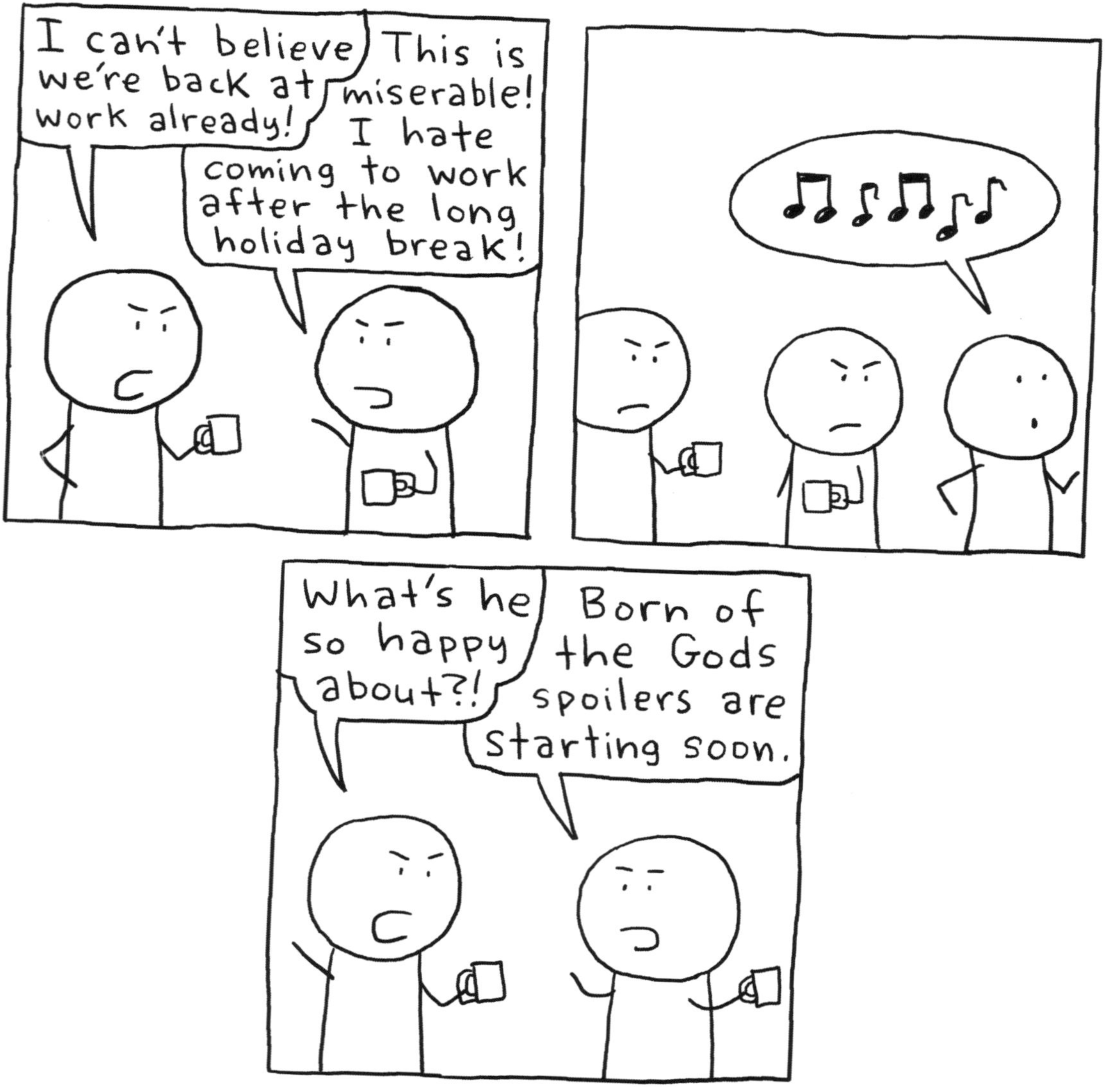
I can't believe we're back at work already!
This is miserable! I hate coming to work after the long holiday break!
What's he so happy about?!
Born of the Gods spoilers are starting soon.

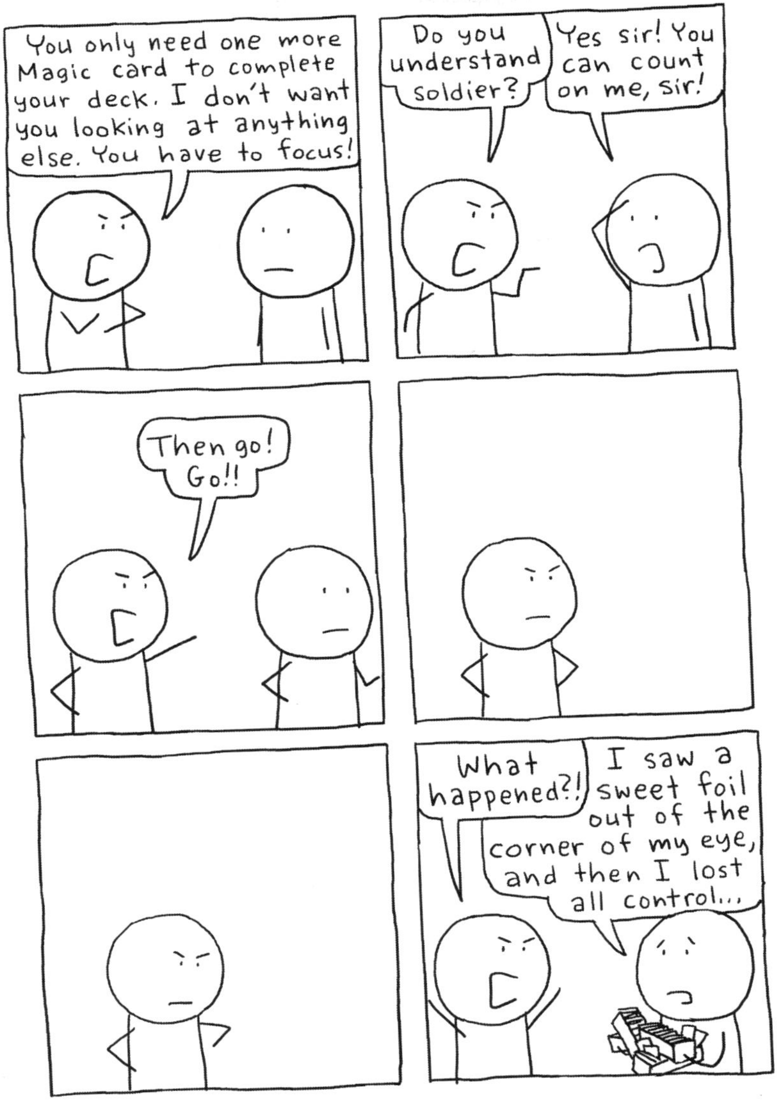
You only need one more Magic card to complete your deck. I don't want you looking at anything else. You have to focus!
Do you understand soldier?
Yes sir! You can count on me, sir!
Then go! Go!!
What happened?!
I saw a sweet foil out of the corner of my eye, and then I lost all control...

What's the matter with you? All you ever do is play Magic cards!
But you told me to.
I did not!
Earlier...
You should live every day like it's your last.
Okay...

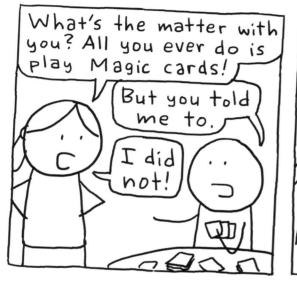

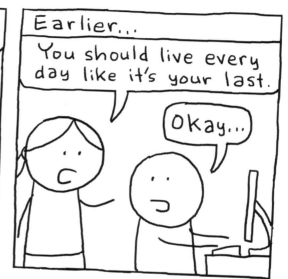

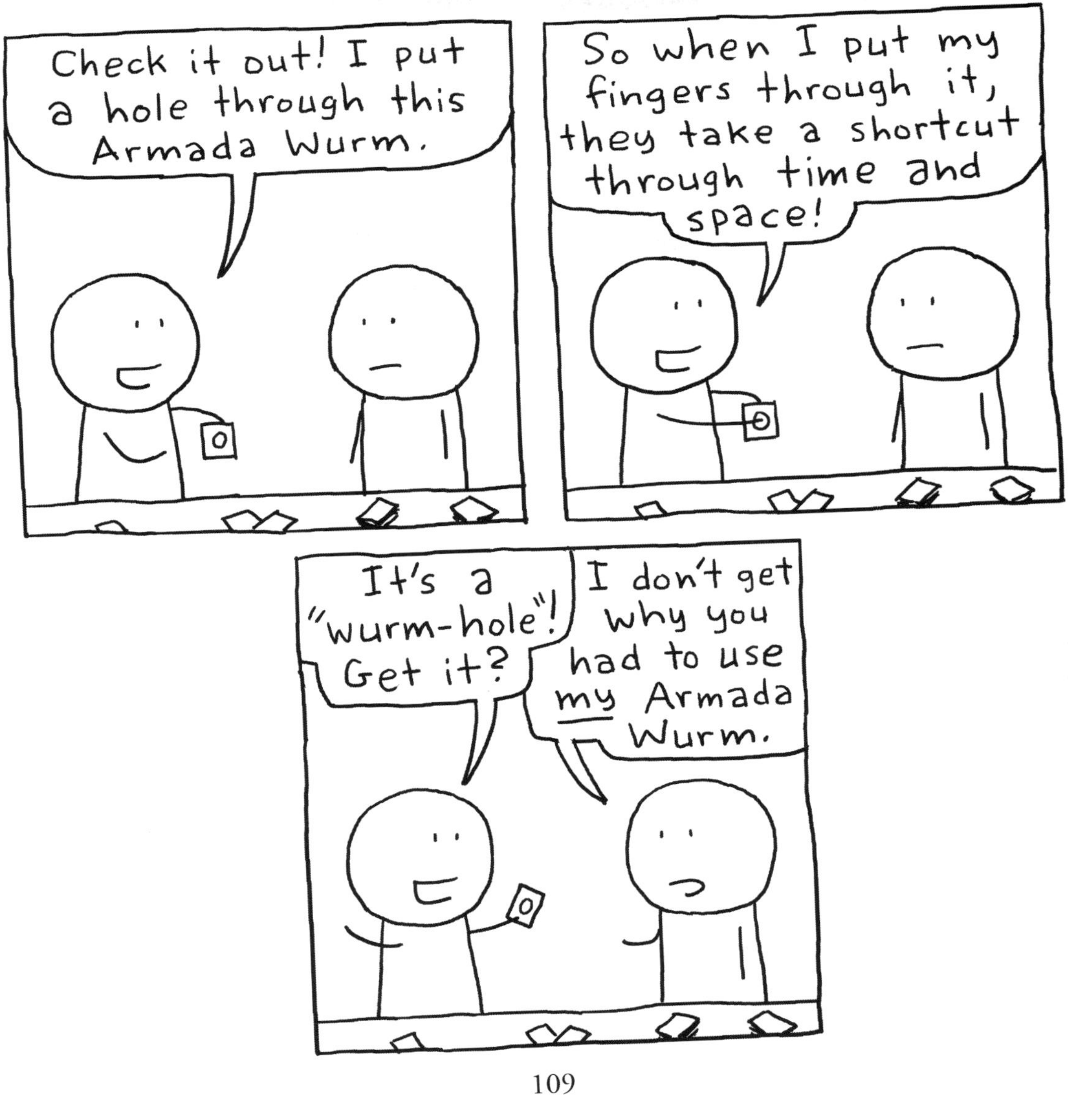

Check it out! I put a hole through this Armada Wurm.
So when I put my fingers through it, they take a shortcut through time and space!
It's a "wurm-hole"! Get it?
I don't get why you had to use my Armada Wurm.

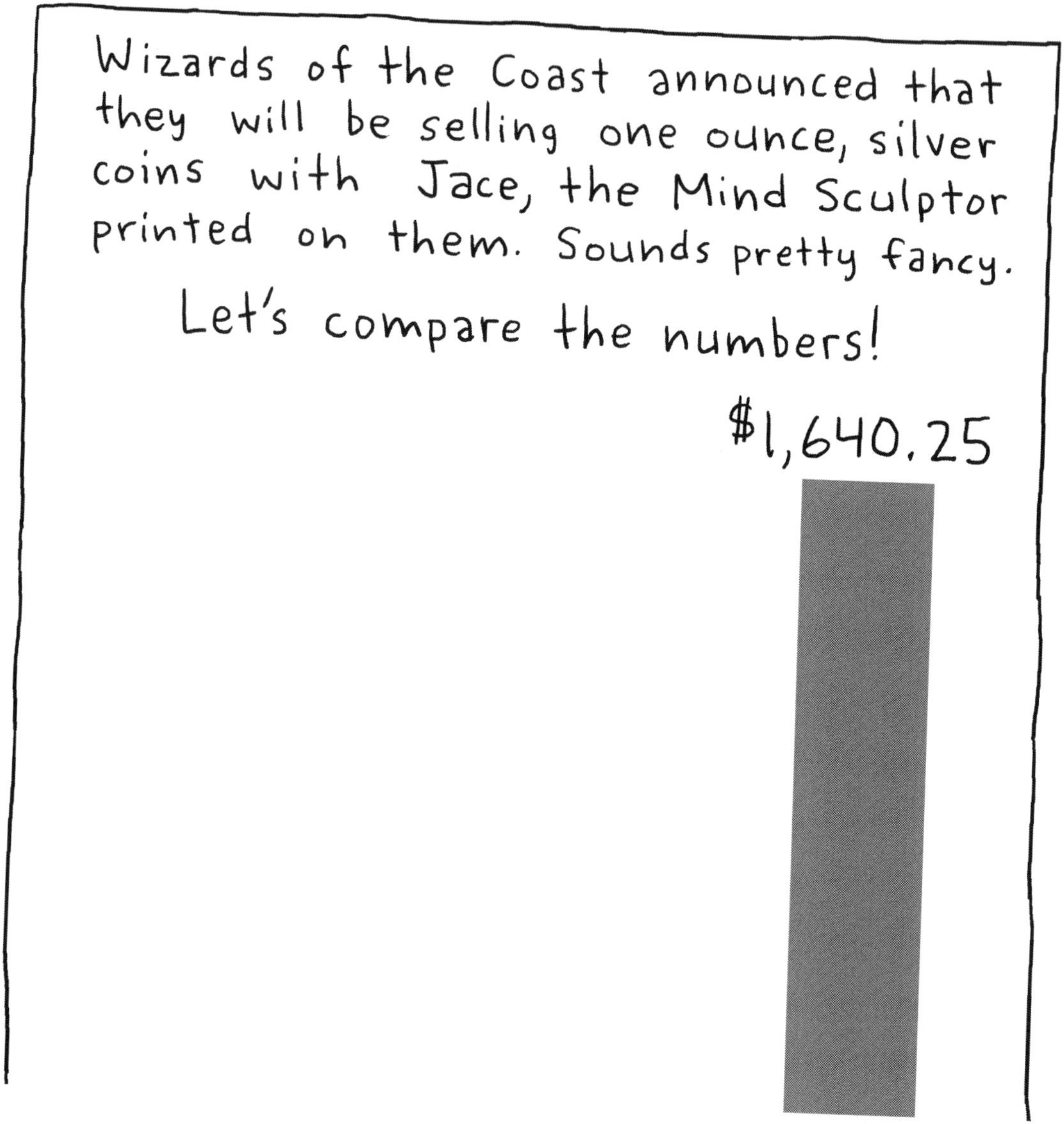
Wizards of the Coast announced that they will be selling one ounce, silver coins with Jace, the Mind Sculptor printed on them. Sounds pretty fancy.
Let's compare the numbers!
$1,640.25

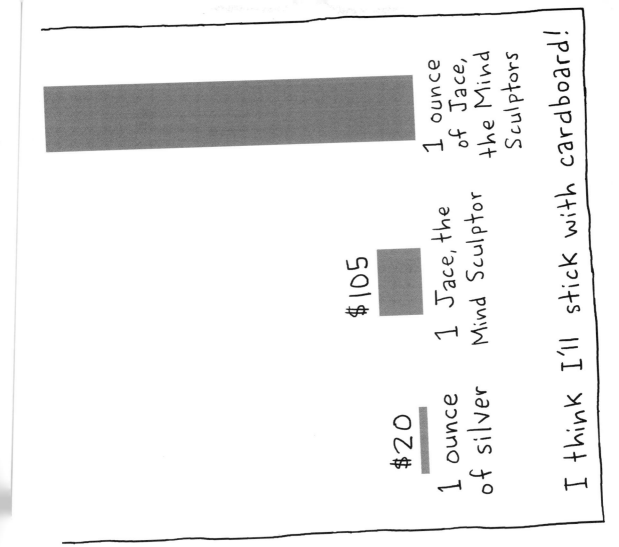

$20
1 ounce
of silver

$105
1 Jace, the
Mind Sculptor

1 ounce
of Jace,
the Mind
Sculptors

I think I'll stick with cardboard!

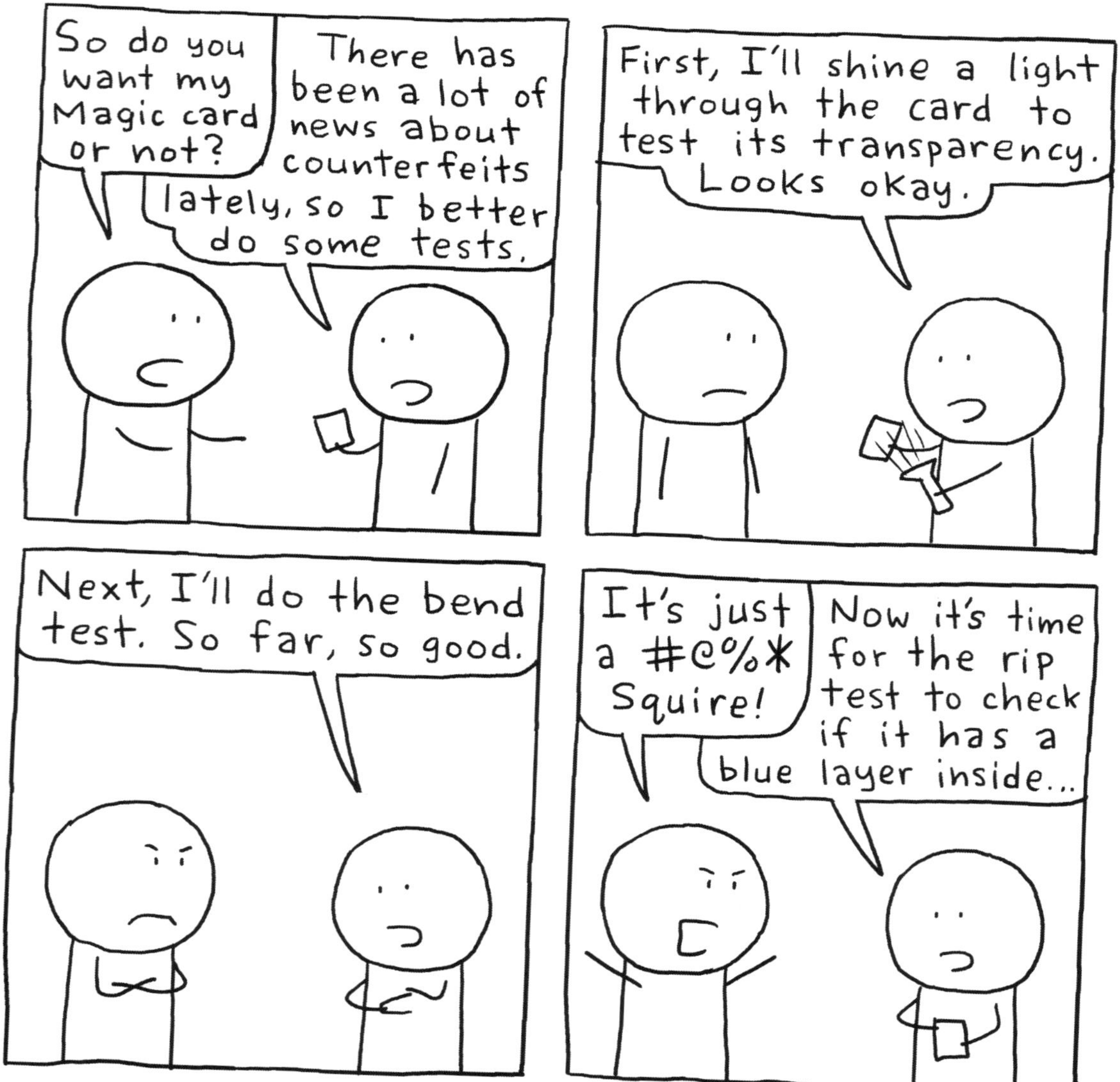
So do you want my Magic card or not?
There has been a lot of news about counterfeits lately, so I better do some tests.
First, I'll shine a light through the card to test its transparency. Looks okay.
Next, I'll do the bend test. So far, so good.
It's just a #@%* Squire!
Now it's time for the rip test to check if it has a blue layer inside...

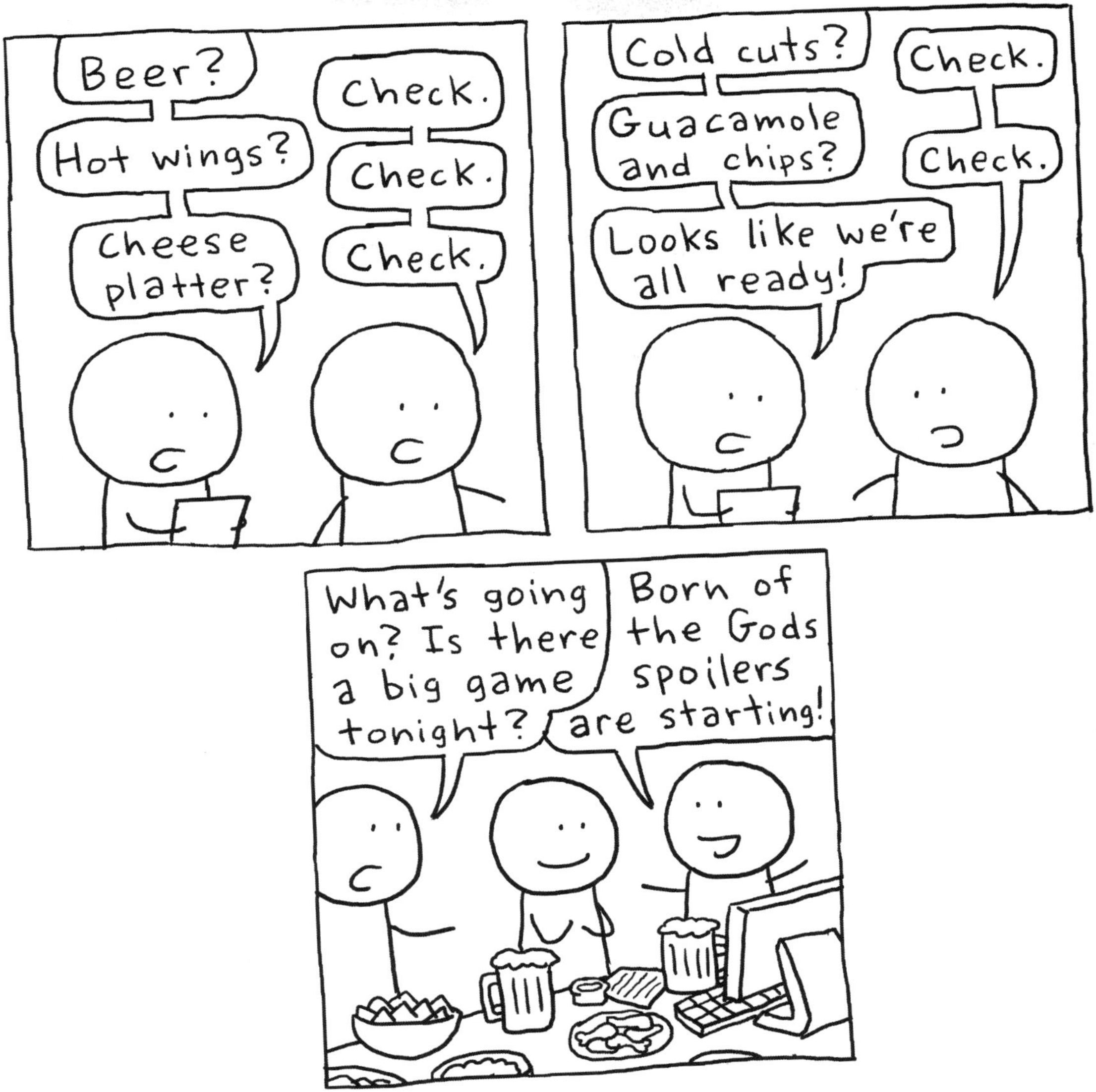
Beer?
Check.
Hot wings?
Check.
Cheese platter?
Check.
Cold cuts?
Check.
Guacamole and chips?
Check.
Looks like we're all ready!
What's going on? Is there a big game tonight?
Born of the Gods spoilers are starting!

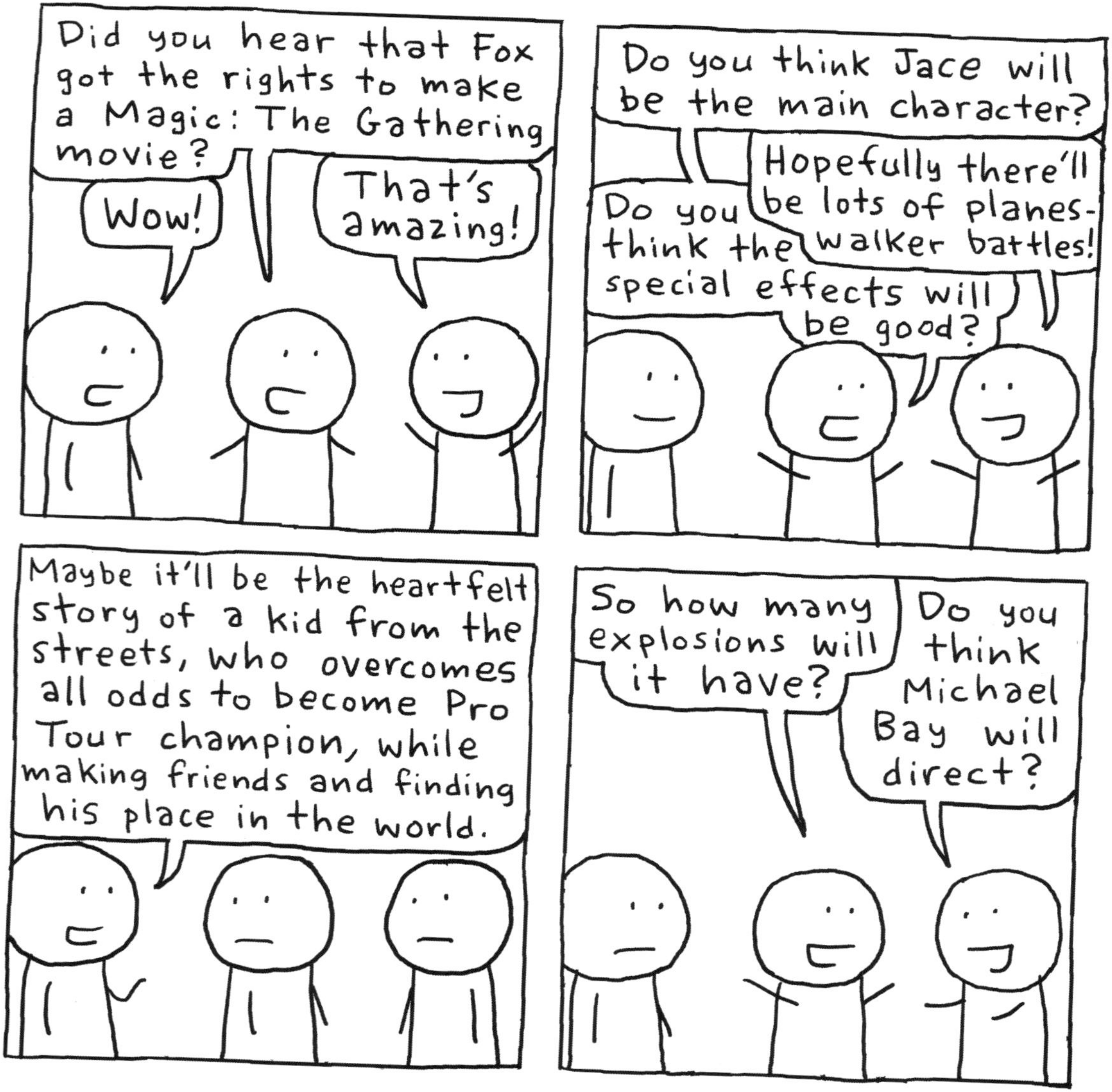
Did you hear that Fox got the rights to make a Magic: The Gathering movie?
Wow!
That's amazing!
Do you think Jace will be the main character?
Do you think the special effects will be good?
Hopefully there'll be lots of planes-walker battles!
Maybe it'll be the heartfelt story of a kid from the streets, who overcomes all odds to become Pro Tour champion, while making friends and finding his place in the world.
So how many explosions will it have?
Do you think Michael Bay will direct?

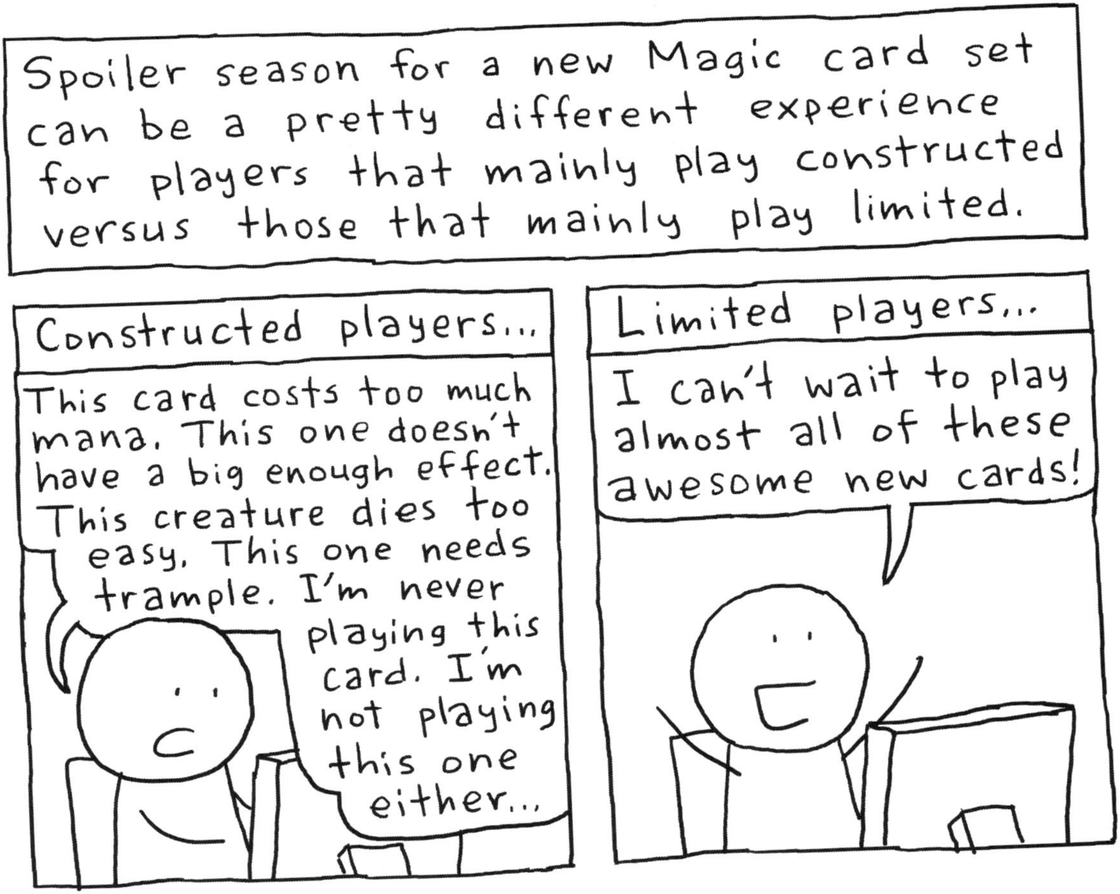
Spoiler season for a new Magic card set can be a pretty different experience for players that mainly play constructed versus those that mainly play limited.
Constructed players...
This card costs too much mana. This one doesn't have a big enough effect. This creature dies too easy. This one needs trample. I'm never playing this card. I'm not playing this one either...
Limited players...
I can't wait to play almost all of these awesome new cards!

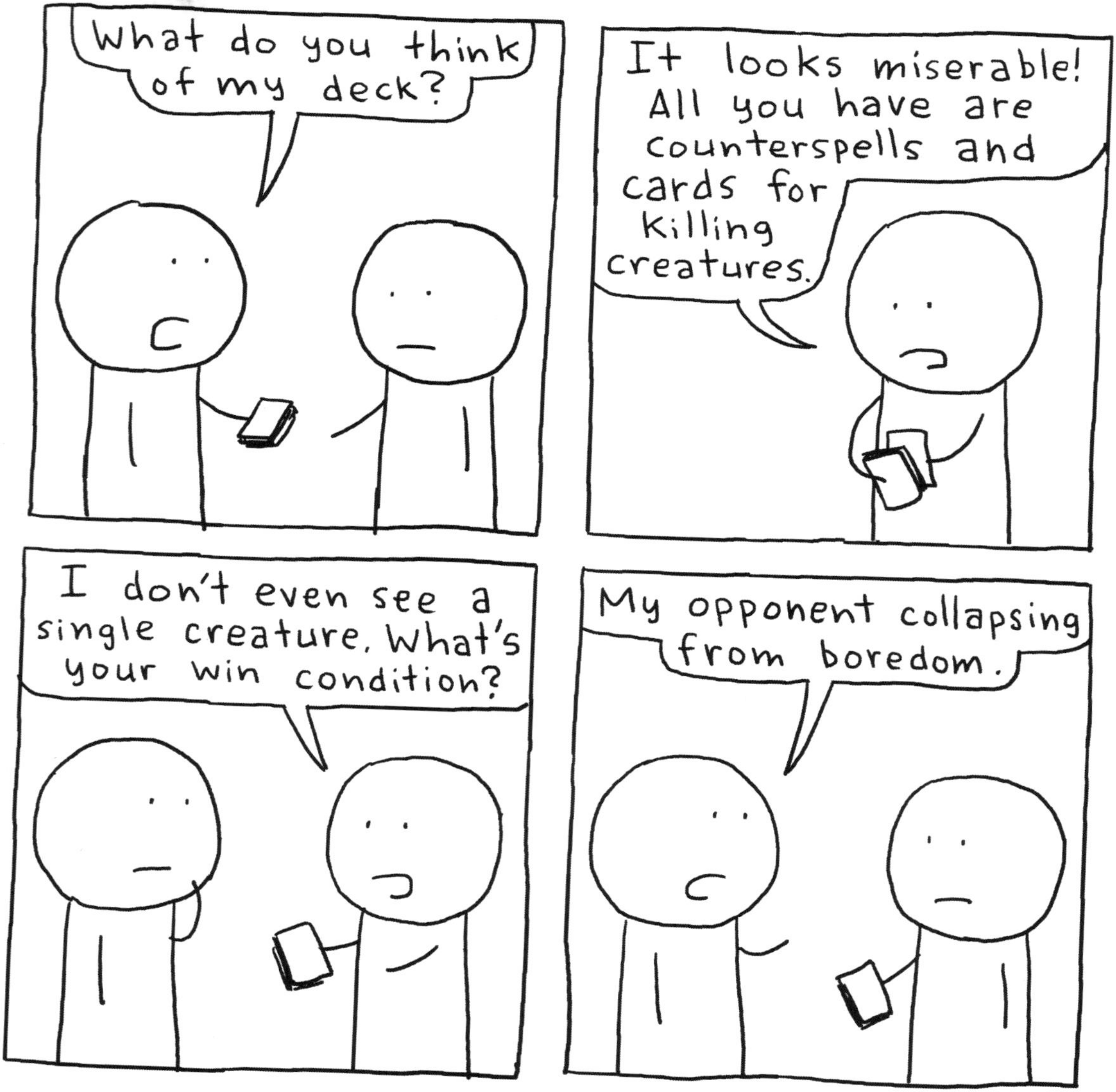
What do you think of my deck?
It looks miserable! All you have are counterspells and cards for killing creatures.
I don't even see a single creature. What's your win condition?
My opponent collapsing from boredom.

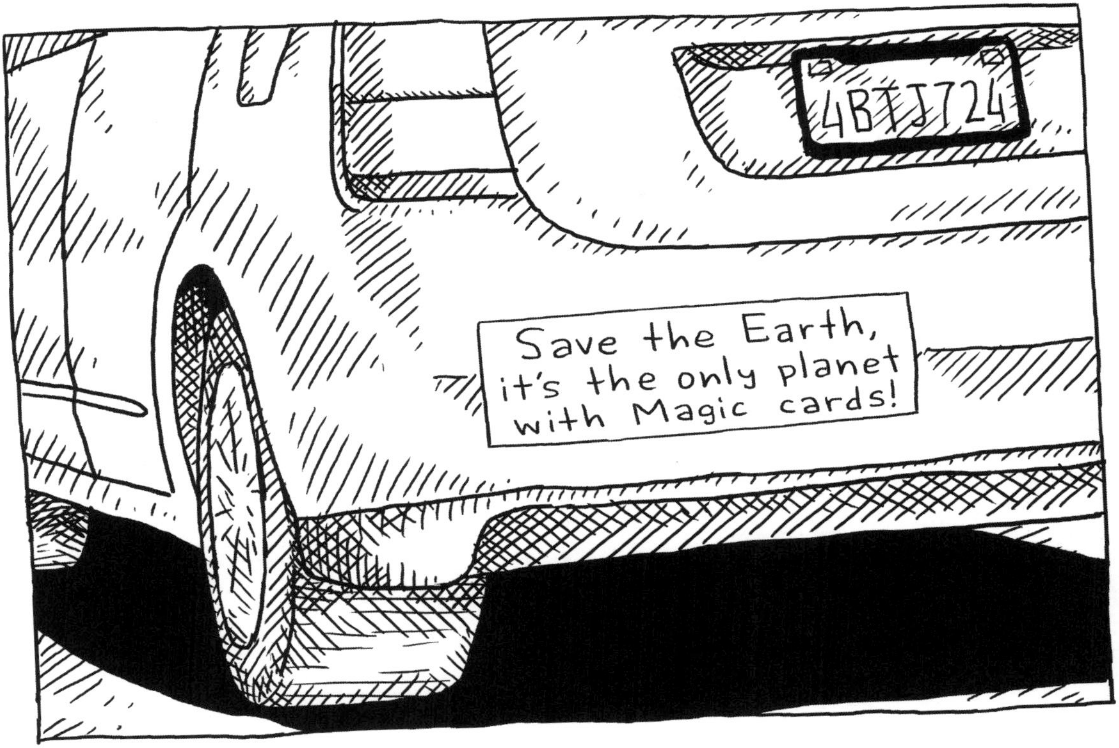
4BTJ724
Save the Earth, it's the only planet with Magic cards!

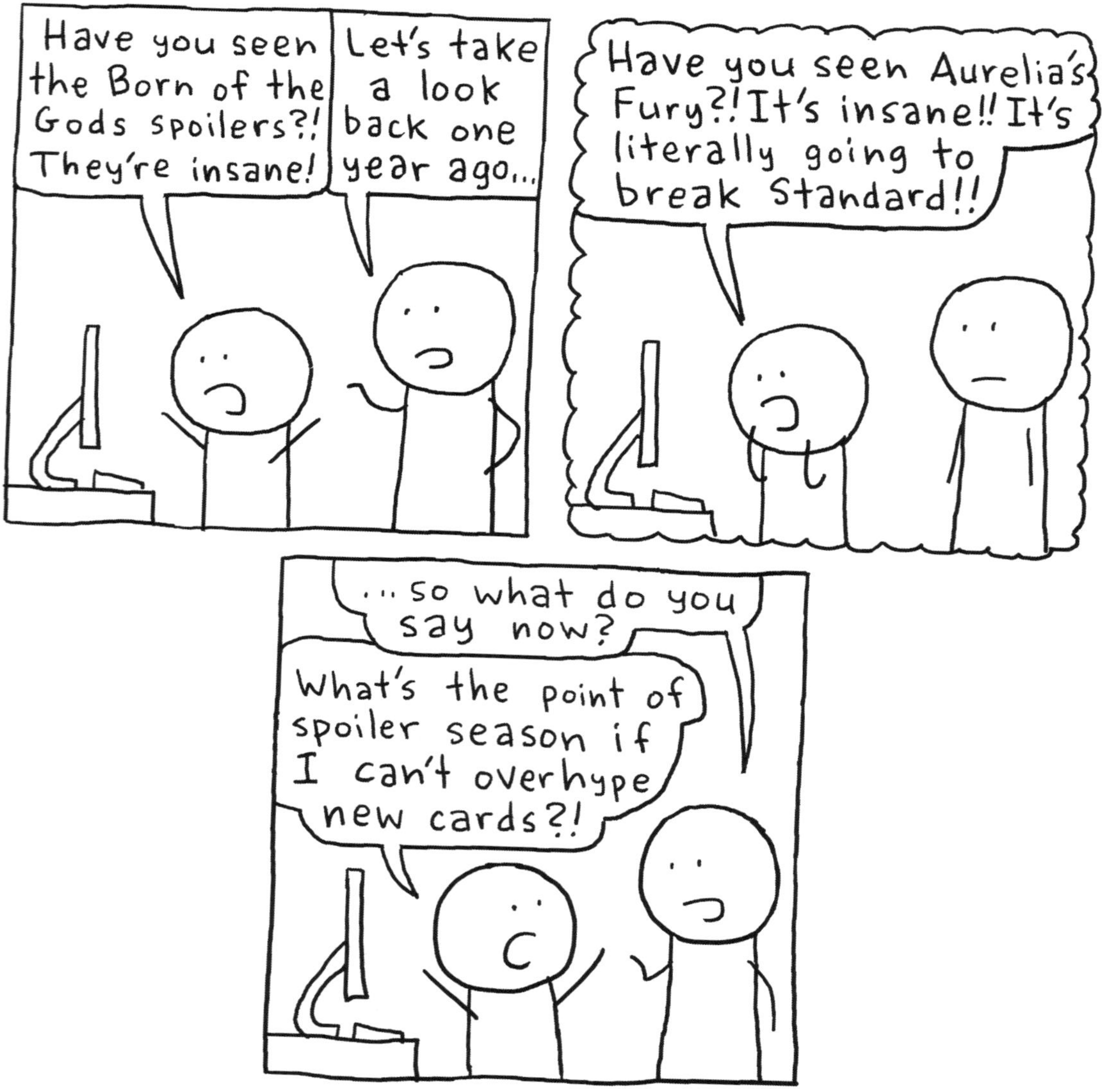

Have you seen the Born of the Gods spoilers?! They're insane!
Let's take a look back one year ago...
Have you seen Aurelia's Fury?! It's insane!! It's literally going to break Standard!!
...so what do you say now?
What's the point of spoiler season if I can't overhype new cards?!

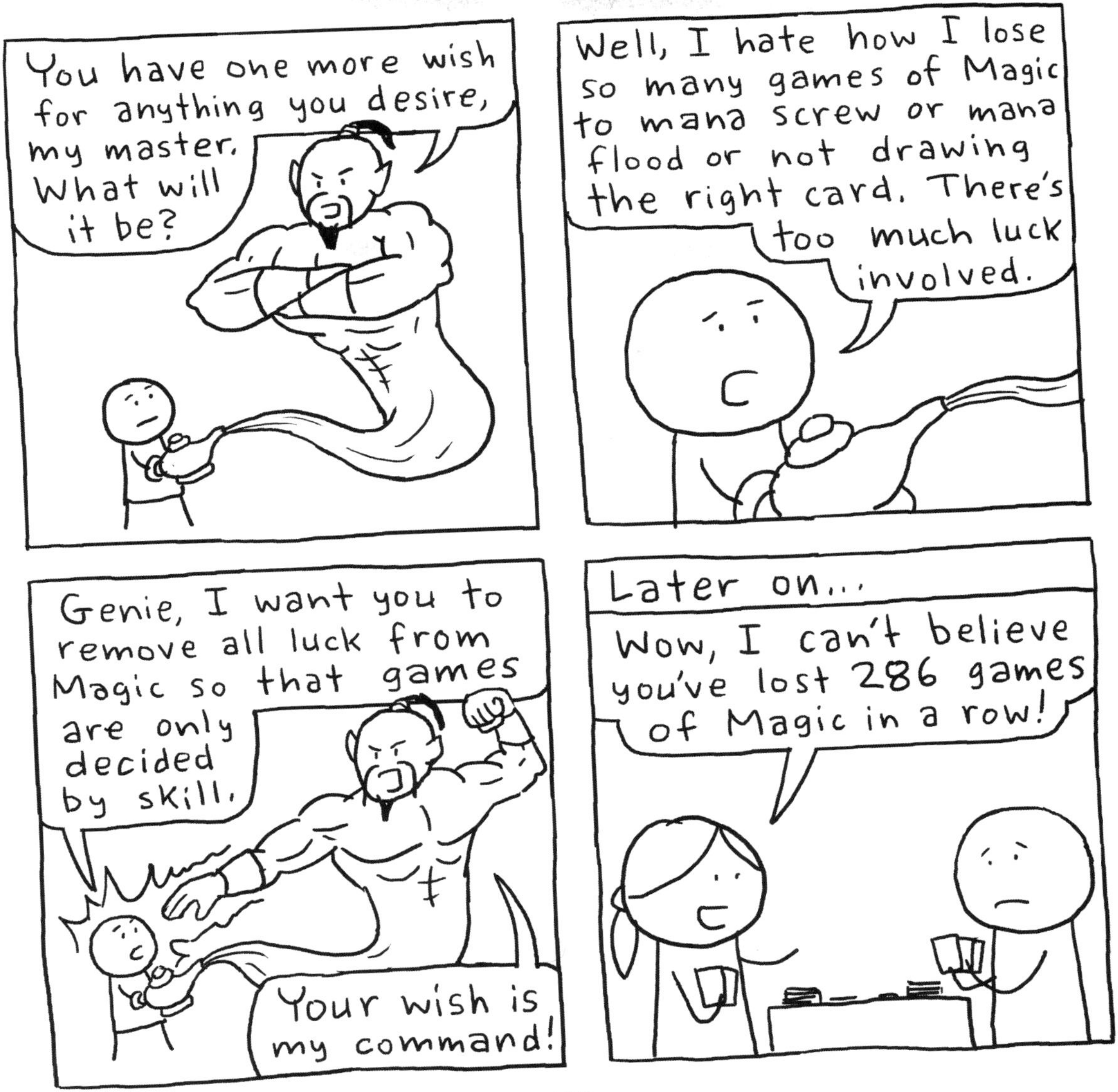
You have one more wish for anything you desire, my master. What will it be?
Well, I hate how I lose so many games of Magic to mana screw or mana flood or not drawing the right card. There's too much luck involved.
Genie, I want you to remove all luck from Magic so that games are only decided by skill.
Your wish is my command!
Later on...
Wow, I can't believe you've lost 286 games of Magic in a row!

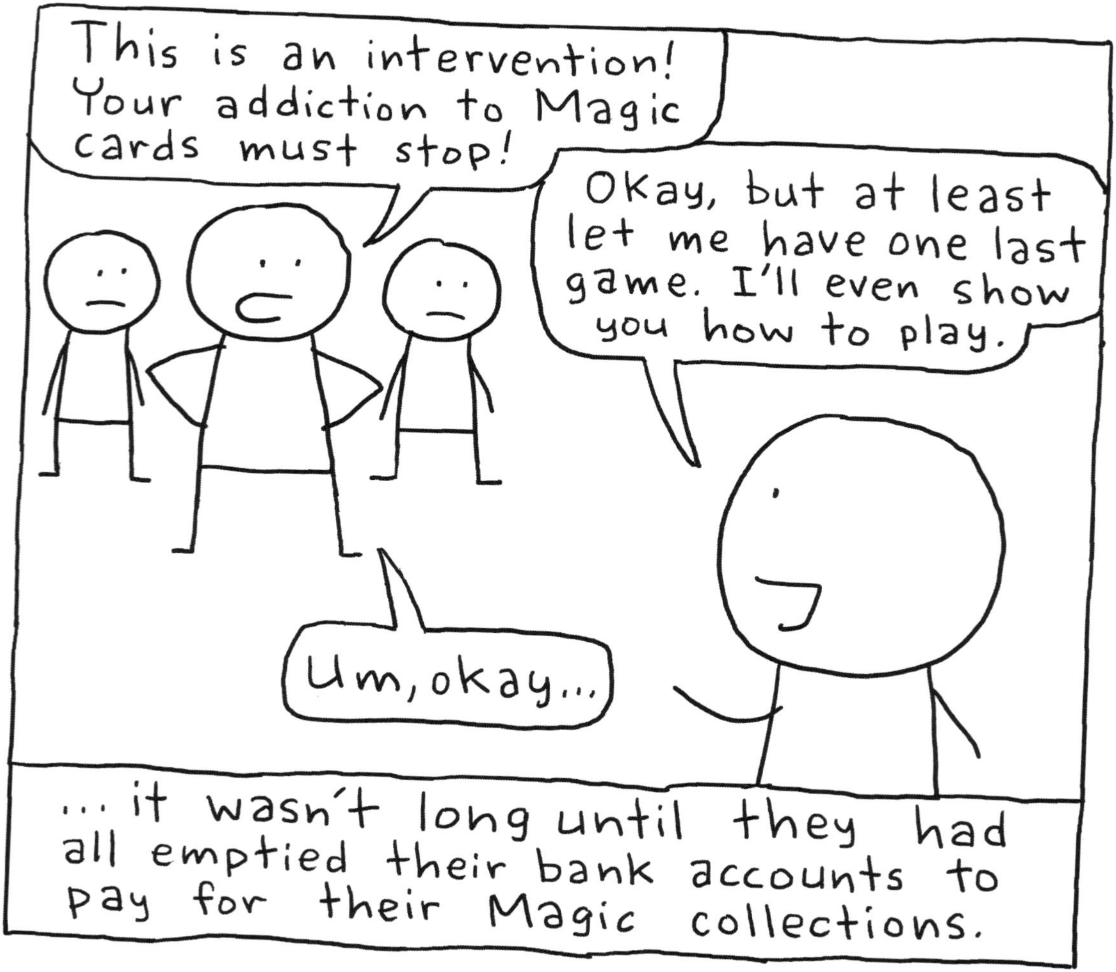
This is an intervention! Your addiction to Magic cards must stop!
Okay, but at least let me have one last game. I'll even show you how to play.
Um, okay...
... it wasn't long until they had all emptied their bank accounts to pay for their Magic collections.

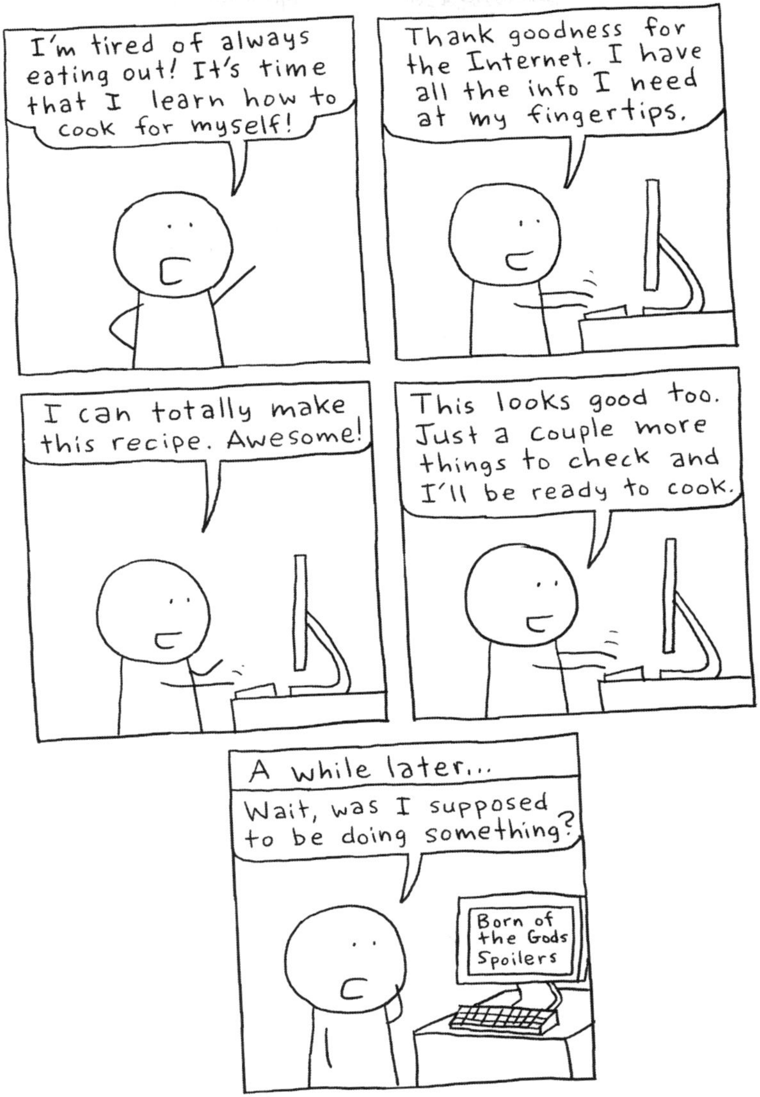
I'm tired of always eating out! It's time that I learn how to cook for myself!
Thank goodness for the Internet. I have all the info I need at my fingertips.
I can totally make this recipe. Awesome!
This looks good too. Just a couple more things to check and I'll be ready to cook.
A while later...
Wait, was I supposed to be doing something?
Born of the Gods Spoilers

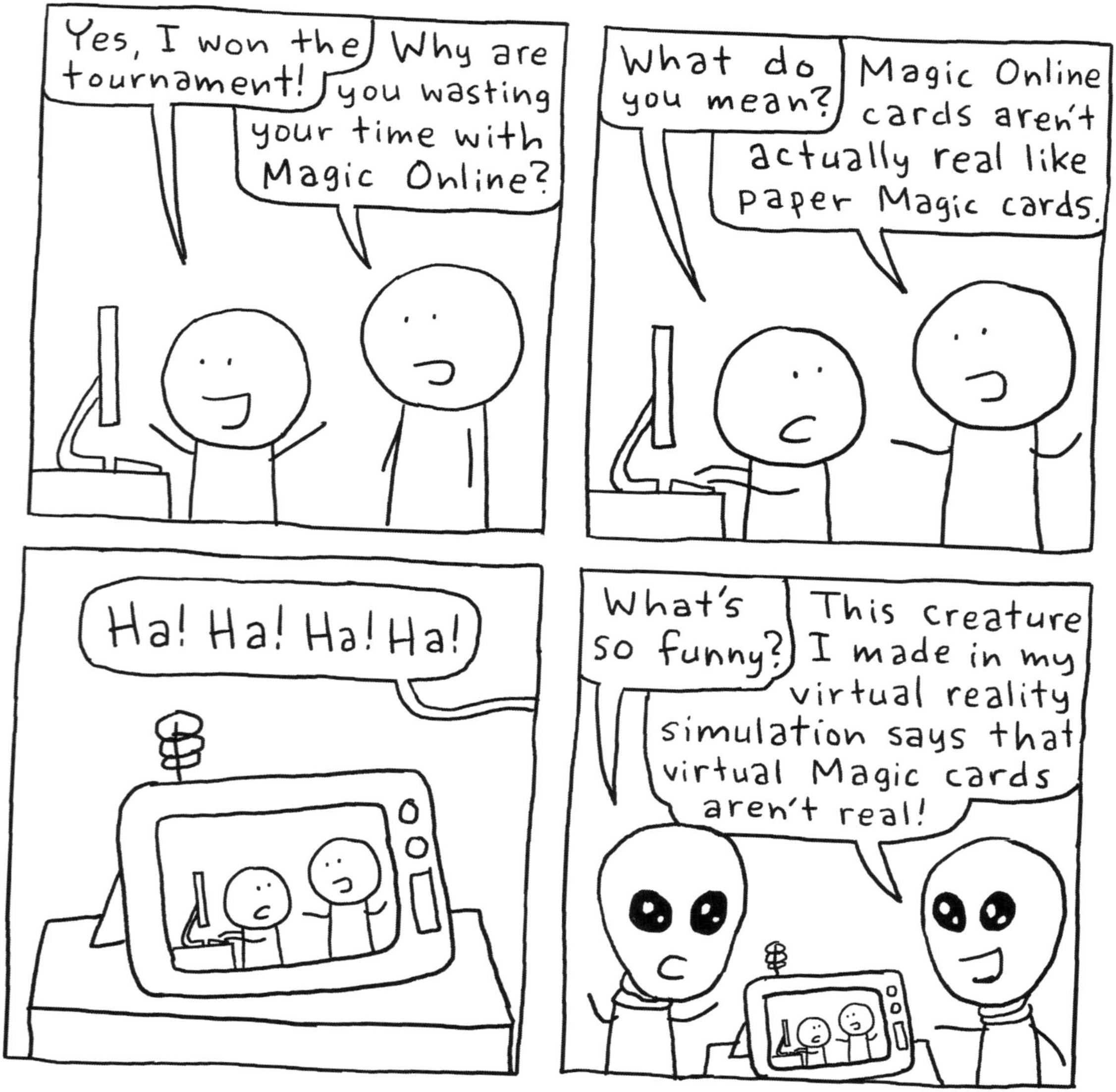
Yes, I won the tournament!
Why are you wasting your time with Magic Online?
What do you mean?
Magic Online cards aren't actually real like paper Magic cards.
Ha! Ha! Ha! Ha!
What's so funny?
This creature I made in my virtual reality simulation says that virtual Magic cards aren't real!

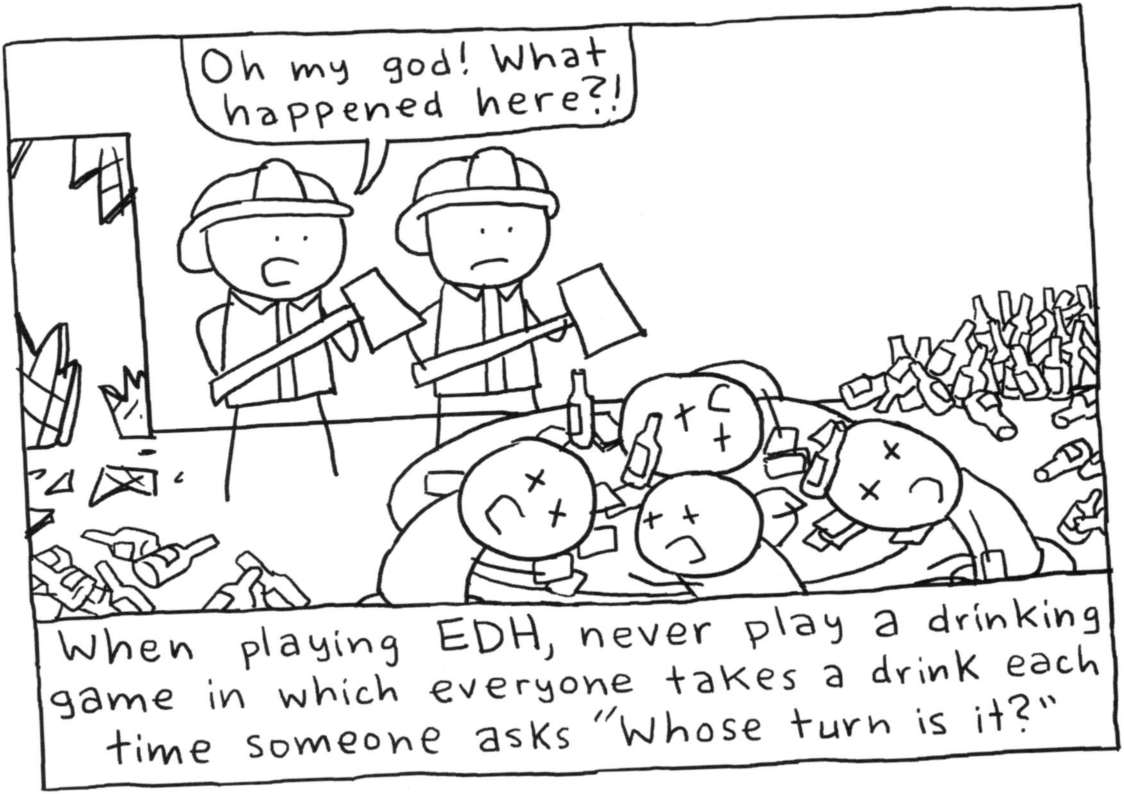
Oh my god! What happened here?!
When playing EDH, never play a drinking game in which everyone takes a drink each time someone asks "Whose turn is it?"

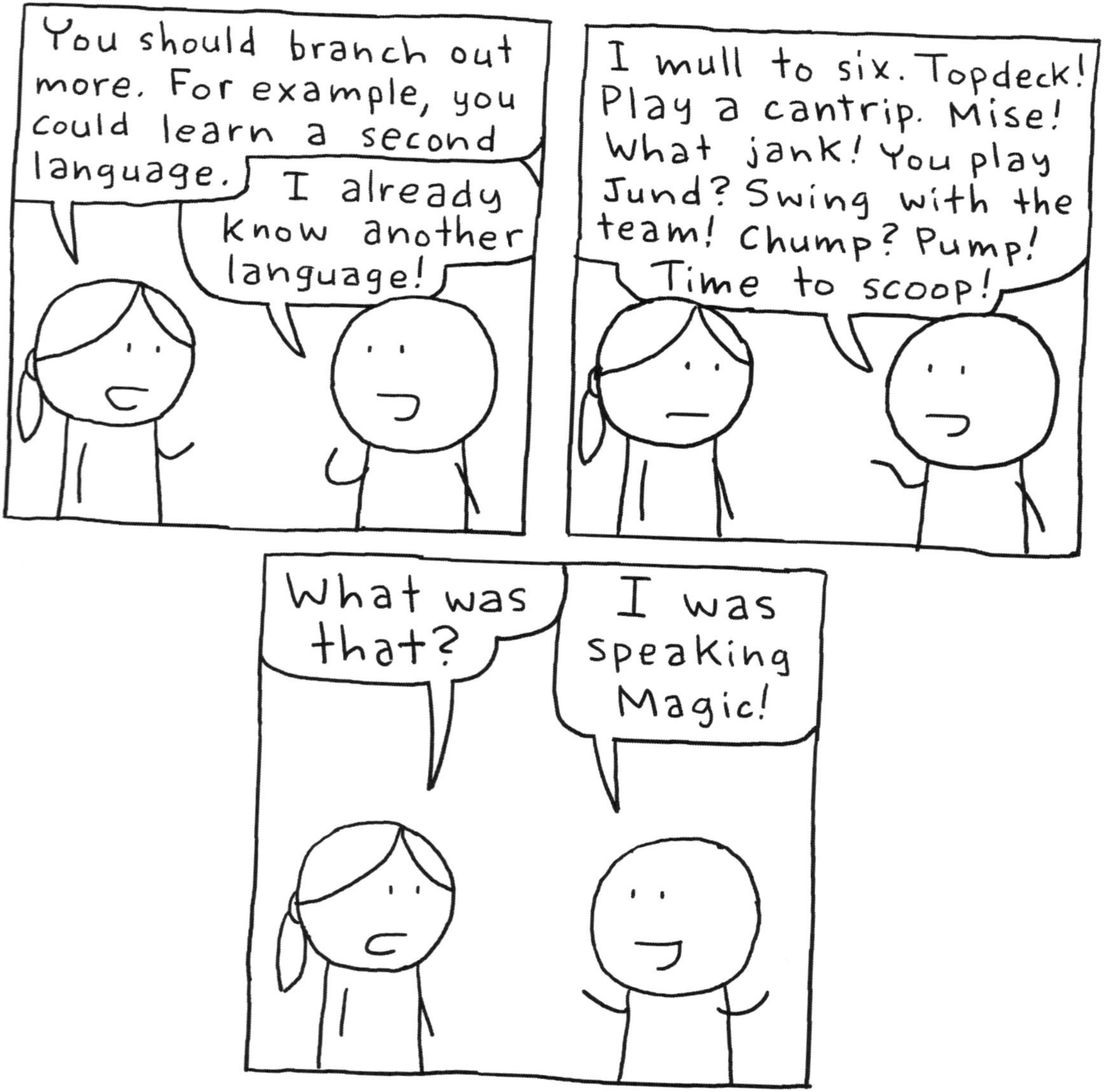
You should branch out more. For example, you could learn a second language.
I already know another language!
I mull to six. Topdeck! Play a cantrip. Mise! What jank! You play Jund? Swing with the team! Chump? Pump! Time to scoop!
What was that?
I was speaking Magic!

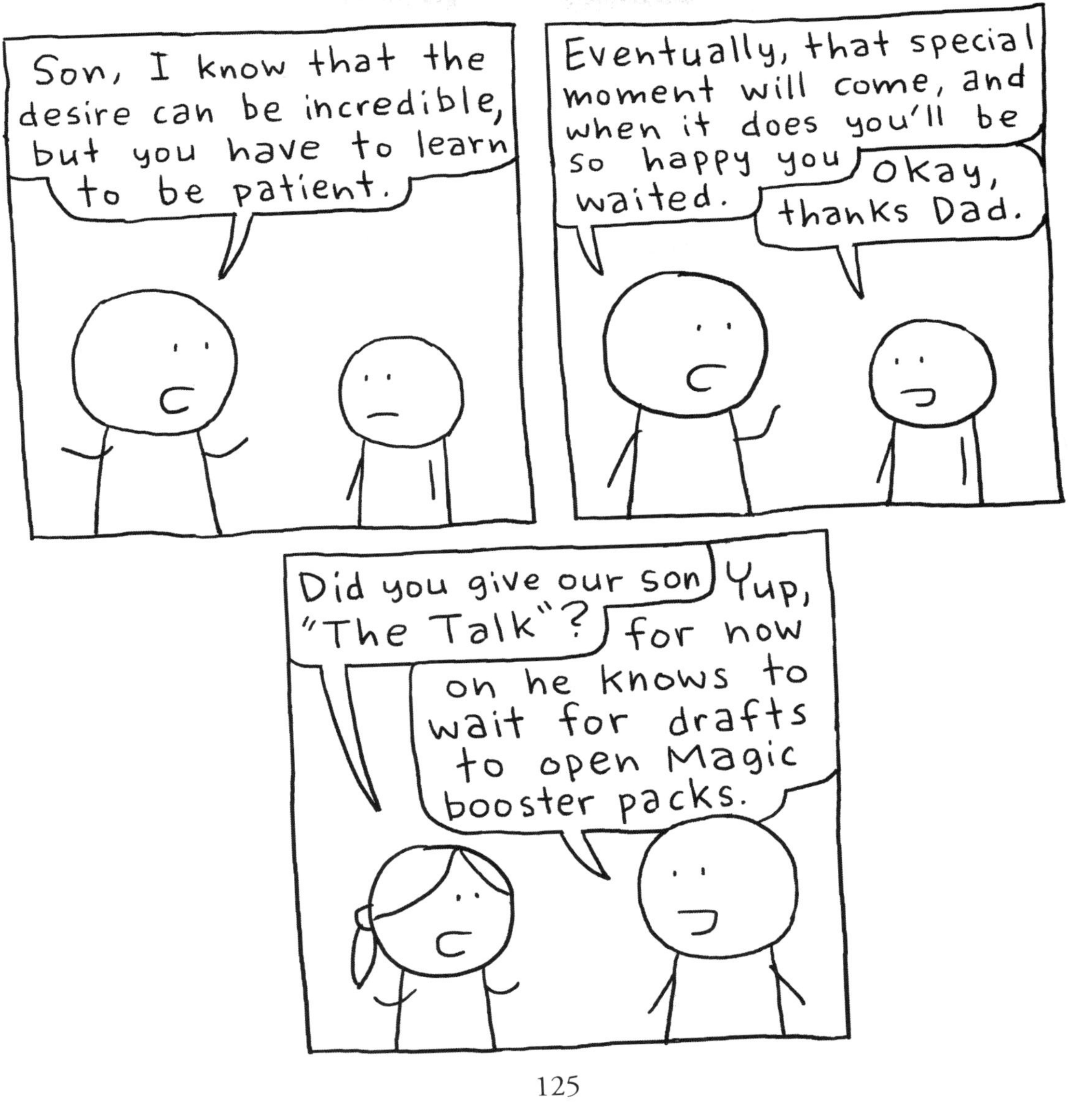
Son, I know that the desire can be incredible, but you have to learn to be patient.
Eventually, that special moment will come, and when it does you'll be so happy you waited.
Okay, thanks Dad.
Did you give our son "The Talk"?
Yup, for now on he knows to wait for drafts to open Magic booster packs.

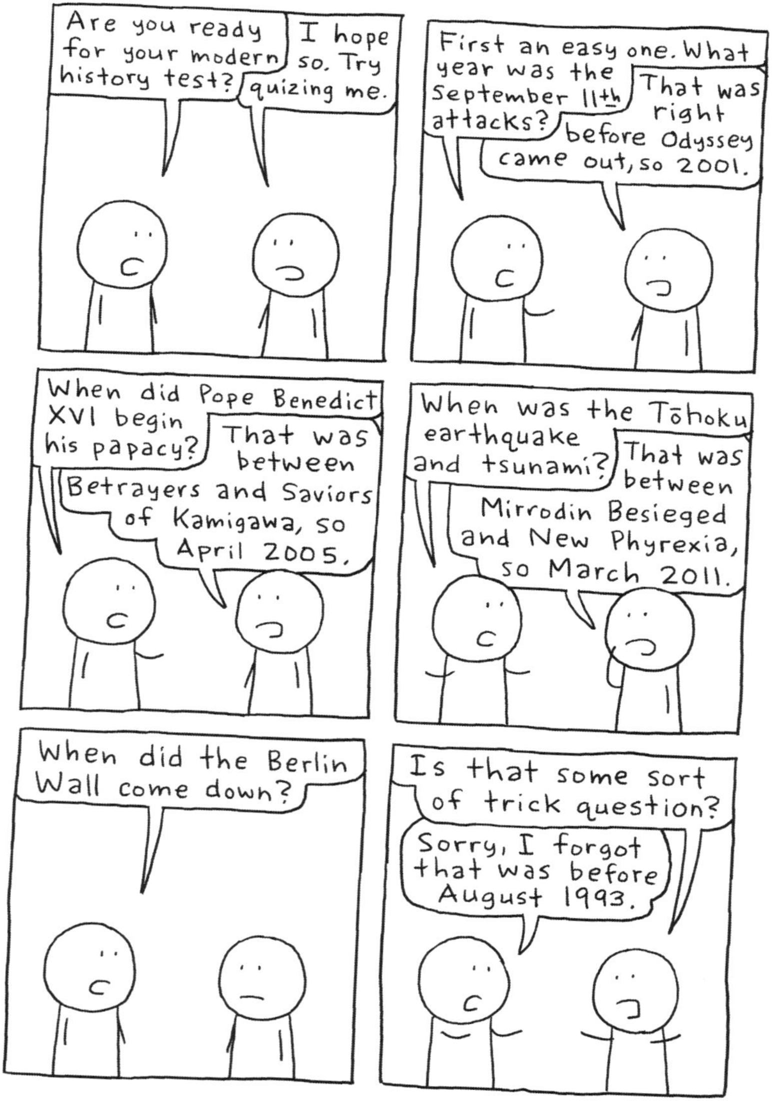
Are you ready for your modern history test?
I hope so. Try quizing me.
First an easy one. What year was the September 11th attacks?
That was right before Odyssey came out, so 2001.
When did Pope Benedict XVI begin his papacy?
That was between Betrayers and Saviors of Kamigawa, so April 2005.
When was the Tōhoku earthquake and tsunami?
That was between Mirrodin Besieged and New Phyrexia, so March 2011.
When did the Berlin Wall come down?
Is that some sort of trick question?
Sorry, I forgot that was before August 1993.

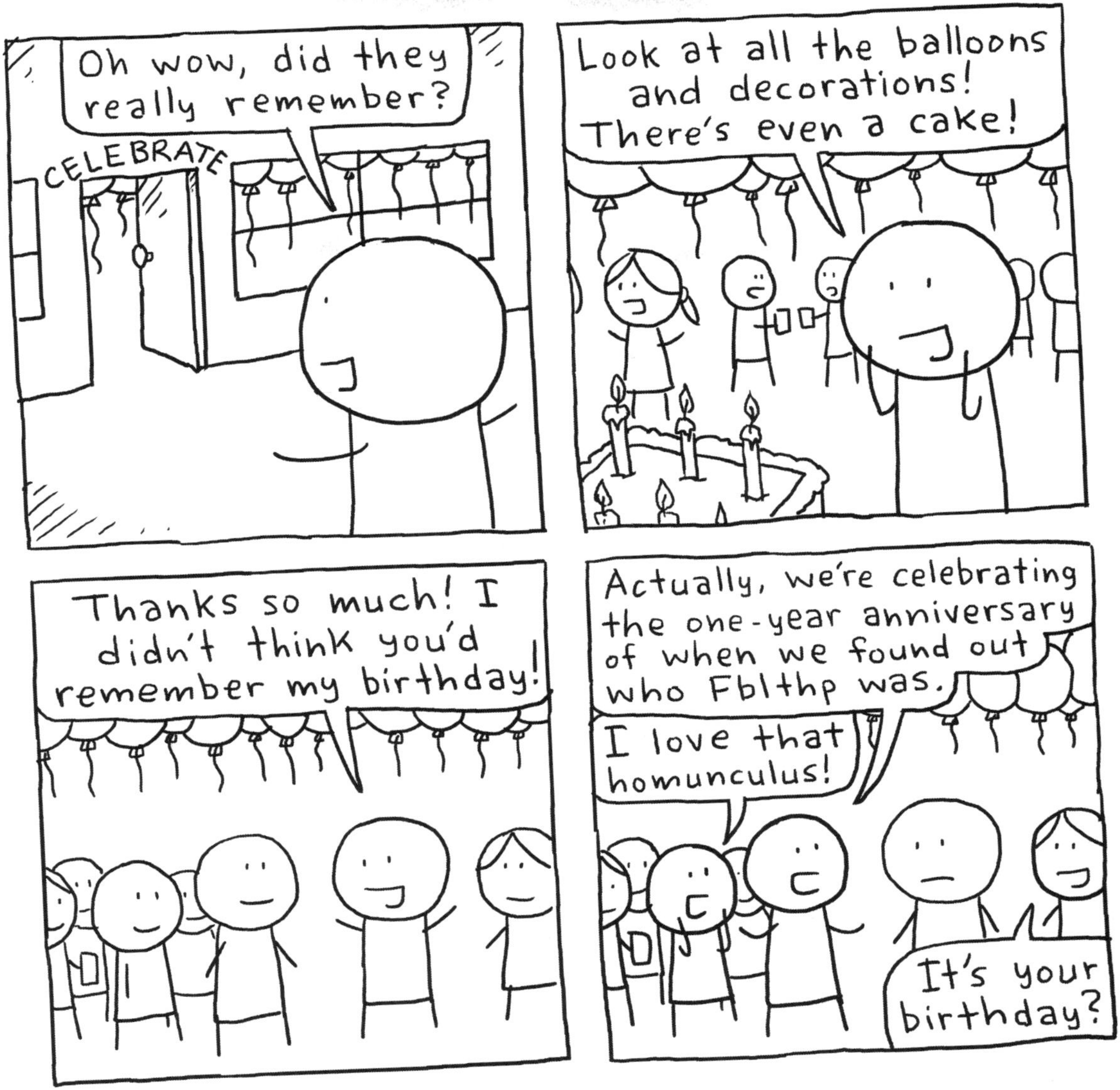
Oh wow, did they really remember?
CELEBRATE
Look at all the balloons and decorations! There's even a cake!
Thanks so much! I didn't think you'd remember my birthday!
Actually, we're celebrating the one-year anniversary of when we found out who Fblthp was.
I love that homunculus!
It's your birthday?

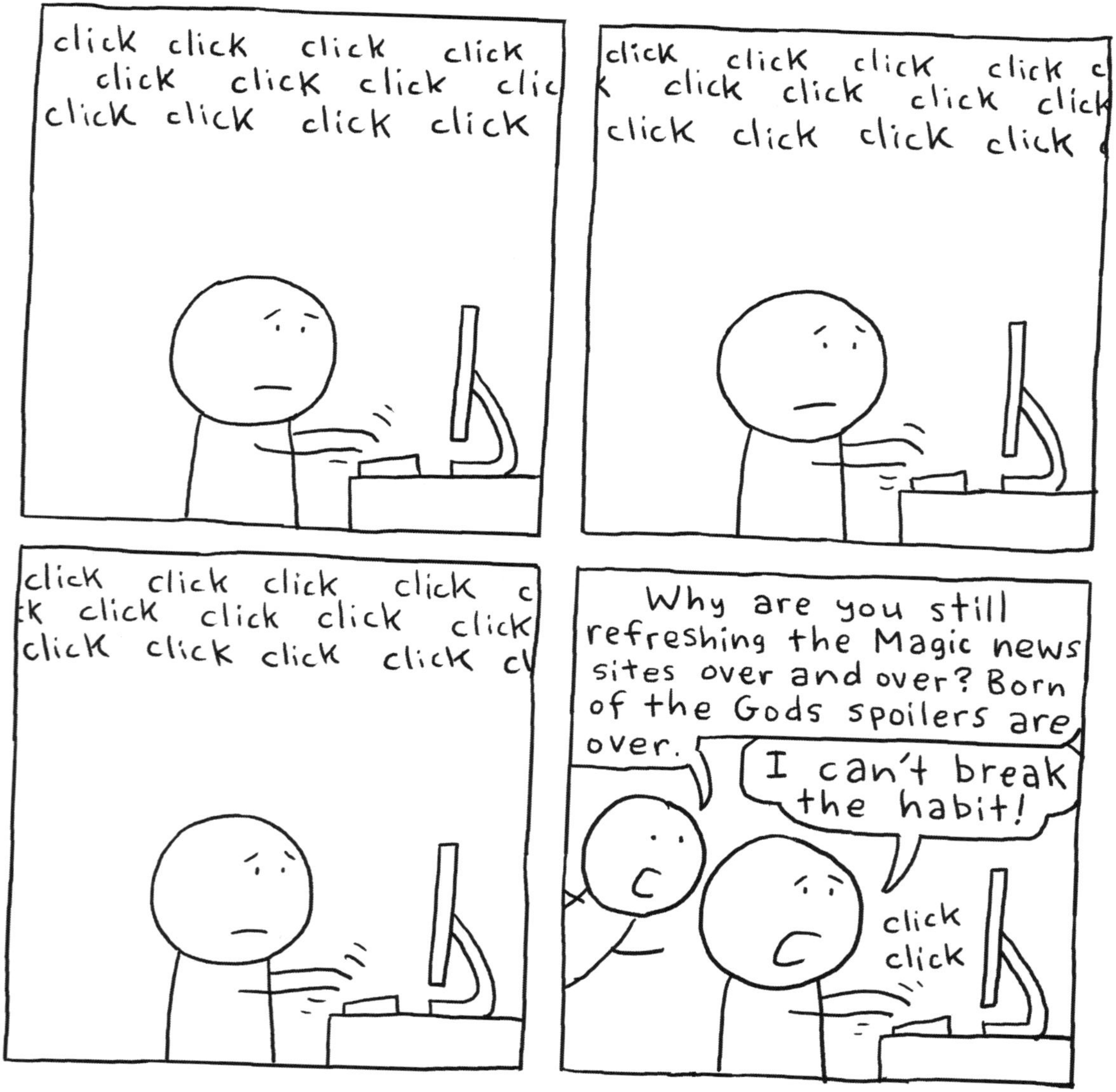
click click click click
click click click clic
click click click click
click click click click c
k click click click click
click click click click
click click click click c
k click click click click
click click click click cl
Why are you still refreshing the Magic news sites over and over? Born of the Gods spoilers are over.
I can't break the habit!
click click

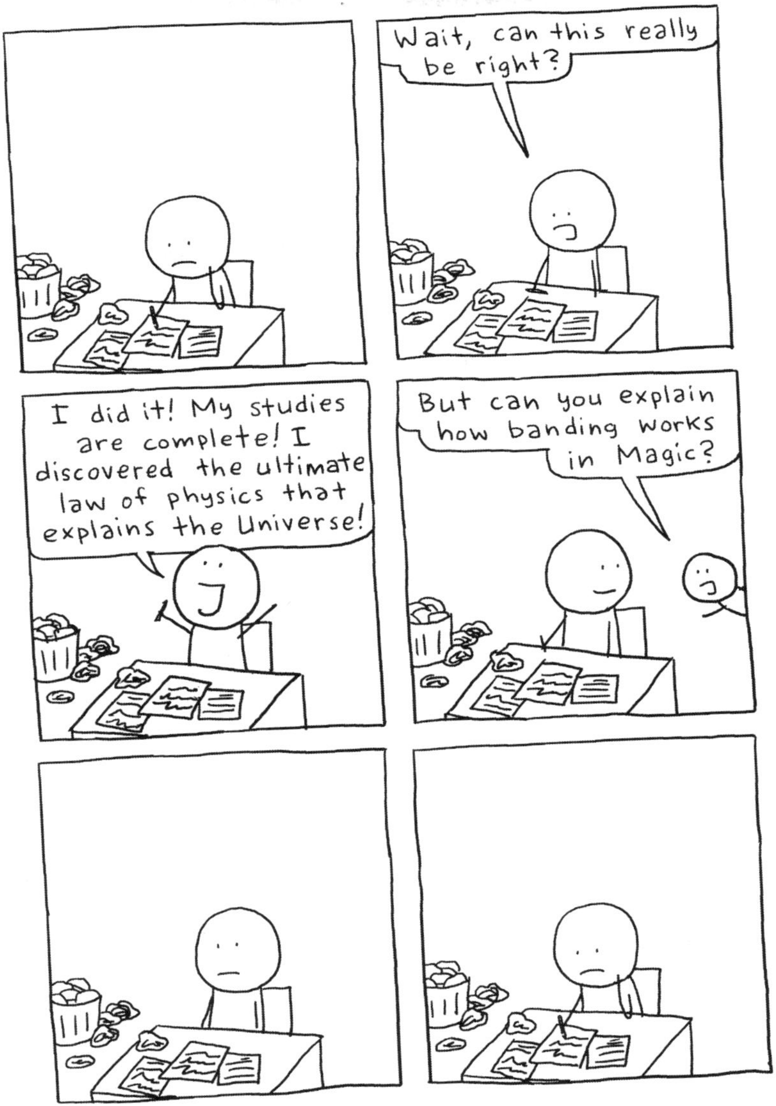
Wait, can this really be right?
I did it! My studies are complete! I discovered the ultimate law of physics that explains the Universe!
But can you explain how banding works in Magic?

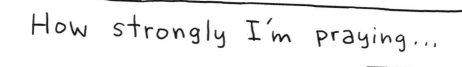

How strongly I'm praying...

...when I see a cop after I've been speeding.

...when I'm late for work and don't want my boss to catch me.

...when I need to draw a second land after keeping a one land hand.

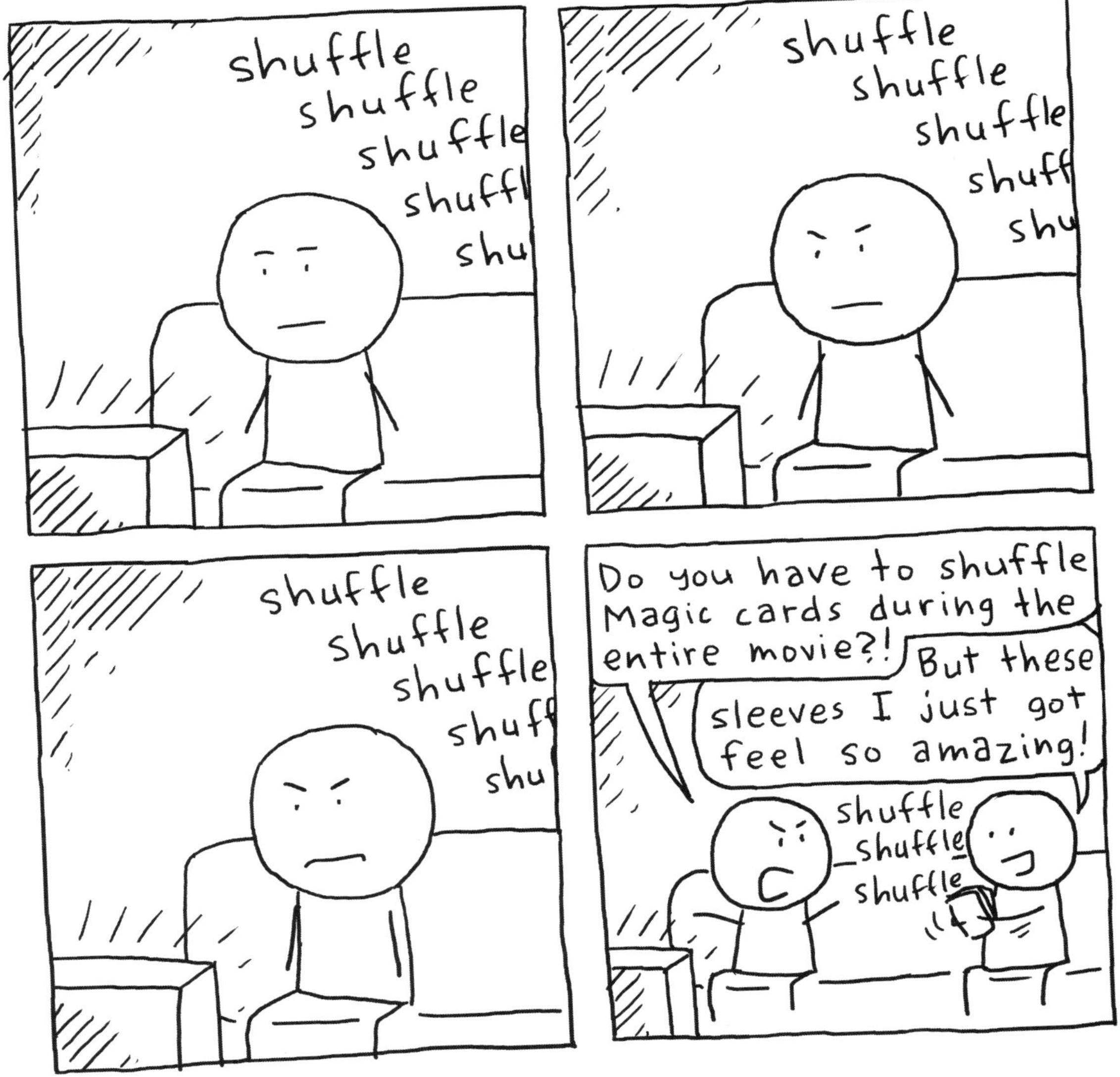
shuffle
shuffle
shuffle
shuffl
shu
shuffle
shuffle
shuffle
shuff
shu
shuffle
shuffle
shuffle
shuff
shu
Do you have to shuffle Magic cards during the entire movie?!
But these sleeves I just got feel so amazing!
shuffle
shuffle
shuffle

Bonus Comics

The following pages feature comics that are exclusive to this book and have never been posted to the Cardboard Crack website. I hope you enjoy the chance to see them here for the first time!

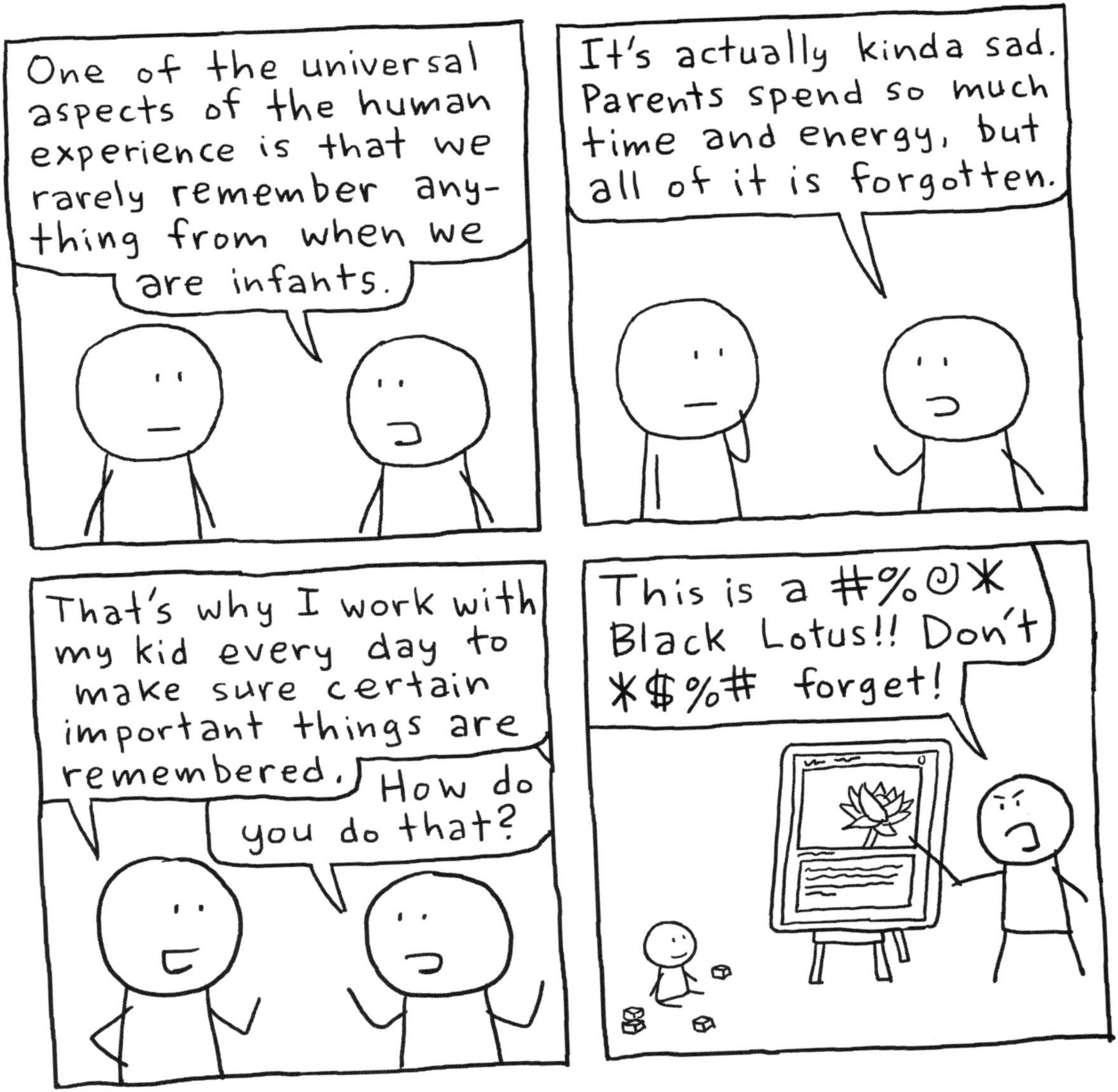
One of the universal aspects of the human experience is that we rarely remember anything from when we are infants.
It's actually kinda sad. Parents spend so much time and energy, but all of it is forgotten.
That's why I work with my kid every day to make sure certain important things are remembered.
How do you do that?
This is a #%@* Black Lotus!! Don't *$%# forget!

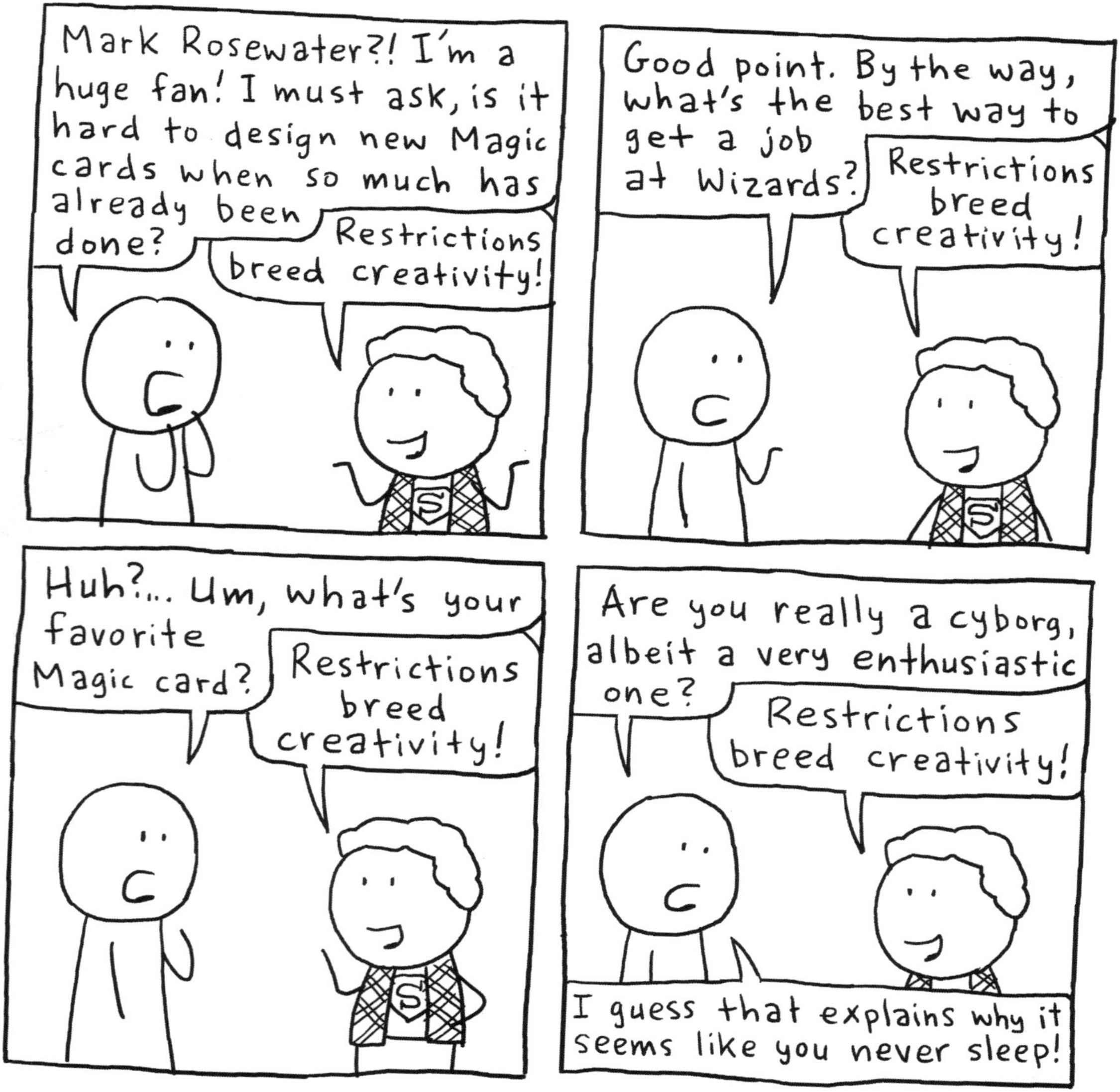
Mark Rosewater?! I'm a huge fan! I must ask, is it hard to design new Magic cards when so much has already been done?
Restrictions breed creativity!
Good point. By the way, what's the best way to get a job at Wizards?
Restrictions breed creativity!
Huh?... Um, what's your favorite Magic card?
Restrictions breed creativity!
Are you really a cyborg, albeit a very enthusiastic one?
Restrictions breed creativity!
I guess that explains why it seems like you never sleep!

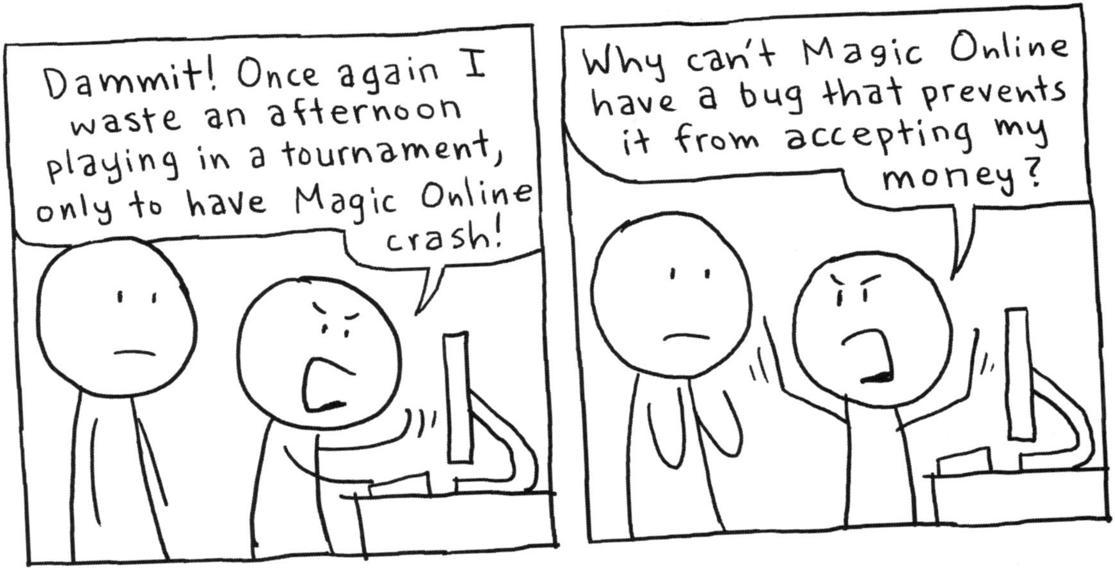
Dammit! Once again I waste an afternoon playing in a tournament, only to have Magic Online crash!
Why can't Magic Online have a bug that prevents it from accepting my money?

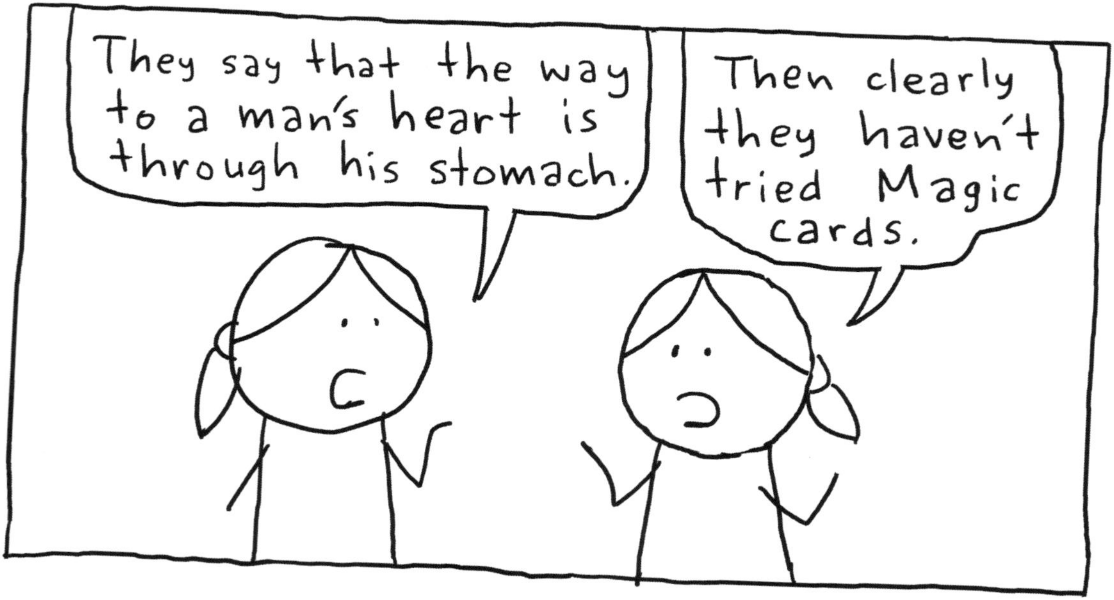
They say that the way to a man's heart is through his stomach.
Then clearly they haven't tried Magic cards.

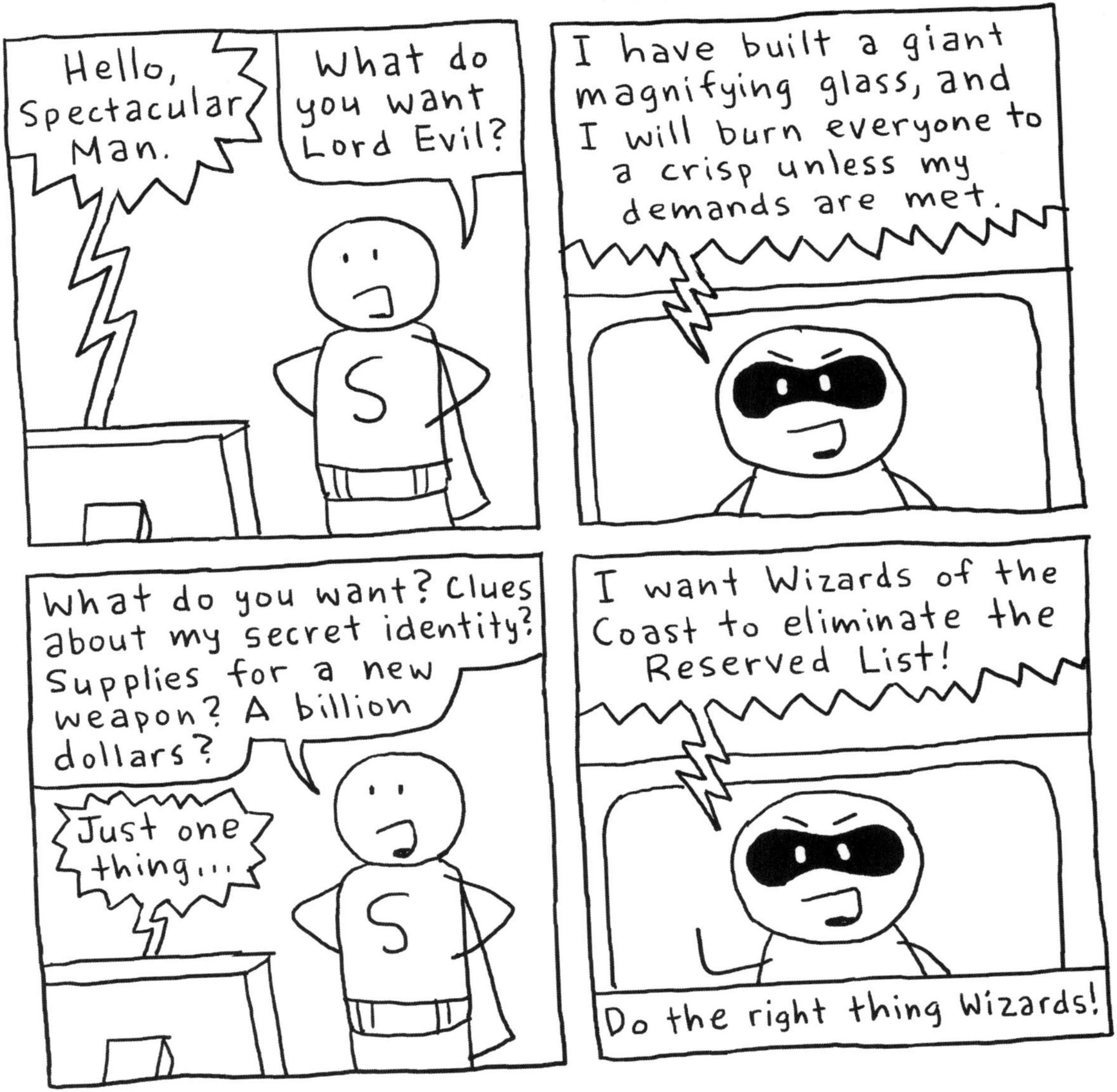
Hello, Spectacular Man.
What do you want Lord Evil?
I have built a giant magnifying glass, and I will burn everyone to a crisp unless my demands are met.
What do you want? Clues about my secret identity? Supplies for a new weapon? A billion dollars?
Just one thing...
I want Wizards of the Coast to eliminate the Reserved List!
Do the right thing Wizards!

You may have won, but deep down you know that it is really just a temporary and pointless victory that has no real impact on our insignificant lives.
Since I suck at Magic, I focus on making my opponent's wins as empty as possible.

Hello little boy. What would you like for Christmas?
I want Wizards of the Coast to stop #%@*-ing with us and print more full art lands!

This last comic has actually appeared on the Cardboard Crack website and should have been included in the previous collection of comics. Unfortunately, I forget to put it in. I guess Fblthp just can't get any respect! For all the completionists out there, I've included this comic here now.

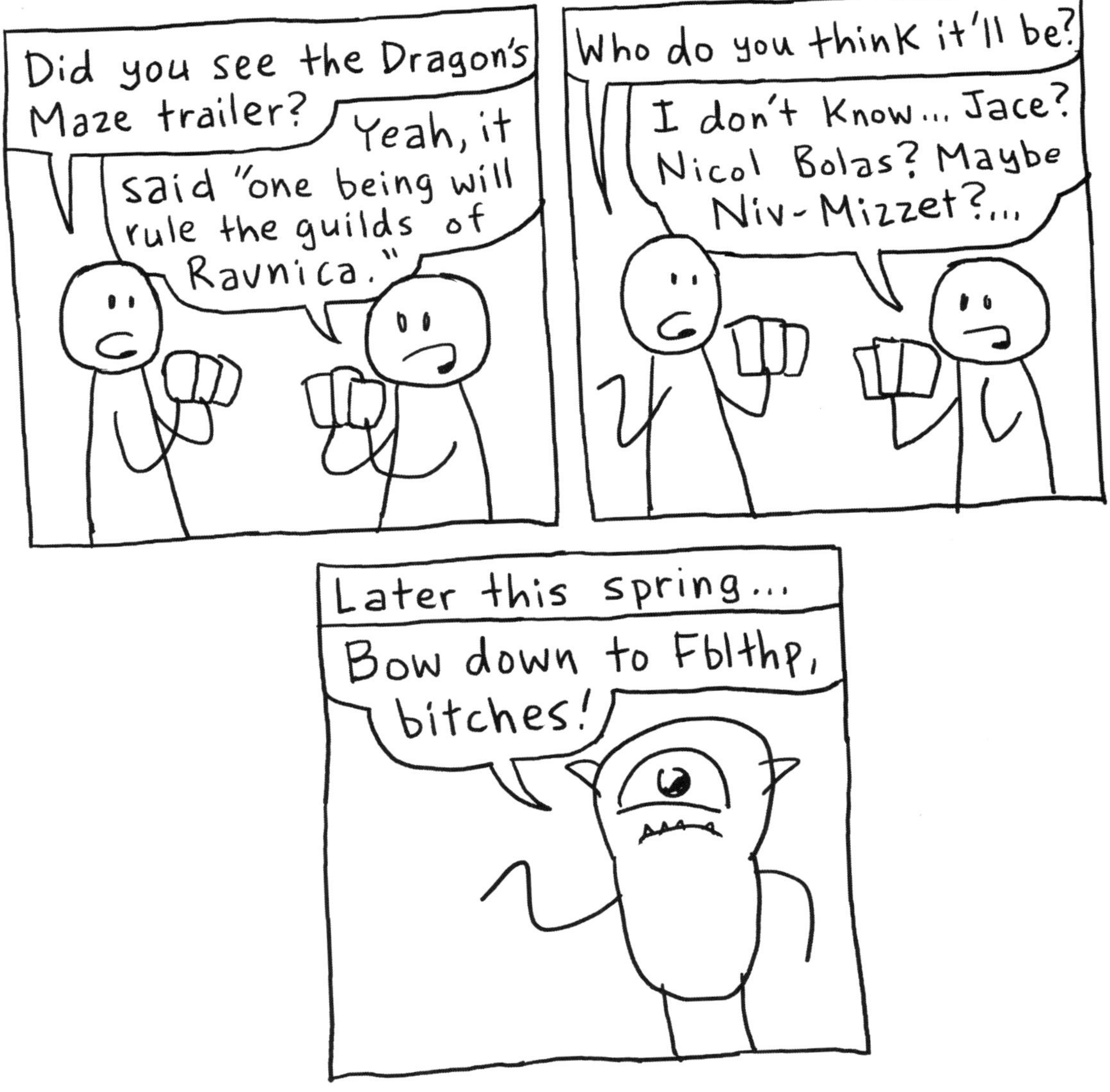
Did you see the Dragon's Maze trailer?
Yeah, it said "one being will rule the guilds of Ravnica."
Who do you think it'll be?
I don't Know... Jace? Nicol Bolas? Maybe Niv-Mizzet?...
Later this spring...
Bow down to Fblthp, bitches!

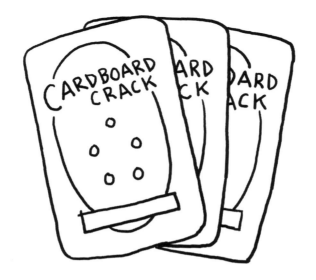

Cardboard Crack has been online since March 25, 2013, exclusively featuring comics about the world's most addictive game, Magic: The Gathering. Since that time, the Cardboard Crack website has gained many thousands of followers and many millions of page views. It has received links from a wide variety of prominent personalities in the Magic community, from Aaron Forsythe (current director of Magic: The Gathering R&D) to Jon Finkel (widely regarded as one of the greatest Magic players of all-time). Cardboard Crack is also featured in the weekly newsletter of StarCityGames.com (the world's largest Magic store).

New comics can be found regularly at:
cardboard-crack.com
facebook.com/CardboardCrack